GEOProcessing 2018

The Tenth International Conference on Advanced Geographic Information Systems, Applications, and Services

March 25 – 29, 2018

Rome, Italy

GEOProcessing 2018 Editors

Claus-Peter Rückemann, Leibniz Universität Hannover / Westfälische Wilhelms-Universität Münster /North-German Supercomputing Alliance (HLRN), Germany
Yerach Doytsher, Technion - Israel Institute of Technology, Haifa, Israel

Printed from e-media with permission by:

Curran Associates, Inc.
57 Morehouse Lane
Red Hook, NY 12571

Some format issues inherent in the e-media version may also appear in this print version.

Printed by Curran Associates, Inc. (2018)

International Academy, Research, and Industry Association (IARIA)
412 Derby Way
Wilmington, DE 19810

Phone: (408) 893-6407
Fax: (408) 527-6351

petre@iaria.org

Additional copies of this publication are available from:

Curran Associates, Inc.
57 Morehouse Lane
Red Hook, NY 12571 USA
Phone: 845-758-0400
Fax: 845-758-2633
Email: curran@proceedings.com
Web: www.proceedings.com

GEOProcessing 2018

Forward

The tenth edition of The International Conference on Advanced Geographic Information Systems, Applications, and Services (GEOProcessing 2018), held in Rome, Italy, March 25 - 29, 2018, addressed the aspects of managing geographical information and web services.

The goal of the GEOProcessing 2018 conference was to bring together researchers from the academia and practitioners from the industry in order to address fundamentals of advances in geographic information systems and the new applications related to them using the Web Services. Such systems can be used for assessment, modeling and prognosis of emergencies

GEOProcessing 2018 provided a forum where researchers were able to present recent research results and new research problems and directions related to them. The topics covered aspects from fundamentals to more specialized topics such as 2D & 3D information visualization, web services and geospatial systems, geoinformation processing, and spatial data infrastructure.

We take this opportunity to thank all the members of the GEOProcessing 2018 Technical Program Committee as well as the numerous reviewers. The creation of such a broad and high-quality conference program would not have been possible without their involvement. We also kindly thank all the authors who dedicated much of their time and efforts to contribute to the GEOProcessing 2018. We truly believe that, thanks to all these efforts, the final conference program consists of top quality contributions.

This event could also not have been a reality without the support of many individuals, organizations, and sponsors. We are grateful to the members of the GEOProcessing 2018 organizing committee for their help in handling the logistics and for their work to make this professional meeting a success.

We hope that GEOProcessing 2018 was a successful international forum for the exchange of ideas and results between academia and industry and for the promotion of progress in geographic information research.

We also hope that Rome provided a pleasant environment during the conference and everyone saved some time for exploring this beautiful city.

GEOProcessing 2018 Chairs

GEOProcessing Steering Committee

Claus-Peter Rückemann, Leibniz Universität Hannover / Westfälische Wilhelms-Universität

GEOPROCESSING 2018

COMMITTEE

Dickson K.W. Chiu, University of Hong Kong, Hong Kong
Sidonie Christophe, IGN/LaSTIG/COGIT, France
Christophe Claramunt, Naval Academy Research Institute, France
Konstantin Clemens, Technical University in Berlin, Germany
Alexandre Corrêa da Silva, HEX Geospatial Technologies, Brazil
Ana Cristina Costa, NOVA IMS - Universidade Nova de Lisboa, Portugal
Christophe Cruz, Université de Bourgogne, France
Monica De Martino, Consiglio Nazionale delle Ricerche - Genova, Italy
Anselmo C. de Paiva, Universidade Federal do Maranhão, Brazil
Cláudio de Souza Baptista, Federal University of Campina Grande, Brazil
Mahmoud R. Delavar, University of Tehran, Iran
Sergio Di Martino, Università degli Studi di Napoli 'Federico II', Italy
Jean-Paul Donnay, University of Liege, Belgium
Yerach Doytsher, Technion - Israel Institute of Technology, Haifa, Israel
Suzana Dragicevic, Simon Fraser University, Canada
Olivier Dubois, OSCARS, France
Surya Durbha, Indian Institute of Technology Bombay, India
Emre Eftelioglu, University of Minnesota, USA
Süleyman Eken, Kocaeli University, Turkey
Javier Estornell, Universitat Politècnica de València, Spain
Nazli Farajidavar, University of Surrey, UK
Marin Ferecatu, Conservatoire National des Arts et Metiers, France
Paolo Fogliaroni, Vienna University of Technology (TU-Wien), Austria
Cidália C. Fonte, University of Coimbra/INESC Coimbra, Portugal
Jérôme Gensel, Université Grenoble Alpes, France
Mauro Gaio, LIUPPA - University of Pau, France
Zdravko Galić, University of Zagreb, Croatia
Georg Gartner, Vienna University of Technology, Austria
Birgit Gersbeck-Schierholz, Leibniz Universität Hannover, Germany
Albert Godfrind, Geospatial technologies/Oracle Server Technologies - Sophia Antipolis, France
Enguerran Grandchamp, Université des Antilles – LAMIA, France, Guadeloupe
Carlos Granell Canut, Universitat Jaume I of Castellón, Spain
Amy Griffin, University of New South Wales | Australian Defence Force Academy, Australia
William Grosky, University of Michigan, USA
Cédric Grueau, Escola Superior de Tecnologia de Setúbal, Portugal
Stefan Herle, RWTH Aachen University, Germany
Erik Hoel, Esri, USA
Bo Huang, The Chinese University of Hong Kong, Hong Kong
Qunying Huang, University of Wisconsin - Madison, USA
Yan Huang, University of North Texas, USA
Sergio Ilarri, University of Zaragoza, Spain
Xunfei Jiang, Earlham College, USA
Shuanggen Jin, Shanghai Astronomical Observatory, China
Didier Josselin, Université d'Avignon, France
Levente Juhasz, University of Florida, USA
Katerina Kabassi, TEI of Ionian Islands, Greece
Hassan A. Karimi, University of Pittsburgh, USA
Izabela Karsznia, University of Warsaw, Poland

delle Ricerche (CNR), Italy
Alexandre Sorokine, Oak Ridge National Laboratory, USA
Mudhakar Srivatsa, IBM T. J. Watson Research Center, USA
Cristian Stanciu, University Politehnica of Bucharest, Romania
Katia Stankov, Synodon Inc., Canada
Leon Stenneth, HERE (BMW, Audi, Daimler), USA
Kazutoshi Sumiya, Kwansei Gakuin University, Japan
Ruby Y. Tahboub, Purdue University, USA
Muhammad Ali Tahir, Institute of Geographical Information Systems (IGIS) - National University of Sciences and Technology (NUST), Islamabad, Pakistan
Zhenghong Tang, University of Nebraska-Lincoln, USA
Ergin Tari, Istanbul Technical University, Turkey
Maguelonne Teisseire, TETIS | Irstea, Montpellier, France
Maristela Terto de Holanda, University of Brasilia (UnB), Brazil
Roger Tilley, University of California, Santa Cruz, USA
Linh Truong-Hong, School of Civil Engineering - University College Dublin, Ireland
Taketoshi Ushiama, Kyushu University, Japan
Marc van Kreveld, Utrecht University, Netherlands
Michael Vassilakopoulos, University of Thessaly, Greece
Monica Wachowicz, University of New Brunswick, Canada
Caixia Wang, University of Alaska Anchorage, USA
Fusheng Wang, Stony Brook University, USA
Jue Wang, Washington University in St. Louis, USA
June Wang, Washington University in St. Louis, USA
John P. Wilson, University of Southern California, USA
Ouri Wolfson, University of Illinois, USA
Zena Wood, University of Greenwich, UK
Jianhong Cecilia Xia, Curtin University, Australia
Ningchuan Xiao, The Ohio State University, USA
KwangSoo Yang, Florida Atlantic University, USA
Xiaojun Yang, Florida State University, USA
May Yuan, University of Texas at Dallas, USA
F. Javier Zarazaga-Soria, University of Zaragoza, Spain
Demetris Zeinalipour, University of Cyprus, Cyprus
Chuanrong (Cindy) Zhang, University of Connecticut, USA
Wenbing Zhao, Cleveland State University, USA
Xun Zhou, University of Iowa, USA
Qiang Zhu, University of Michigan, Dearborn, USA

Copyright Information

Table of Contents

Geographic Decision Making in Urban Management - A SOLAP Tool for the Analysis and the Management of Public Lighting in the City of Oran 1
Ahmed Saidi, Mohamed Faycal Khelfi, Abdellah Mebrek, and Abdelhak Trache

Cultural Metro at Rome A Sustainable Transportation Example Extending Public Transportation System in Rome 8
Michele Angelaccio and Lucia Zappitelli

Analyzing Spatio-Temporal Effects of Social-Economic Factors on Crime 11
Sebastian Baumbach, Nikita Sharma, Sheraz Ahmed, and Andreas Dengel

GeoCubes Finland - A Unified Approach for Managing Multi-resolution Raster Geodata in a National Geospatial Research Infrastructure 18
Lassi Lehto, Jaakko Kahkonen, Juha Oksanen, and Tapani Sarjakoski

Coupling an Unstructured NoSQL Database with a Geographic Information System 23
Amandine Holemans, Jean-Paul Kasprzyk, and Jean-Paul Donnay

ClusterWIS - A Decentralized Forest Information and Management System for the Cluster Forestry and Wood 29
Jurgen Rossmann, Michael Schluse, Martin Hoppen, Gregor Nagele, Tobias Marquardt, Christoph Averdung, Werner Poschenrieder, and Fabian Schwaiger

Assessing and Evaluating Standard Compliance with a State and Local Government GIS Metadata Profile in Large Geospatial Databases 36
Timothy Mulrooney

Methodology of Knowledge Mapping for Arbitrary Objects and Entities: Knowledge Mining Knowledge Mining and Spatial Representations - Objects in Multi-dimensional Context 40
Claus-Peter Ruckemann

Using Smart A* Algorithm to Solve TSP Navigation Problem 46
Hatem Halaoui

A Spatial Decision Support System for Waste Management in Municipal Society of Lahore City 52
Muhammad Haris and Beenish Fatima

National Geoinformation System Development in the Republic of Uzbekistan 56
Muzaffar Djalalov

Motion Planning in 3D Environments Using Visibility Velocity Obstacles 60
Oren Gal and Yerach Doytsher

A Case Study for a Multitemporal Segmentation Approach in Optical Remote Sensing Images 66
Wanderson Costa, Leila Fonseca, Thales Korting, Margareth Simoes, and Patrick Kuchler

An Approach for Assessing Array DBMSs for Geospatial Raster Data 71
Janne Kovanen, Ville Makinen, and Tapani Sarjakoski

Towards Modelling Privacy Risks in Geo-Social Networks 77
Alia Abdelmoty

Geographic Decision Making in Urban Management

A SOLAP Tool for the Analysis and the Management of Public Lighting in the City of Oran

Ahmed Saidi
Université Oran 1 Ahmed Benbella
Centre des Techniques Spatiales Arzew
Oran, Algeria
email: ha_saidi@yahoo.fr

Mohamed Fayçal Khelfi
Université Oran 1 Ahmed Benbella
Oran, Algeria
email: mf_khelfi@yahoo.fr

Abdellah Mebrek
Centre des Techniques Spatiales
Arzew Oran, Algeria,
email: mebrek_abdellah@hotmail.com

AbdelhakTrache
Centre de Développement de Satellites
Oran, Algeria
email: trache_a@yahoo.fr

Abstract— **Approaches to business intelligence provide data mining techniques offering a new vision in multidimensional information analysis. This is particularly true when it comes to information with spatial reference. The procedures leading to the creation of Data Warehouses (DW) are inefficient when it comes to integrating the spatial dimension. Indeed, deriving a Spatial Data Warehouse (SDW) suggests the use of methods able to process complex geographical information, taking several aspects into account. If the archive character of the data is relatively easy to identify for each aspect, it is not obvious to detect this criterion in a global view of the geographic entity. We present in this paper an experiment showing a Geo-Decisional methodology of SDW construction, integrated in the functionalities of a Geographic Information System (GIS), to have a general procedure providing an information database and the specific tools to initiate spatial Data mining operations. An experimentation of this methodology to manage public lighting in the city of Oran is presented.**

Keywords - Data Warehouse; Data mining; SOLAP; GIS.

I. INTRODUCTION

Any activity on a territory generates data and information with spatial reference. The abundance of information on the space that we occupy shows the great interest various actors of territorial administration have on geographic information. New information technology has produced an exponential increase of data and information in almost all organizations. This has led to an improvement in management and better accuracy in the decisions made. In the field of economic activity, data processing proposes decision making approaches (Business Intelligence - BI) able to analyze non-volatile archived data over a fixed time period. Emanating from business intelligence, this approach is intelligent and produces particular inductions, unsuspected and undetected by traditional methods. Properties, trends and findings not revealed by classical approaches are updated and contribute greatly to making a more judicious decision. These tools are structured around the DW concept. They allow an exploratory search of data (Data mining). However, when the geographic information is concerned, these approaches are helpless and sometimes not well adapted.

Geographic information, the base of any characterization of territory, is complex and has multidimensional aspects in its definition. The geometric and topological aspect expresses metric characteristics like localization, shape, surface, and also all spatial relations between objects. It is coupled with attributive aspects describing intrinsic information of its theme. This duality in definition of geographic information is not taken into account by these new approaches. The GIS are excellent tools to characterize information with spatial reference. They offer a range of solutions to manage geographic information and to make deterministic spatial analysis. However, these systems do not make a spatio-temporal and oriented-subject analysis of the archived data. That represents the predominant constraint over their ability to provide an analysis using data mining.

Our study aims to present a methodology by enriching and adapting DW and Data mining approaches in the spatial context for the management of public lighting in the city of Oran. A Spatial On Line Analytical Processing (SOLAP) is developed. The specificity of this tool is dictated by the complexity of geographical information and especially its diversity. It is unrealistic at current state of research to claim to develop universal tools SDW or SOLAP. Each geographical theme is specific. Hydrology, agriculture, transport, waste management or public lighting are not treated in the same manner. Objects have different geometric and topological aspects. For this reason, the few SOLAP experiments identified in the world are all specific and target a defined theme. The application we have developed here is integrated into the GIS environment to allow visualization and mapping of the results.

II. The Problem of the Spatial Analysis

A. DW and Spatial DW:

A DW is a derivation of existing data structures such as databases to produce a structure containing archived data not subject to change.

Bill Inmon [7], considered as the founding father of DW, defines them as follows: "*A Data Warehouse is a collection of subject-oriented, integrated, not volatile, historical and organized data for decision-making.*" (Figure 1)

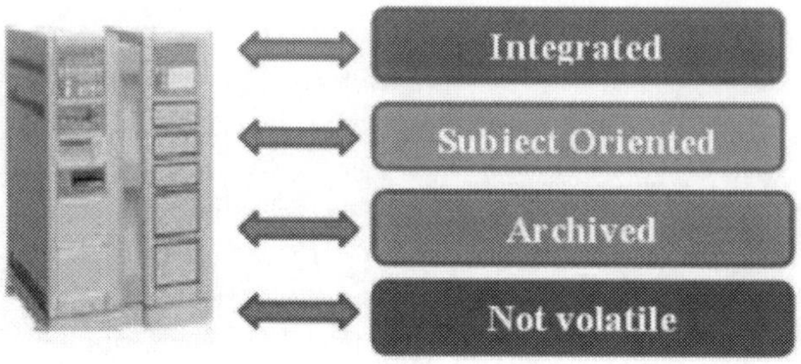

Figure 1. Data Warehouse

This definition assumes that data is stored in its most elementary level for basic and flexible use, making it easy and fast to analyze the information.

Accessing and processing the DW data are done by using a set of tools called Data Warehousing (Figure 2). In Data Warehousing, data is modeled as a data-cube, when the number of data does not exceed three dimensions. Each dimension is represented by one table. If the cube exceeds three dimensions, it is called hyper-cube.

By integrating the spatial dimension, Spatial DW is defined (SDW).

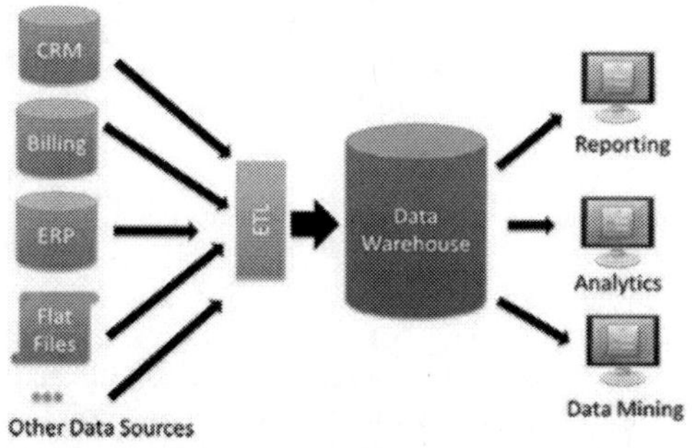

Figure 2. Manipulating tools of DW: The DWing

It is recognized that analytical processes do not use the full potential of data when they do not integrate the spatial component. However, this spatial dimension is mostly present in territory information defining, location, address, postal code, GPS location, region or country, position, territorial reference, etc.

It is currently estimated that 80% of data stored in corporate databases have spatial reference [5]. Sometimes, the spatial component comes in several elements in addition to position, like a shape, an orientation and a size. Simple visualization of spatial components allows providing first understanding of phenomenon in relation to its space (Figure 3). So, the simple fact of displaying spatial data gives an idea of their location in territory, their extent, their distribution (concentrated, dispersed, grouped, random, regular, etc.). This visualization action makes it possible to discover information not available by traditional OLAP tools.

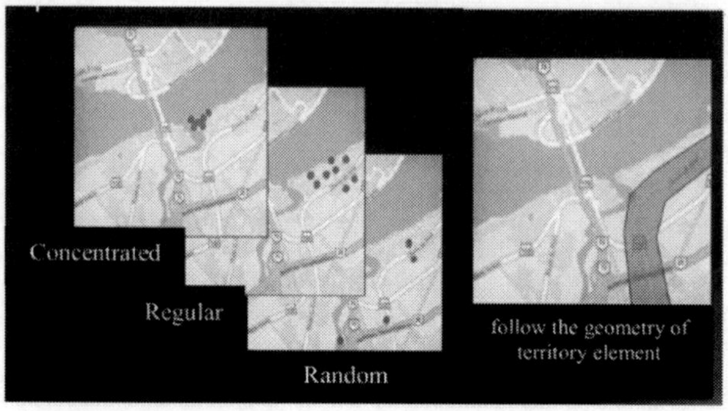

Figure 3. Spatial distribution of phenomenon

B. Data mining – OLAP - SOLAP:

The set of methods requiring analysis using DW is grouped into the concept called OLAP [6]. It opposes to transactional analytical approaches offered by DBMS tools. If we are interested in the spatial component of information, we are in the presence of a Spatial OLAP approach (Figure 4). Distinction between the two concepts is fundamental. The introduction of spatial component as dimension in analysis requires a method combining a geometric approach with a more classical, literal and attributive process in relation to the reference theme.

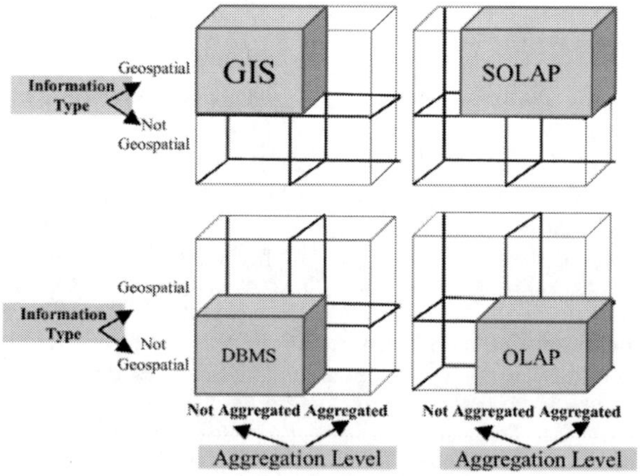

Figure 4. Type of Spatial Analysis

Any spatial Data mining is dependent on the existence of updated, stable and coherent SDW. This results from need to process space data in order to extract knowledge by exploratory means (Statistical, excavation, visualization, etc.).

SOLAP application is presented as "*A type of software that allows fast and easy navigation in spatial databases and offers several levels of granularity of information, several themes, several epochs and several modes of synchronized or non-synchronized display: Maps, charts and diagrams* "[3].

A SOLAP technology suggests new decision support functions, not available in traditional GIS tools or OLAP tools. This technology allows cartographic visualization of data, cartographic navigation on the map itself or in symbols displayed on the map, according to different types of drilling. In SOLAP technology, the creation of the results maps is dynamic, unlike some OLAP visualization software (e.g., Cognos Visualizer) where each spatial navigation operation (e.g., drilling) has to be predefined in application and associated with a map. This limitation of OLAP makes it more complex to update geometric data, by distributing information on several maps. The SOLAP tool manages adequately the mapping rules for analysis results on maps [4].

According to its definition, SOLAP does not require an expert person for its use. The user can create a multitude of different maps by some clicks. In presentation of results, SOLAP uses same semiological rules (e.g., color, frame, contour) for all displays. This makes it possible to have a visual synchronization between various modes of presentation and to have homogeneous panorama. Graphical semiology used for various types of display (i.e. tables, graphs and maps) remains synchronized during drilling or other operations, preserving perceptual continuity, necessary for discovery of correlations [9].

Three possible architectures exist for a SOLAP tool [1] (Figure 5).

- Predominant OLAP: This kind of solution proposes all features of an OLAP tool. It is implicit that such solution uses capacities of OLAP server. On the other hand this solution will integrate few functions of GIS, generally the functions of displaying, cartographic navigation and selection of geometric elements. The functions of space analysis, space synchronization, etc., are not available. Sometimes some minimal functions of space drilling can be offered and then make it possible to develop interesting SOLAP applications.

- Predominant GIS: OLAP server can be simulated inside a relational database by means of star model. When volumes of data are relatively low, this solution can be very advantageous. The requests can be adapted according to the needs of a particular project. For example, this action can be done while avoiding calculating, some non-significant aggregations or while making it possible to join tables implied in the requests in a way more flexible than OLAP servers allow it usually. On the other hand, this solution must include, in database, elements making it possible realization of OLAP operations such as drilling and the reassembly. The predominant GIS solutions offer all the features of GIS functions, but only one small subset of OLAP tool. This solution couples relational database simulating OLAP server with a GIS software or any tool for visualization of space data. The graphic interface for user and functions of semantic and spatial drilling must be programmed.

- Hybrid or Mixed Solution: This type of solution, integrate GIS functionalities and OLAP tools with the same proportions. It could be described as a centric-geospatial application, where spatial reference of objects is used constantly in the exploration and analysis of data. This type of solution is useful when the application must be integrated in Geomatic environment with a high data flow. It offers an OLAP server and a GIS tool. Then, it is possible to develop an OLAP extension to integrate in the GIS software. A SOLAP technology allows to group or to enrich both functionalities OLAP and GIS. The graphical interface provides the user with both spatial and semantic drilling functions, spatial analysis functions, mapping functions and so on. Tools of map navigation allow you to drill into maps according a synchronized manner with other types of displays (e.g. tables and diagrams).

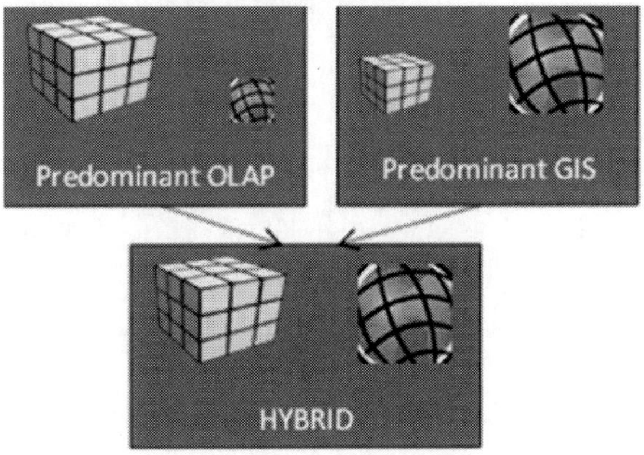

Figure 5. Architectures of SOLAP Solutions

Finally, SOLAP applications must be distinguished from SOLAP technologies. A SOLAP technology is a generic technology specially built to offer basic or more advanced SOLAP functions without the need of programming. A SOLAP application is a business application that provides the user with a number of SOLAP features and can be constructed with SOLAP technology or with combinations of non-SOLAP technologies (eg. GIS and OLAP and a self-programing code, or with other technologies) [2].

Our work is the development of a SOLAP application named "public lighting" integrated into GIS environment with software ArcGis in the city of Oran.

III. THE PROBLEM OF PUBLIC LIGHTING IN ORAN

A. *Current situation of public lighting in Oran :*

Oran is defined as a medium-sized city of Mediterranean territory (Figure 6). It is located in north-west of Algeria, and is considered the second largest city of the country. It has a population of 1.5 million. It is spread over an area of about 105 km² and incorporates a set of buildings combining several architectural types ranging from Arabic-Moorish to Haussmannian and Modern.

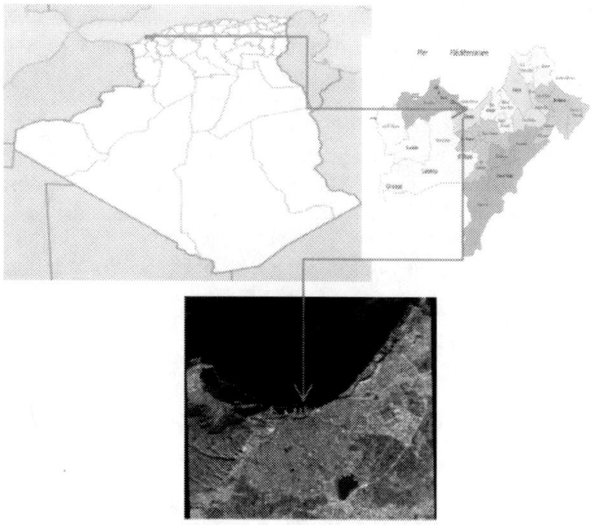

Figure 6. The City of Oran

Public lighting for city of Oran is a common problem and at center of many economic, social and political stakes. There is today a strong expectation, expressed by the populations in terms of urban lighting. These challenges of urban lighting especially security of properties and people, security of movement, valorization of city and economic development are well understood by elected officials and their citizens. A well illuminated city will be more pleasant to live in, more attractive to its visitors and more marked in its night identity. Today, the image and the living environment are essential conditions of attractive business for the city.

B. The statistics of public lighting in ORAN :

Oran has a significant public lighting network. It consists of:

- more than 42,000 luminaires,
- more than 3,600 switch cabinets,
- more than 916 control stations,
- Beyond 1,956 Km of cable,

Several companies, public and private, manage the network of lighting. The main operator remains ERMESSO which governs more than 60% of network of territory of Oran, and all control on the town of Oran. This operator has recently introduced mapping and modern technological tools in network management (GIS, GPS, etc.).

Frequent breakdowns are announced on the network generating a growing dissatisfaction of the population because of the deficiency of lighting generated by these incidents.

The potential causes of these incidents are not always identified. Operators in charge of management of network operate according to a policy of event-driven maintenance. Indeed, the teams of maintenance, they have the role of mitigating incidents which have occurred on the territory following the request of security services, communal services or of citizens. The only actions undertaken in this situation is replacement of defective devices (lamp, lighting, cupboard, cable, etc.). This situation is one of the main causes which motivate us to implement a SOLAP application to analyze the network, to diagnose nonobvious causes of incidents and to decide on a policy of adequate maintenance.

C. Elaborating the SDW "Public lighting Oran":

The SDW is generated from an existing database at ERMESSO. It is a collection of geographic data organized in specific system (GIS), dealing with public lighting on territory of city of Oran. The different components of the Database are layers of information structured around the territory and reference entities relating to the topic of study. The main ones are:

- Luminaires: A set of lighting post with their technical characteristics.
- Cabinets: The energy distribution cabinets to which the luminaires are connected,
- Lines : Connection Cables between the luminaires and the Cabinets,
- Road Network: The streets of Oran organized in categories, type, flow, road surface type, etc.
- Administrative Division: The different boundaries identifying territory of municipalities, urban areas and neighborhoods.
- A satellite image (SPOT 6) with resolution of 1,5 meters, taken in March 2015.

D. Different components of the SDW:

All referred entities in the database of the GIS will be represented in our SDW. However, light versions of entities will be produced to achieve efficient and coherent SDW. The problem lies in the choice of the entities components, candidate for the SDW. We target in our approach, the relevance, simplicity and stability of the information for the elements making up the SDW. The elaborated procedure aims precisely discrimination of the fields of objects and to keep only those that meet these criteria.

- *Stability:*

The SDW concentrates stable and nonvolatile data. This supposes data which undergo the least possible updates and modifications. The measurement of stability is ensured by installation of a flag for each entity in GIS database, and counting the number of updates with date of the last update over one given period (3 months, 6 months, or a year). A standardized classification is operated on the entities to calculate rate of update. The rate of update reflects for us the variability of information and its temporal stability. Consider the case of the entity distribution cabinet (Figure 7).

Fields, like daily consumption, agent code and electric charge are volatile entities when variability is daily. They cannot claim to integrate the SDW.

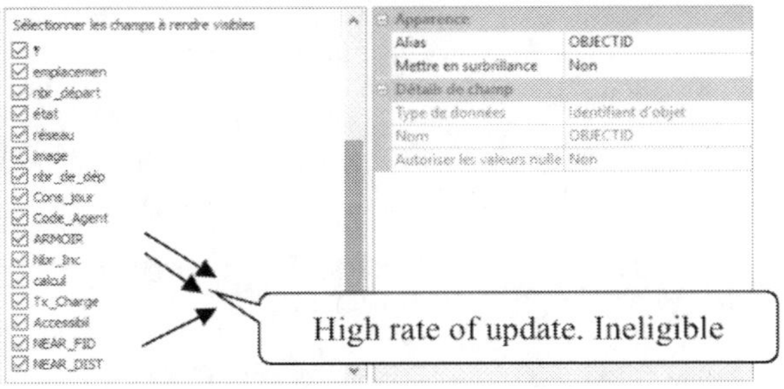

Figure 7. Energy Distribution cabinets

Below, we present the procedure for the calculation of functional stability.

```
Procedure Stability
Begin
    Fmj [] : intger Variable = number of update
    Tmj[] : Normalized rate of update
    Candidate : logical variable
    /* Calculation the number of update
    For each coverage of entity
        do
            For each entity Ei of the coverage in
        the period time
                do
                If Update
                    then
                        Fmj[Ei]=Fmj[Ei]
                +1
                        Stamp the date
                Endif
                End
        End
    /* Calculation of the stability of the update rate
    For each coverage of information do
        For each entity Ei of the referenced coverage
        do  Calculate Tmj[Ei]
          if Tmj[Ei] < critical value
           then Candidate = "true" /* field eéligible for
    SDW
            Else
              Candidate ="false" /* Non éligible, à
        exclure
          Endif
          End
```

With the execution of this operation, we will have eligible information and other non-eligible ones to join the SDW. For the user, non-eligible fields will not be displayed. He will have leisure to choose among eligible components those which he decides to put in SDW.

- *Spatial Relevance:*

The objective of this property is to identify among all the information eligible for the SDW, those that will be relevant for future spatial analysis. It is a very complex operation. Indeed, the component that does not influence a phenomenon today; can be preponderant in its variability in the future. It is developed to determine the potential correlations existing between objects. Generally it is the result of analysis that can lead to suspect the effect of component on the phenomenon. Our approach focuses initially only on the spatial relations. The spatial junctions like crossing type, connection, proximity and inclusion are detected and their significant advent is assessed. If the relationship is robust, then the entity is judged able to integrate with SDW.

This procedure is dynamic in our choice. Inclusion or exclusion in SDW is not fixed. The user is given the opportunity to reintegrate into the SDW a component that may fail in the Relevance procedure. This is generally observed when execution of SOLAP does not lead to significant results.

```
Procedure Spatial Relevance
Objects = {Set of the stable objects}
Begin
        For each entity Ei ∈ Objects
            Do
            Compute spatial relationship in Objects
            If ∃ relation robuste
                Then
                    Accept for SDW
            Endif
            End
End
```

- *Space Coherence:*

We understand by space coherence an expression of the reality compared to its space modeling. It means determination geometrical and semantic and spatial constraints of objects. If an object is regarded as a zone, we must make sure that it is well represented by a closed polygon generating a surface, a boundary, an interior and an outside. For a linear object, it will not contain a priori surface but only one length, as well as the point object which will not derive other information except its position.

```
Procedure Space Coherence
Objects = {Set of stable and relevant objects}
Begin
        For each Object Oi ∈ Objetcs
         do /* Geometric and topologic constraint
                Case : point
                Verift (position)
                Case : linear
                Verify (Length, non-overlap)
                Case : surface
                Verify  (surface, non-degenerative)

                End
                End
End
```

E. SDW Generating:

The procedures established above make it possible to purify the data coming from database and to keep only those that will feed the SDW. Since we have opted for a GIS-predominant solution, we will assimilate the SDW to a particular geodatabase that will be injected into GIS tool.

F. SOLAP Operations: Definition:

There is a panoply of OLAP operations allowing Data mining. We can gather them in two groups [10]:

1. Operators of drilling:
   - Aggregation (or Roll-Up): this operation concerns calculation for one or more dimensions. It makes it possible to climb in hierarchies by incorporating measurements.
   - To drill (or Roll-down or drill-Down): drill-down is operation of zoom down. It makes it possible to obtain information on a level of finer detail by disaggregating measurements.
2. Slice operators:
   - Slicing: A slice is a section or a subset of a multidimensional array. It allows you to focus on a particular area of event.
   - Dicing: dice is the selection of certain values of dimension. It makes it possible to restrict dimension of the hypercube.
   - Rotating: this operation makes it possible to change orientation of the cube, for example by inter-changing rows and columns of result.

In case of SOLAP, these same operations will require, in addition to informational search, a cartographic representation showing the result. It is the transcription of this action into the GIS functionality that determines the specificity of the SOLAP tool.

IV. Experimentation

A. Data mining and diagnosis of publicl lighting:

A first aggregation operation shows that the mapping of the number of incidents per district over a period of one quarter, displays a certain disparity between certain districts deemed stable and others very disturbed. The districts "Hai Hamri" and "Hai Ghoualem" are considered to be very degraded (over 80 incidents). The maintenance budgets are precisely calculated on incident thresholds and distributed equitably between districts of the same class (Figure 8).

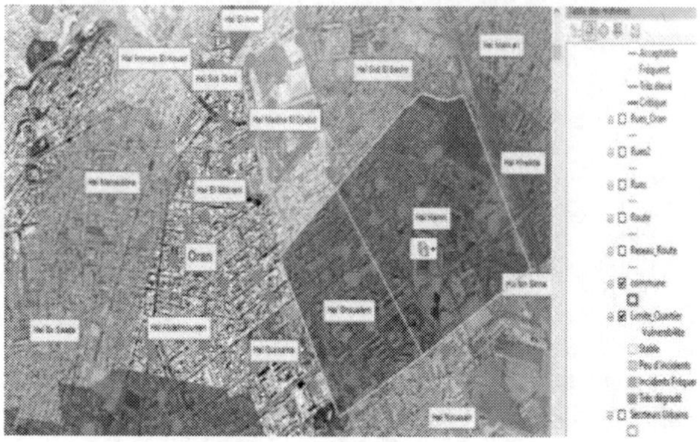

Figure 8. Mapping the districts by incidents number

At the executing of our application SOLAP, we can see that in the "Hai Hamri" district, only two cabinets are problematic with a high frequency of incidents (Figure 9) [8]. The other cabinets are relatively stable. Conversely, district "Hai Ghoualem" is degraded. The majority of its distribution cabinets have frequent incidents (Figure 10).

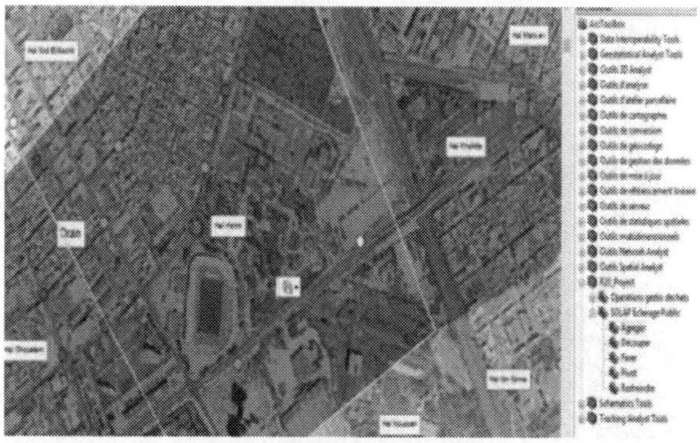

Figure 9. Situation of cabinet of district Hai Hamri

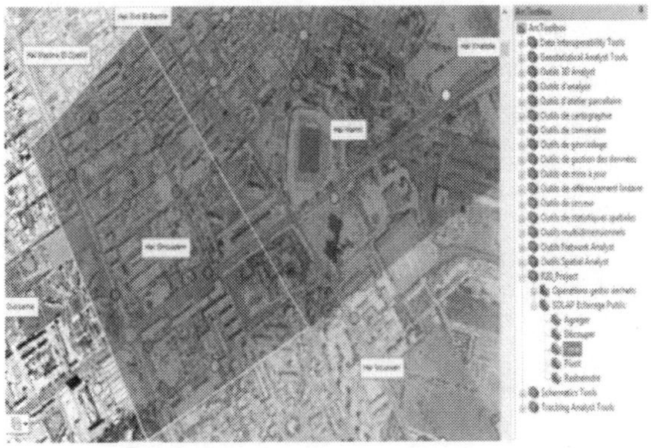

Figure 10. Situation cabinet of Hai Ghoualem

This shows that classification of districts, performed by usual functionalities of GIS is erroneous, and suffers from inaccuracy in actual diagnosis of the state of the lighting. This observation cannot be detected by classical tools of spatial analysis. The advantage of SOLAP is that it can navigate through archived data in several dimensions and views, to arrive at non-obvious findings by deterministic analysis.

B. Synthesis:

Visualization of the results of Data mining of public lighting showed the limits of diagnoses already stopped by the company in charge of the network. The exploitation of observations carried out by operations of SOLAP tool makes it possible to contribute effectively to a precise and rational management of network and especially to refine and better specify the different decisions.

V. CONCLUSION

The contribution of spatial Data mining like a technique, like a discipline and especially like a methodology, confers a better apprehension of phenomena having an anchoring on territory. Deductive inductions resulting from their procedure often inform about states and trends, unsuspected and not detected by usual techniques of space analysis, too restrictive and too deterministic.

The SOLAP approach developed in this experiment highlighted a true and capital knowledge for effective management of a lighting network. The notable fact is that this tool is quickly adopted by the persons responsible for management of public lighting, due to the fact that it does not require any special prerequisites for its use or significant training. With the contribution of other information characterizing the territory, the SDW can produce an informational base even more useful for the Data mining process.

IV. REFERENCES

[1] Y. Bédard, S. Larrivée, M. J. Proulx, P. Y. Caron, F. Létourneau, "Geospatial Datawarehousing: Positionnement technologique et stratégique," Rapport préparé pour le Centre de recherche de la défense de Valcartier, Université Laval, 79 pp. 1997. [in English: Geospatial Datawarehousing: Technological and strategic positioning". Report for the Research center of Defense of Valcartier, Laval University]

[2] Y. Bedard, S. Rivest, M. J. Proulx, "Spatial On-Line Analytical Processing (SOLAP): Concepts, Architectures and Solutions from a Geomatics Engineering Perspective", Robert Wrembel & Christian Koncilia (ed(s)), Data Warehouses and OLAP : Concepts, Architectures and Solutions,Chap.13, IBM Press-Idea Group, 2007.

[3] Y. Bédard, 2010, "Le géodécisionnel: origine, évolution, état de l'art, enjeux, R&D", École Nationale Supérieure des Mines de Paris– Centre de recherche sur les Risques et les Crises [in English: "The Geodecisonal: origin, evolution, state of the art, stakes, Research & Development", National School of Mines of Paris, Research Center on Risks and Crisis], Sophia-Antipolis, France, Octobre 2010.

[4] S. Bimonte, M. Bertolotto, J. Gensel, O. Boussaid, "Spatial OLAP and Map Generalization: Model and Algebra.", IJDWM, 2012 .

[5] C. Franklin, "An Introduction to Geographic Information Systems: Linking Maps to Databases", Database, April 1992, pp. 13-21.

[6] J. Han, M. Kamber, "Data Mining: Concepts and Techniques", Morgan Kaufmann Publisher, Inc, 2001.

[7] W. H. Inmon, "Building the Data Warehouse", Jon Wiley and Sons Editions, ISBN: 0471569607, 1st edition 1992.

[8] C. T. Lu, X. Tan, S. Chawla, S. Shekhar, R. R. Vatsavai, "MapCub: A visualisation tool for spatial Data Warehouses", Geographic Data Mining and Knowledge Discovery, London: Taylor and Francis, 2000.

[9] "Le Géodécisionnel, Les SIG au service du géodécisionnel". Projet Bibliographique dans le cadre du Mastère ASIG, Ecole Nationale des Sciences Géodésiques. [in English: "The GeoDecisional, GIS to serve geodecisional", Bibliographic Project as part of the Master ASIG, National School of Geodesic Science]. France 2008.

[10] M. D. Van Damme, "Entrepôts de données dans le domaine spatial pour l'inventaire forestier", Conservatoire National des Arts et Métiers Cnam – Région Centre. Centre d'Enseignement Principal d'Orléans. ["Spatial datawarehouse for forest inventory", Thesis for a diploma of Cnam engineer degree. Central Region. Center of Main education of Orleans]. Sept. 2010.

Cultural Metro in Rome

A Sustainable Transportation Example Extending Public Transportation System in Rome

Michele Angelaccio, Lucia Zappitelli

Department of Enterprise Engineering
Smartourism Lab
University of Rome Tor Vergata
Rome, Italy
Email: angelaccio@dii.uniroma2.it, lucia.zappitelli@gmail.com

Abstract—**This work introduces a georeferenced model that aims to yield a sustainable transport system located in a part of the city of Rome. This is achieved by considering two urban walks as transport lines connecting existing metro stops in order to improve the transportation system in a sustainable way, thus reducing vehicular traffic. In addition, the proposed solution is designed according to a cultural heritage perspective in the sense that the paths introduced have been defined by following ancient Roman roads leading us to call them *Metro Cultural Heritage (Metro-CH) paths*. As an additional result, we obtain the advantage to improve the touristic flow and social life in the suburbs that now are poorly exploited areas compared with the heart of Rome. From the overview map definition, we derive a geo based mobile application system used to implement a local Web mobile application system tailored for the Metro-CH without any additional infrastructure. As discussion, we show how the solution is in line with the principles of European Convention of Faro for the Cultural Heritage and with the national Italian guidelines of historical paths.**

Keywords–Cultural Heritage; Sustainable Mobility; Map Integration.

I. INTRODUCTION

Sustainability is requiring a strong revision of technologies and studies related to the improvement of the quality of urban life. This is especially true for those urban areas rich in cultural heritage sites, but having poor quality of life, like the suburbs of Rome. In this case, a possible strategy to remedy the situation could be to consider a new form of smart tourism which can lead to a sustainable economic and social improvement [3]. In particular, in this paper we introduce a georeferenced sustainable mobility model that integrates existing natural paths and urban paths revisited in accordance to slow cultural tourism patterns. This mobility model has been used in order to follow old roman roads, such as the one close to the famous ancient Via Appia, thus connecting in a safe way the railway metro stations by walking there. The description is obtained by deriving a virtual map from the existing railway map through a virtual extraction of such ancient roads after a preliminary walking study and Web map annotation. The final characterization is strongly based on cultural heritage preservation in the sense that it is inspired by literary works of the famous writers Goethe and Gregorovius. Moreover, the model could be applied to other transportation systems such as local trains providing connections to other touristic areas close to Rome.

A. Dynamic Revision of Cultural Heritage

From a general point of view, the main purpose of the proposed Cultural Metro is strongly related to the principles of European Faro Convention established in 2005 on the value of Cultural Heritage for the Society. Starting from the principle of Cultural Heritage as a set of resources inherited from the past upon which values and knowledge are expressed by the help of people living close to it (Art. 2 of the Faro Convention), we think that there is the need to propagate such a cultural asset to subsequent generations in order to guarantee a good evolution. This will be accomplished by enriching its knowledge and studying its value (Artt. 4 and 5 of Faro Convention in [7]).

B. On the Sustainable Cultural Tourism

Improving new type of tourism in a sustainable way is a key factor for increasing the knowledge not only for historical monuments but also for all facts and issues related to living styles and traditions which are very rich in interpretations and with new aspects to be transmitted to future generations.

In particular, the increasing interest for slow tourism gives the chance to have a better interaction with hidden monuments and local traditions. Hence, our purpose is to combine slow tourism with existing public transport system by highlighting the ancient roads with their monuments nearby. It is important to note that this approach is effective because all roads are safe for walking and they respect the guidelines of Italian walking paths introduced at national level [9].

II. CULTURAL METRO DESCRIPTION

The southern suburbs of Rome contain several walking tours of particular interest from a historical point of view which offer a strong potential in terms of slow tourism. With respect to the hearth of Rome often plenty of cars and people moving in a pletora of shops, museums etc., the suburbs offer a different perspective with many hidden interesting places. Our model aims therefore to cope with such issues trying to optimize public transport and to contribute to hidden cultural values extraction (see the integration schema proposed in Figure 1).

The interested area has been outlined on the Official Rome Transport Map as shown in Figure 2.

It corresponds to the south-east part of the city in which there are two main subway lines A and C with their starting stations.

Figure 2 gives the resulting integration schema with green lines evidencing the Cultural Metro lines (a sort of urban cultural trekking paths).

Figure 3 shows in a more focused way, by means of typical transport icons and graphical elements, how this concept is used to optimize the transportation system in a sustainable way.

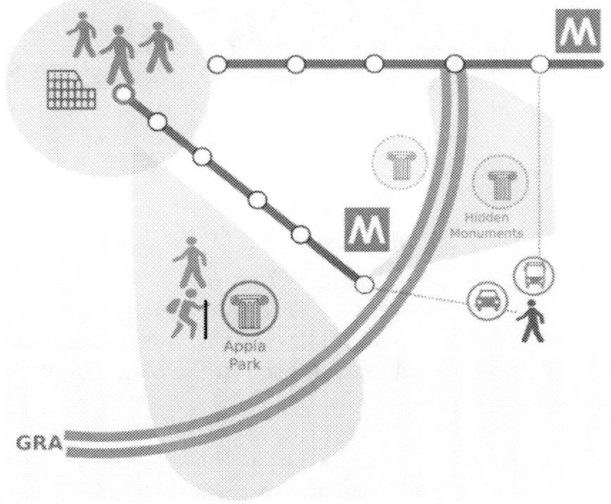

Figure 1. Cultural Metro Introduction Schema

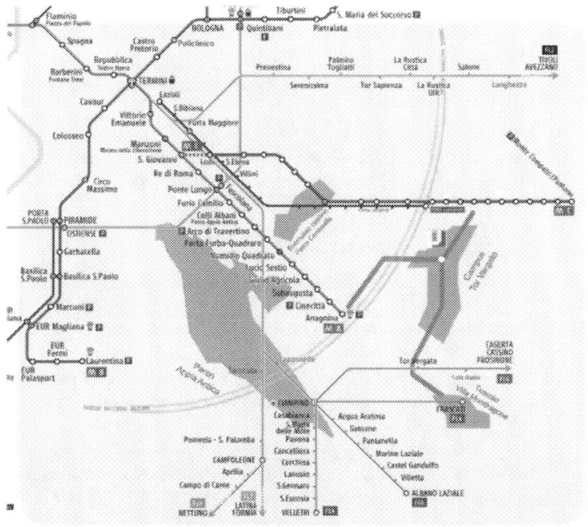

Figure 2. The Metro Map of Rome with the green areas related to Cultural Metro proposal

These pathways are organized by selecting ancient paths close to *old Appia roman* street located to north-east of the Appia itself. They are named Goethe line and Gregorovius line respectively, in accordance to cultural heritage concept because, in the XIX century, they were extensively used by such famous writers. In fact, in the past they themselves have traveled the routes checking in person and recording in their studies / diaries what was catching their attention. In this way the proposed Cultural Metro system might be considered a way to preserve cultural heritage by handing down to posterity

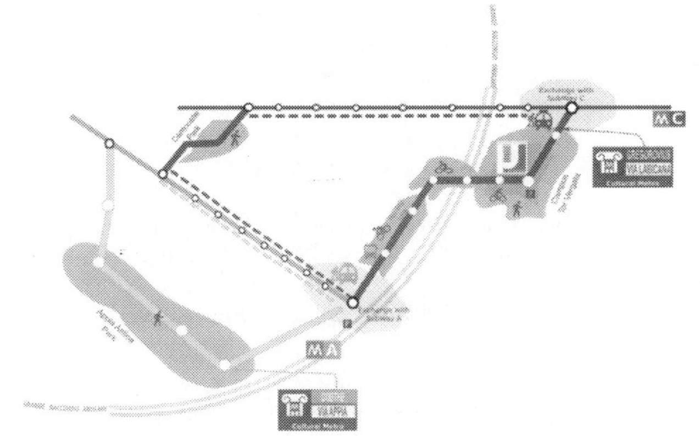

Figure 3. Focus with graphical symbols and sustainable paths integrated with railway metro lines

[Was du erebt von deinen Vatern hast,erwirb es, um es zu besitzen!. . . (What you have inherited from your fathers, get it to own it!) (Goethe-Faust)].

- Goethe Line for the pathway along Appia and old Latina road towards Tuscolo Area.
- Gregorovius Line for the pathway corresponding to Labicana road close to Prenestina road.

The proposed general schema for the Cultural Metro might be organized by considering as terminus of the subway lines the Tor Vergata Campus (Figure 3). All of these lines allow to reach Metro lines A and C of the Rome Metro Railway system.

Each line of the Cultural Metro is a walking pathway designed in the area surrounding the Campus of University of Rome Tor Vergata. The Gregorovius Line has been associated to the old Labicana roman road while the Goethe line corresponds to eastern roman road such as via Appia and via Latina. In this way, such walking paths are very interesting from an historical point of view, providing a nice experience from the people.

A. Map Building Activity Description

From the Metro description, we can see that the map definition could be obtained by deriving the walking routes in a standard format for each path and adding to them the occurring annotations (building information and monuments, next stop station close to the current position, etc). The adopted map building strategy is defined as follows:

1) Starting from the campus and walking towards metro C in a way similar to the walking routes from Goethe and Gregorovius travel books, we have marked points of interest on the map with the purpose to use them also as reference poinst like metro stations, leading to a virtual metro line composed of a sequence of cultural metro stops placed at regular intervals between the starting point and railway Metro C (Gregorovius Line).
2) Again, after starting from Via Appia Park close to metro A (Villa dei Quintili), we executed another traced route by walking towards the Metro A and by following ancient monuments like Acquedotto

Claudio and ancient roads connecting Romana Appia to other roads to the North (Goethe line).

3) Hereafter, GPS (Global Positioning System) routes and monuments informations have been included on digital maps downloaded from Open Street Map website (www.openstreetmap.org). Green areas extracted by OSM (Open Street Map) map in form of shapes have been checked and compared with GPS tracks in order to guarantee that there is a good chance to obtaining a well sustainable complete walking path.

B. Description of Pedestrian Walking System in Cultural Metro

The map shows that every line is defined as a sequence of small walking paths (each of them long from 10 to 100 meters), without any slope and easy to be crossed due to presence of sidewalks on all busy roads. In addition, the presence of a public bus on the campus might be used to replace some walking paths.

III. A Light Mobile Information System for Cultural Metro

In order to optimize the cultural value of the proposed Cultural Metro, it is important to introduce a mobile application system that could be used to help people while walking in Cultural Metro, thus leading to a particular innovative *cultural navigational digital system*. The main advantage of considering walking paths as a metro line for walking people is the fact that its implementation requires only that each path must be available for pedestrians and does not require external infrastructure except for an adequate infosystem able to show what are the nearest stop and physical route towards the next stop. Figure 4 shows an example of Mobile Application View with Augmentity Reality (AR) Interface (called MetroGO) to navigate towards subway metro stop of Line A.

The main idea is to consider that visual annotations on the screen can be used not only for explaining old monuments, but also for helping to move towards next metro station.

It is important to note that the AR solution provided by MetroGO APP is more sustainable with respect to other solutions based on localization devices (or tags/beacons) in the sense that environment is respected and there is no need to make use of additional things or hardware often considered for intercepting monuments and helping to find direction. For instance in the works [1] and [2] it has been introduced a geo tag based info model named **Street Web** characterized by local wifi internet able to support mobile smartphones of visitors in a context based navigation useful in places rich of monuments and for which is hard to obtain the same result through 4G connections. Hence this work can be considered a new way to make use of AR for cultural navigational system and it is first example of this type to our knowledge.

IV. Conclusions

Improving the quality of urban life in Art cities like Rome according to Smart City paradigm, requires a careful design to avoid dangerous effects (traffic congestion and pollution). Moreover the need to involve citizen must be kept onto account especially in the case of Art Cities. A sustainable approach is to consider Human Smart City in which cultural areas hidden to citizen can be reused in terms of smart tourism and slow tourism. In this work we showed a preliminary example designed with the aim to reach a tourism-based slow transportation system enforcing the emerging styles of slow tourism for which touristic walking tours close to big cities must be re-discovered and used in the planning systems of the urban future.

Figure 4. MetroGO APP with AR of cultural types

References

[1] M. Angelaccio, "Street Web A Framework for -Web on the Road - Smart Services", Proceedings of the 12th International Conference on Web Information Systems and Technologies, WEBIST, Volume 1, Rome, Italy, April 23-25, 2016. SciTePress, ISBN 978-989-758-186-1

[2] M. Angelaccio, B. Buttarazzi and C. Gnessi, "Smart Mobility and Cultural Tourism: The Termini-Centocelle Train Museum, an Example of Smartourism Project in Rome", IARIA SMART, June 25, 2017 to June 29, 2017, pages: 44 to 48, Venice, (Italy)

[3] M. Angelaccio, L. Zappitelli, "Social Smartourism" Journal of Tourism, June 25-27 2016, Athens, (Greece)

[4] J. Y. Kim , J. Y. Lee, "Development of Local Cultural Resources Based on the Concept of Ecomuseum, Focusing on Cheorwon, Gangwon Province", International Journal of Multimedia and Ubiquitous Engineering, Vol.8, No.5 (2013), pp.297-302

[5] N. Viswanadham, S. Kameshwaran,"Ecosystem Aware Global Supply Chain Management", World Scientific 2013

[6] Dr.P.D. SireeshaKumari, Mosalikanti.Subha Lakshmi, "Internet of Things (IoT) gateway to smart villages", International Journal of Innovative Research in Advanced Engineering (IJIRAE) ISSN: 2349-2763, Issue 12, Volume 3 December 2016

[7] "Convenzione Quadro del Consiglio Europeo 27 Febbraio, 2013 (European Convention)". http://conventions.coe.int/Treaty/EN/Treaties/Html/199.htm

[8] "Internet of Things: Converging Technology for Smart Environments and Integrated Ecosystems", (River Publishers series in Information Science and Technology), Editors Ovidiu Vermesan and Peter Fries, June 2013

[9] "Atlante dei Cammini d'Italia", ("Italian Historical PathWays Atlas") http://www.turismo.beniculturali.it/home-cammini-ditalia/atlante-dei-cammini-ditalia/ [accessed March 2018]

Analyzing Spatio-Temporal Effects of Social-Economic Factors on Crime

Sebastian Baumbach
German Research Center for Artificial Intelligence (DFKI)
Technische Universität Kaiserslautern
Kaiserslautern, German
Email: sebastian.baumbach@dfki.de

Nikita Sharm
Technische Universität Kaiserslautern
Kaiserslautern, German
Email: nikita.sharma1108@gmail.com

Sheraz Ahmed
German Research Center for Artificial Intelligence (DFKI)
Kaiserslautern, German
Email: sheraz.ahmed@dfki.de

Andreas Dengel
German Research Center for Artificial Intelligence (DFKI)
Technische Universität Kaiserslautern
Kaiserslautern, German
Email:andreas.dengel@dfki.de

***Abstract*—Rampant increase in crime incidents has led to the need of crime analysis in greater detail. Existing crime analysis approaches focused on higher spatial granularity (i.e., country or state levels) and consider each data observation independent of each other. However, data can exhibit spatial and temporal relationships among them. Such interrelationships must be taken into consideration if precise crime analysis is intended. Therefore, a two-stage approach is proposed for predicting crime by analyzing its relationship with socio-economic factors: the first stage applies a spatio-temporal analysis on the data and these results are utilized for the spatio-temporal prediction, which forms the second stage. For evaluation, more than 450 different socio-economic factors and crime data for county level in Germany were analyzed. The evaluation results exhibit a mean absolute percentage error of 6.79% for spatio-temporal crime predictions, outperforming traditional regression techniques with an error rate of 37.1% - 37.8%.**

Keywords–Staptio-temporal Data Mining; Crime Analysis; Prediction Models; Location Factors;

I. Introduction

Crime has been a recurrent activity since the beginning of society evolution. Crime incidents can be traced to as early as imperial era in history. As McCollister et al. stated in their work [1], such incidents have been a deterrent to social harmony and have affected the development of communities. The authors specified the effects of crime in society in terms of economic development, as well as society integration and suggest effective measures for government policies to reduce criminal activities.

A detailed insight on crime is required as concluded in [1], as it can benefit the inland security services for effective police force deployment. Cunningham et al. [2] described that crime analysis is necessary to provide better law enforcement in a region and maintain integrity as well as peaceful environment of the society. Crime analysis assists surveillance forces to make preemptive decisions and hence, ensures better vigilance and control of a crisis situation [1] [2].

Consequently, crime analysis is an active research field. There are numerous studies like [3] [4] that explored social media data (e.g., from Twitter) to predict crime. These works conducted sentiment analysis on Twitter posts collected to predict crime at a specific location. There is a wide range of works studying effect of social-economic factors on crime [5] [6]. For instance, Chainey et al. [7] assessed the relationship between crime and social-economic factors at the state level in the USA. Similarly, Entorf and Spengler [8] analyzed the effects of social-economic data on crime at state level in Germany. Caruso and Schneider conducted a similar analysis in their work [9] by focusing on crime trends at a higher geographical level, i.e., comparing crime trends between different European countries.

All the above-mentioned work focused either on higher spatial granularity (e.g., [9]) or on data content, such as analysis of social media data for sentiment detection (e.g., [4]). None of these studies focused on the detailed relationship of crime and its influencing factors at lower spatial and temporal granularity. Neither of these researchers assessed the interrelationship that exists in crime data.

Referring to the problem stated for the existing approaches, there arises the need for analyzing crime data on a deeper spatial and temporal granularity. Additionally, there is the *First Law Of Geography* by Walder Tobler' which says "*everything is related to everything else, but near things are more related than distant things*" [10]. Thus, the proposed two-stage approach utilizes spatial and temporal data correlations to predict crime intensity and applies it at lower spatio-temporal granularity. The first stage, spatio-temporal analysis, focuses on validating the existence of spatio-temporal relationships in data and allows for the selection of the best feature subset for crime prediction. The second stage, spatio-temporal prediction, exploits the spatio-temporal proximity in data and predicts crime rate by utilizing spatio-temporal prediction models. The evaluation was carried out on a county level collection of social-economic factors and crime data.

Summarizing, the main contributions of this paper are defined as follows: i) a spatio-temporal analysis approach that gives a detailed insight into crime and social-economic data trends in space and time domain, ii) a significant improvement of 32% in crime prediction over existing regression approaches by utilizing spatio-temporal prediction, and iii) a spatio-temporal prediction approach, which can predict crime at county level in Germany. Consequently, spatio-temporal relations in a dataset decrease the error rate in crime prediction and enhance the performance of existing prediction models.

The rest of this paper is organized as follows. Section II summarizes and assesses the state-of-the-art in crime data analysis by focusing on the explored data sources, as well as utilized methodologies. Section III presents the proposed approach for analyzing crime with a high spatio-temporal granularity. Section IV depicts the applied crime dataset together with the socio-economic location factors, which are used in this paper for evaluating the proposed approach. Section V presents the findings of this paper, stating that spatio-temporal data interactions increase the prediction capability for crime analysis. Finally, Section VI discusses and summarizes the results.

II. Related Work

In the scientific community, there is a vast range of work on crime analysis. The existing approaches focused on enhancing traditional regression techniques or deep learning for crime analysis and prediction. Their authors focused on tuning these models based on crime relationship with influencing factors, such as Twitter data, social-economic factors, or background data of criminals. However, each observation in these datasets is considered as independent, i.e., these approaches consider no relation to be existing between individual records in the dataset.

A. Exploring Data Sources for Crime Analysis

Data sources, such as social media, criminal records, or ideological beliefs of listed terrorist organizations, were explored in various studies to gain detailed insights into crime trends. Acquiring social media data with a high spatial granularity is difficult as geo-referenced social media content is hardly available [11]. Furthermore, analyses of crime with social media data, criminal data, and their ideological beliefs are based on subjective analysis. The sentiments respective the intentions of people are evaluated based on a list of words termed as 'hate' words. These approaches do not necessarily amount to crime intentions.

1) Social Media Content: Wang et al. [3] applied semantic analysis and natural language processing on Twitter data to find topics of discussion on social media. The authors proved that these topics can be indicators of future crime incidents by analyzing previous crime incidents and the topics of discussion on social media at their time of occurrence. Gerber [4] used a Twitter-specific linguistic analysis and a statistical topic modeling to automatically identify discussion topics across a major city in the United States. Other studies [12] [13] focused on determining the general population's sentiment in a certain regions by conducting sentiment analysis on microblogging sites like Twitter.

2) Social-Economic Data: Caruso and Schneider [9] performed an empirical evaluation on social-economic determinants of crime. Their work was based around the hypothesis stating that social-economic factors (such as population, migration, and poverty) determine factors of crime. Edmark [5] explored the relation between unemployment and crime using regression methods. Freytag et al. [6] applied regression techniques to conclude whether social-economic factors have an impact on crime. Entorf and Spengler [8] utilized panel regression on social-economic and crime data to predict crime incidents at state level in Germany.

3) Crime Data and Criminal Beliefs: There exists a number of researches that explored past records of criminals and their ideological beliefs to analyze crime. Martinez et al. [14] assessed the relationships between past actions of criminals and their associated behavior. This relationship was utilized to predict actions based on the current observed behavior of criminals. Sampson and Groves [15] measured the society integration, i.e., how well people are connected and integrated in a community. The authors explored the direct relationship of social integrity with the number of crime incidents as listed by the Federal Bureau of Investigation, USA.

B. Methodologies of Crime Analysis

Traditional regression techniques and neural networks are based on a frequentist approach and rely on a large data sample to train, learn and estimate crime incidents. Thus, Bayesian approaches have their advantages over neural network and other probability based regression techniques (frequentist approach) when it comes to the analysis of (spare) crime datasets. Bayesian approaches add a degree of uncertainty to the prediction methods and thus, emulate a real world situations closely compared to the frequentist approach.

1) Regression Techniques: A range of work on crime prediction is based on regression analysis. Edmark [5] performed a panel regression on data from Swedish counties over the time period 1988 - 1999. The author focused on analyzing the impact of unemployment on crime. Entorf and Spengler [8] utilized logarithmic panel regression on demographic and economic data of German states to predict crime. Caruso and Schneider [9] applied a negative binomial regression on social-economic panel data of western European countries. Freytag et al. [6] applied the same approach on data of 110 countries to test the hypothesis that poor socio-economic development leads to rise in terrorism.

2) Neural Network Techniques: A large section of studies in the research community analyzed crime with neural network techniques. Olligschlaeger [16] incorporated the predictions with neural networks by using a geographical information system to forecast the emergence of drug hot-spot areas. The input data are the number of distress calls made to security department in a certain region which were fed to a pre-trained neural network to predict crime prone areas. Caulkins [17] compared the performance of neural network based approaches over statistical methods for crime analysis. The dataset used is an information set about offenders and criminals that includes their imprisonment terms, level of punishments, number of crimes committed. Palocsay et al. [18] researched on neural network approaches to locate recidivists from a dataset of criminals and listed offenders.

C. Spatial Temporal Analysis

A vast range of work on crime analysis applied visual exploration approaches to understand crime patterns and used the derived information to predict crime occurrences. Cheong and Lee [13] performed visual analysis of Twitter data to generate insights on how Twitter data could be a facilitator of crime. Nakaya and Yano [19] conducted an exploratory analysis of crime to facilitate the visualization of the geographical extent and duration of crime clusters.

Wang and Brown [20] proposed the Spatio-Temporal Generalized Additive Model (S-T GAM) to discover the underlying factors related to crime and predict future crime incidents. Wang et al. [20] extended the S-T GAM approach by adding Twitter analysis and concluded that the additive Twitter analysis enhance the predictive performance of S-T GAM.

Other research works emphasized that it is important to find external factors that facilitated the varying spatial or temporal crime patterns. Ivaha et al. [21] devised a crime prediction model that incorporated the effects of weather conditions on changing crime patterns in space and time. Townsley et al. [22] focused on discovering space and time dependencies with crime. The authors investigated the relation between crime incidents that have spatial and temporal proximity. They concluded that the existing proximity relationship between crime data can be used to forecast future crime locations and time of occurrence.

III. Proposed Approach for Crime Analysis

To perform crime analysis with a high spatio-temporal granularity, the proposed approach consists of two sub-processes: Spatio-Temporal Analysis and Spatio-Temporal Prediction. Figure 1 presents the workflow of the proposed approach.

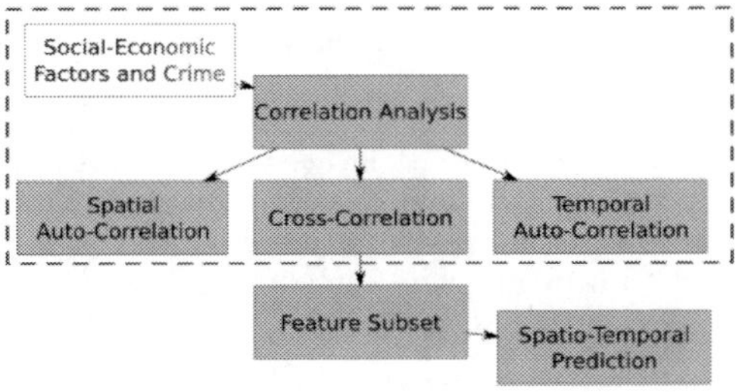

Figure 1. Workflow for proposed approach.

A. *Correlation Analysis*

The first stage is the spatial and temporal data analysis, for which the spatial, temporal, and cross-correlations are discussed.

1) Spatial Auto-correlaion Analysis: Spatial auto-correlation is an analysis process that measures the association of a variable with itself along the spatial dimension. There exists a number of statistical measures that can be computed for spatial analysis. Moran's I was chosen for this work [23]. The statistical measures for spatial analysis are based on a spatial weight matrix that defines the intensity of the distance relationship among observations (crime data) in a geographical space. The Moran's I ranges from -1 to $+1$ depending on whether the observations are spatially dispersed or clustered.

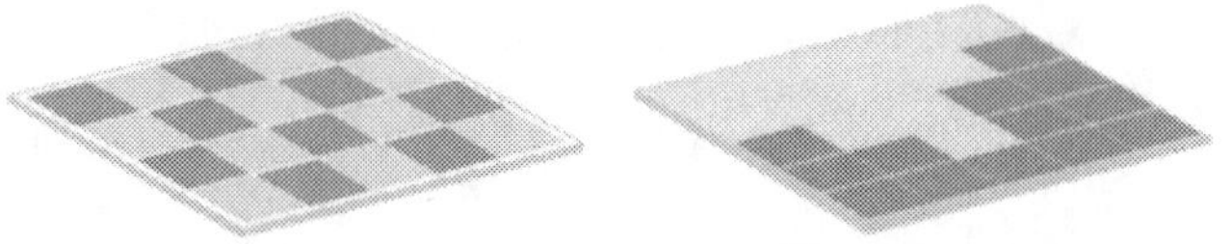

(a) Negative Auto-correlation. (b) Positive Auto-correlation.

Figure 2. Example of observations with Spatial Autocorrelation.

Figure 2a displays an example of observations with negative spatial auto-correlation. In this case, Moran's I is close to -1 for such values because geographically nearby locations exhibit negative relationship, i.e., they are dispersed and do not form a cluster. Similarly positive auto-correlation is depicted in Figure 2b, where data from geographically close locations form a cluster. In general, an observation dataset with Moran's I close to $+1$ indicates a positive auto-correlation. Moran's I with a value 0 indicates no spatial auto-correlation.

2) Temporal Auto-correlation Analysis: Temporal auto-correlation is a measure of how data at one timepoint is related to data at other timepoints. Figure 3 explains the temporal auto-correlation plot for the social-economic factor "Migration data". The plot depicts how migration data are related to itself at time lags of $0, 1, 2, 3$, and 4. There is a positive correlation at lag 1, i.e., the relation between migration data at consecutive timepoints is a positive slope. The blue dashed line denotes the significant level of correlation. Correlation at any lag that is intersecting this line is defined to be a significant auto-correlation at this lag. The lag with a positive temporal auto-correlation is used in spatio-temporal prediction models as an input parameter.

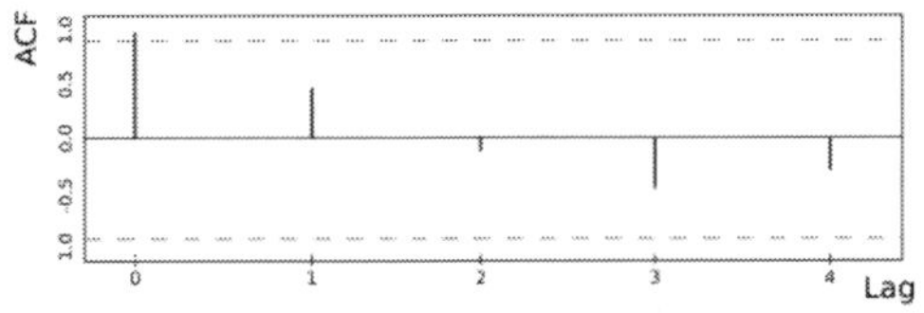

Figure 3. Temporal Auto-correlation for Migration Data Time Series.

3) Cross-Correlation Analysis: Cross-Correlation between two time series is a measure of the lateral effect of one time series over the other. Correlations are calculated between every social-economic factor at timepoint t_{+h} and crime at timepoint t for $h \in \mathbb{N}, h \leq 0$. A negative value for h is a correlation between a social-economic factor at a time before t and the crime variable at time t. When a time series x with h negative are predictors of a time series y at t, it is referred to as x leads y.

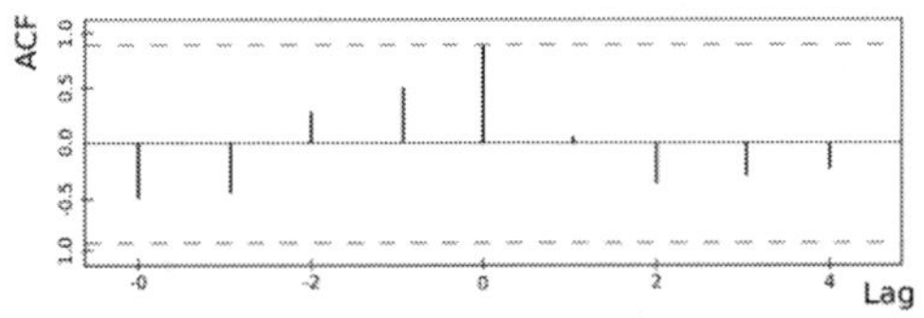

Figure 4. Cross-correlation between Migration and Crime Data Time Series.

Figure 4 depicts an example of cross-correlation between migration data and crime series from the current dataset. At lag -1 and -2, the plot shows a positive cross-correlation. This concludes that at time $t-1$ and $t-2$, migration data can be a positive influence in predicting crime data at time t.

B. *Spatio-Temporal Prediction*

The proposed approach utilizes spatio-temporal models, which can be categorized into general and dynamic models.

1) General Spatio-Temporal Models: General spatio-temporal models are of 3 types, which differs in the choice of distribution for the process stage model.

Gaussian Process Models are defined as follows:

$$Z_t = O_t + \epsilon_t, \quad (1)$$

$$O_t = X_t\beta + \eta_t, \quad (2)$$

where ϵ_t is the independent normally distributed nugget effect or the pure error term at time unit t and η_t denotes the spacial-temporal random effects following an independent normal distribution. Z_t depicts the observed spatio-temporal data while O_t represents the overall random effects. For the p covariates and n number of observations, X_t denotes the $n \times p$ covariate matrix. $\beta = (\beta_1, ...\beta_p)$ denotes the $p \times 1$ vector of regression coefficients.

To perform predictions at location s at time t, the posterior predictive distribution for $Z(s,t)$ is defined as an integration over the parameters with respect to the joint posterior distribution as:

$$\pi(Z(s,t)|z) = \int \pi(Z(s,t)|O_l(s,t), \sigma_\epsilon^2, z) \\ \pi(O(s,t)|\theta)\pi(\theta|z)\partial O(s,t)\partial\theta \quad (3)$$

where $\theta = (\beta, \sigma_\epsilon^2, \phi, \nu)$ denotes all the model parameters.

Auto-Regressive Models are defined as follows:

$$Z_t = O_t + \epsilon_t, \quad (4)$$

$$O_t = \rho O_{t-1} + X_t\beta + \eta_t, \quad (5)$$

where ρ denotes the unknown temporal correlation parameter assumed to be in the interval $(1, 1)$. The initial value for O_0 is assigned a prior distribution with independent spatial model with mean μ and the covariance matrix $\sigma^2 S_0$.

To perform predictions at location s at time t, the posterior predictive distribution for $Z(s,t)$ is defined as an integration over the parameters with respect to the joint posterior distribution as:

$$\pi(Z(s,t)|z) = \int, \pi(Z(s,t)|O_l(s,t), \sigma_\epsilon^2, z) \\ \pi(O(s,t)|\theta, z^*)\pi(\theta, z^*|z)\partial O(s,t)\partial z^*\partial\theta \quad (6)$$

where $\theta = (\beta, \sigma_\epsilon^2, \phi, \nu)$ denotes all the model parameters. z^* refers to the missing data while z refers to the non-missing data [24].

Gaussian Predictive Model introduces random effects $\eta(s,t)$ at a smaller number, m, of locations, called the knots, and then use kriging to predict those random effects at the data and prediction locations. Hence, the basic Gaussian predictive process model can be represented as:

$$Z(s) = \mu(s) + \eta(s) + \epsilon(s), \quad (7)$$

where, Z(s) denotes vector of observed data for a location s at all timepoints, $\mu(s)$ is the mean function at location s. The residuals are represented in two parts: $\eta(s)$ is the spatially correlated error with a distribution of zero mean and stationary Gaussian process. The second part is the $\epsilon(s)$ which is a non-spatial uncorrelated pure error also distributed normally with mean zero and variance $\sigma_\epsilon^2 I$, where I is the identity matrix [24]. The posterior predictive distribution of an unknown location s^* as described in [24] is defined as:

$$\pi(Z(s^*)|z(s)) = \int \pi(Z(s^*)|\theta, z(s))\pi(\theta|z(s))\partial\theta \quad (8)$$

2) Dynamic Spatio-Temporal Models: Bayesian frameworks have the advantage of working with short time series data and can also deal with uncertainties in data by introducing the concept of priors. A detailed explanation of Bayesian modeling can be found in [25]. Bayesian modeling is a statistical inference approach where the Bayes theorem is used to update the probability of unknown variables as more data become known. The Bayesian models involve drawing inference from the posterior distribution of unknown parameters which is proportional to the likelihood of data times a prior knowledge of various model parameters [26], which as can be seen in (9).

$$posterior \propto likelihood \times prior \quad (9)$$

With respect to the crime dataset, Bayesian modeling can be explained as follows: let $x = x_1....x_n$ be the observed social-economic data and $Q = Q_1....Q_p$ be the model parameters with an assumed prior distribution of $\pi(Q)$, the posterior distribution of parameters can be defined as follow:

$$\pi(Q|x) \propto f(x|Q) \times \pi(Q) \quad (10)$$

where $f(x|Q)$ is a likelihood function which determines the probability of observing the data for different values of Q.

Spatial-Temporal processes contain observations in space and time with varying spatial and temporal support and complicated underlying dynamics [27]. Because of the complexity of these processes, hierarchical models are deemed suitable because of their ability to represent joint covariance relationships among process and model parameters into disjoint covariance structures at lower level of the hierarchy model. There are two main variants of Bayesian spatio-temporal process.

General Spatio-Temporal Models are beneficial when data are available across time and space domain. A general spatio-temporal model focuses on spatio-temporal interactions by modeling a joint space-time covariance structure [28]. However, due to high dimensional and complexity of non-linear spatio-temporal behavior, formulating joint covariance structures is highly complicated.

Dynamic Spatio-Temporal Models represent spatio-temporal interactions in a hierarchical framework. The current state of the process is evaluated as a function of previous states [29]. The joint spatio-temporal process Y can be factored into conditional models based on a Markovian assumption. That is,

$$[Y|\theta_t, t = 1, ..., T] = [y_0]\prod_{t=1}^{T}[y_t|y_t - 1, \theta_t] \quad (11)$$

where $y_t = (y(s_1, t), ...y(s_n, t))$ with $y(s_n, t)$ is the process at spatial location s and time t. The conditional distribution $[y_t|y_t - 1, \theta_t]$ depends on a vector of parameters θ_t which govern the dynamics of the spatio-temporal process of interest. Arab et al. gives a detailed explanation of these models in [30].

IV. Dataset

Crime data were obtained from the Federal Criminal Police Office of Germany. The dataset contains the total number of offences for different crime categories per year and location. These data are only publicly available for counties belonging to cities with more than $100,000$ inhabitants. In Germany, there are only a total of 81 sites beyond this population count, which were taken into consideration for this paper. Ultimately, crime data were modeled as a time series for a constant time period from 2009 to 2013.

Furthermore, more than 450 socio-economic location factors were assessed, which are offered by the Federal Statistical Office of Germany. For the evaluation in this paper, 18 social-economic factors were selected based on expert knowledge [6] [8] [9]. These factors include, among others, Gross Domestic Product (GDP), population division, migration population, index of health services, social secured and insured population, literacy level, employment rate, birth and death rate, number of enterprises and businesses, and index of child day care facilities.

V. Evaluation

The conducted evaluation aimed to prove that spatio-temporal data interactions enhance the prediction capability of existing approaches. Thus, a similar comparison approach is followed as described in [31] [32]. The existing models are tested against the given dataset and a comparison is drawn between the error in crime prediction of the proposed approach and existing state-of-the-art approaches.

A. Prediction Evaluation and Ground Truth

The ground truth for this evaluation was generated by two traditional regression models [33]. Ordinary Least Square (OLS) Regression was performed by minimizing the sum of the squares of the differences between observed and predicted values [34]. Panel Regression was calculated over panel data (cross-sectional data across space and time). Table I shows the prediction efficiency of OLS regression and Panel regression on the socio-economic and crime dataset, measured in Mean Absolute Percentage Error (MAPE).

TABLE I. PREDICTION RESULTS FOR GROUND TRUTH MODELS.

	OLS Regression	Panel Regression
MAPE	38%	37.1%

B. Spatio-Temporal Correlation Evaluation

The spatio-temporal analysis' results allowed to reject the null hypothesis, which states that there is no spatial or temporal auto-correlation between observation data and the data spread is random. Hence, spatio-temporal auto-correlation indicates the presence of spatial and temporal interactions and thus, validates the choice for using spatial-temporal models for prediction.

1) Local Spatial Auto-correlation of Crime: Spatial auto-correlation was depicted by visualizing the Local Interactions of Spatial Association (LISA) cluster maps [35]. LISA maps were generated based on the neighborhood weight matrix that represents the relation between locations based on their distance proximity. The spatial association of a region is plotted based on the significance of its Local Moran's I.

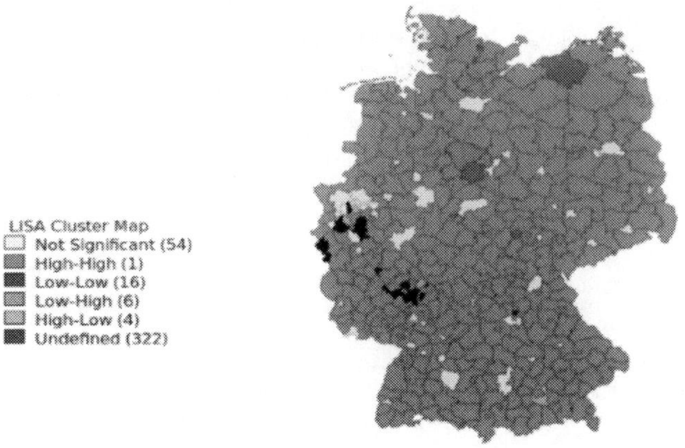

Figure 5. LISA Map for Crime Data of 81 County Sites of Germany.

Figure 5 shows the LISA cluster map for 81 county sites of Germany. The weight matrix is based on a fixed distance band (average distance between two farthest location within the same state). There were 27 such locations with significant spatial clustering. 17 locations depicted a positive spatial correlation and consists of the categories high-high and low-low. Ten regions fell under the category of high-low and low-high and hence, depict a significant negative spatial auto-correlation. For the remaining sites in Germany labeled as "not significant", there were not enough data available to draw conclusions.

2) Temporal Auto-correlation of Crime: Figure 6 shows the temporal auto-correlation in crime data, which is positive at lag 1. Thus, crime occurrence at time $t - 1$ has a positive effect on crime at time t. However, it is below the significant level. The reason for that is most likely that the given time series only have 5 time points. For this research, the lag of 1 for prediction was taken into consideration. However, more data is necessary to eventually clarify this fact.

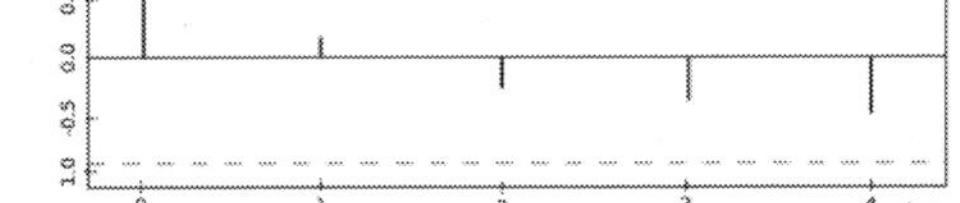

Figure 6. Temporal Auto-correlation Plot for Crime Data of Germany.

3) Cross-Correlation of Crime and Social-Economic Factors: Figure 7 visualizes cross-correlation between the social-economic factor "disposable income" and crime rate in Germany. It depicts the positive correlation between the disposable income of households in Germany and crime rate at the temporal $lag - 1$ and $lag - 2$.

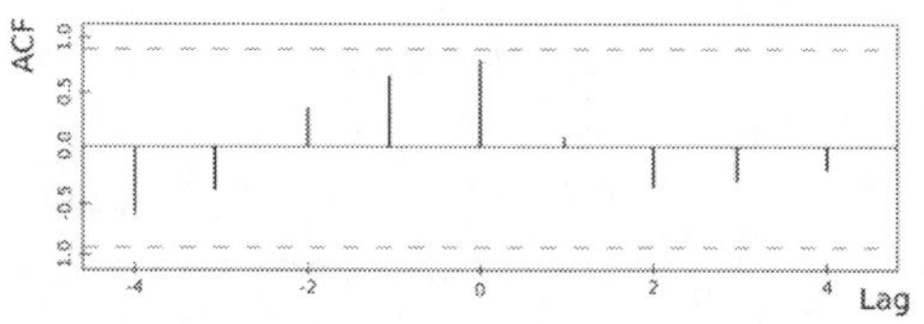

Figure 7. Cross-correlation between Disposable Income and Crime Rate in Germany.

Table II presents the resulting factors selected from a subset of 450 social-economic attributes. These factors have a significant cross-correlation with crime data at various temporal lags. A factor was selected if there was a significant correlation (close to 1 or -1) at lag 0. When there was a weak correlation at lag 0, subsequent cross-correlations at lag -1 and -2 were taken into consideration.

TABLE II. CROSS-CORRELATION BETWEEN SOCIAL-ECONOMIC FACTORS AND CRIME.

Factors	**Lag 0**	**Lag -1**	**Lag -2**	**Lag -3**	**Lag -4**
Migration Data	0.819	0.483	0.252	-0.366	-0.482
Population Data	0.214	-0.425	-0.749	0.420	0.248
Disposable Income	0.741	0.563	0.285	-0.271	-0.580
No. of Employees	0.801	0.596	0.161	-0.388	-0.453
No. of Employer	0.830	0.570	0.131	-0.380	-0.442
No. of Enterprises	-0.058	0.696	0.584	-0.116	-0.586
GDP	0.670	0.554	0.366	0.225	-0.631
No. of Hospital Beds	-0.783	-0.282	-0.358	0.472	0.352
Real Estate Price	0.319	0.469	0.423	0.170	-0.775
Graduate/Dropout Ratio	-0.581	0.134	0.449	0.472	-0.453
No. Social Insured Persons	0.932	0.389	0.048	-0.259	-0.445

C. *Evaluation of General Spatio-Temporal Models*

This section evaluates the crime prediction efficiency of three Gaussian processes and compares it with the ground truth.

Table III shows the result for the Gaussian process model, which produced a MAPE of 36% with the given dataset. Comparing the results with the ground truth, there is not much improvement in the prediction results with Gaussian model.

TABLE III. PREDICTION RESULTS OF GAUSSIAN PROCESS MODEL.

Models	**MAPE**
OLS Regression	38%
Panel Regression	37.1%
Gaussian Process Model	**36%**

Table IV presents the comparison between the ground truth and the Gaussian predictive process model, which gave a MAPE of 37.1%. This model showed a mere improvement of 0.5% over OLS regression. The prediction accuracy was, however, less than for the panel regression and the Gaussian process model.

Table V shows the performance of the auto-regressive model and the comparison with the ground truth. The auto-regressive models produced a MAPE of 28.23%. Comparing the results with the ground truth, auto-regressive models perform better over traditional regression models. Among the spatio-temporal prediction models, auto-regressive models produce the best prediction result.

TABLE IV. PREDICTION RESULTS OF GAUSSIAN PREDICTIVE PROCESS MODEL.

Models	**MAPE**
OLS Regression	38%
Panel Regression	37.1%
Gaussian Predictive Process Model	**37.5%**

TABLE V. PREDICTION RESULTS OF AUTO-REGRESSIVE MODEL.

Models	**MAPE**
OLS Regression	38%
Panel Regression	37.1%
Auto-regressive Model	**28.23%**

D. *Evaluation of Dynamic Spatio-Temporal Models*

Table VI displays the comparison between these models and the ground truth. As a result, the dynamic spatio-temporal model outperforms all other spatio-temporal prediction models and the traditional regression models referred in the ground truth.

TABLE VI. PREDICTION RESULTS OF DYNAMIC ST MODEL.

Models	**MAPE**
OLS Regression	38%
Panel Regression	37.1%
Dynamic Spatio-Temporal (ST) Model	**6.79%**

VI. CONCLUSION AND FUTURE WORK

The proposed approach validated general and dynamic spatio-temporal models for crime prediction. The results showed that the relationships among this spatio-temporal data i) have a positive impact on the prediction accuracy and ii) can be utilized to analyze crime data with a high spatial and temporal granularity. The conducted experiments, however, are only a proof of concept for spatio-temporal predictions at lower spatial granularity.

Upstream spatio-temporal analysis improved the spatio-temporal predictions. The spatial analysis yielded that some locations have a spatial-relation with their neighbors. The temporal analysis confirmed positive correlations between consecutive year's crime incidents. Cross-correlation further identified social-economic factors having relations with crime.

Taking these spatio-temporal patterns into account, the proposed prediction approach outperformed traditional OLS and panel regression that ignores any spatio-temporal relationships in the data. In detail, the dynamic spatio-temporal Bayesian model lowered the error rate in prediction by 31.6% when compared with the ground truth. In contrast, Gaussian based prediction models and auto-regressive models only decreased the error rate by 1% respective 7% (compared with ground truth).

In the future, evaluations have to be extended with more complete data from all geographical hierarchy levels. In practice, however, these data are hard to obtain. Furthermore, more complex analysis models can be designed that accommodate a larger number of independent variables (social-economic factors) for predictions. Having more complete datasets, network models like Bayesian neural networks and LSTM can be evaluated. Especially LSTM archived high time series prediction accuracies when applied on large datasets.

Additionally, the proposed approach can be combined with social media analysis to create a hybrid prediction model that consider the prediction results from two different data sources (social-economic dataset and social media). This way, statistical data (i.e., social-economic factors) anonymously describing (large) groups of people are combined with concrete and precise information about individuals and thus, likely enhance prediction performance.

REFERENCES

[1] K. E. McCollister, M. T. French, and H. Fang, "The cost of crime to society: New crime-specific estimates for policy and program evaluation," Drug and alcohol dependence, vol. 108, no. 1, 2010, pp. 98–109.

[2] W. C. Cunningham, J. J. Strauchs, and C. W. VanMeter, Private security trends, 1970 to 2000: The Hallcrest report II. Butterworth-Heinemann Boston, MA, 1990, vol. 2.

[3] X. Wang, M. S. Gerber, and D. E. Brown, "Automatic crime prediction using events extracted from twitter posts," in International Conference on Social Computing, Behavioral-Cultural Modeling, and Prediction. Springer, 2012, pp. 231–238.

[4] M. S. Gerber, "Predicting crime using twitter and kernel density estimation," Decision Support Systems, vol. 61, 2014, pp. 115–125.

[5] K. Edmark, "Unemployment and crime: Is there a connection?" The Scandinavian journal of economics, vol. 107, no. 2, 2005, pp. 353–373.

[6] A. Freytag, J. J. Krüger, D. Meierrieks, and F. Schneider, "The origins of terrorism: Cross-country estimates of socio-economic determinants of terrorism," European Journal of Political Economy, vol. 27, 2011, pp. S5–S16.

[7] S. Chainey, L. Tompson, and S. Uhlig, "The utility of hotspot mapping for predicting spatial patterns of crime," Security Journal, vol. 21, no. 1-2, 2008, pp. 4–28.

[8] H. Entorf and H. Spengler, "Socioeconomic and demographic factors of crime in germany: Evidence from panel data of the german states," International review of law and economics, vol. 20, no. 1, 2000, pp. 75–106.

[9] R. Caruso and F. Schneider, "The socio-economic determinants of terrorism and political violence in western europe (1994–2007)," European Journal of Political Economy, vol. 27, 2011, pp. S37–S49.

[10] W. R. Tobler, "A computer movie simulating urban growth in the detroit region," Economic geography, vol. 46, no. sup1, 1970, pp. 234–240.

[11] A. Beltran, C. Abargues, C. Granell, M. Núñez, L. Díaz, and J. Huerta, "A virtual globe tool for searching and visualizing geo-referenced media resources in social networks," Multimedia tools and applications, vol. 64, no. 1, 2013, pp. 171–195.

[12] X. Chen, Y. Cho, and S. Y. Jang, "Crime prediction using twitter sentiment and weather," in Systems and Information Engineering Design Symposium (SIEDS), 2015. IEEE, 2015, pp. 63–68.

[13] M. Cheong and V. C. Lee, "A microblogging-based approach to terrorism informatics: Exploration and chronicling civilian sentiment and response to terrorism events via twitter," Information Systems Frontiers, vol. 13, no. 1, 2011, pp. 45–59.

[14] V. Martinez, G. I. Simari, A. Sliva, and V. S. Subrahmanian, "Convex: Similarity-based algorithms for forecasting group behavior," IEEE Intelligent Systems, vol. 23, no. 4, July 2008, pp. 51–57.

[15] R. J. Sampson and W. B. Groves, "Community structure and crime: Testing social-disorganization theory," American journal of sociology, vol. 94, no. 4, 1989, pp. 774–802.

[16] A. M. Olligschlaeger, "Artificial neural networks and crime mapping," Crime mapping and crime prevention, 1997, pp. 313–348.

[17] J. Caulkins, J. Cohen, W. Gorr, and J. Wei, "Predicting criminal recidivism: A comparison of neural network models with statistical methods," Journal of Criminal Justice, vol. 24, no. 3, 1996, pp. 227–240.

[18] S. W. Palocsay, P. Wang, and R. G. Brookshire, "Predicting criminal recidivism using neural networks," Socio-Economic Planning Sciences, vol. 34, no. 4, 2000, pp. 271–284.

[19] T. Nakaya and K. Yano, "Visualising crime clusters in a space-time cube: An exploratory data-analysis approach using space-time kernel density estimation and scan statistics," Transactions in GIS, vol. 14, no. 3, 2010, pp. 223–239.

[20] X. Wang and D. E. Brown, "The spatio-temporal generalized additive model for criminal incidents," in Intelligence and Security Informatics (ISI), 2011 IEEE International Conference on. IEEE, 2011, pp. 42–47.

[21] C. Ivaha, H. Al-Madfai, G. Higgs, and J. A. Ware, "The dynamic spatial disaggregation approach: A spatio-temporal modelling of crime," in World congress on engineering, 2007, pp. 961–966.

[22] M. Townsley, S. D. Johnson, and J. H. Ratcliffe, "Space time dynamics of insurgent activity in iraq," Security Journal, vol. 21, no. 3, 2008, p. 139.

[23] M. Tiefelsdorf and B. Boots, "The exact distribution of moran's i," Environment and Planning A, vol. 27, no. 6, 1995, pp. 985–999.

[24] K. S. Bakar, S. K. Sahu et al., "sptimer: Spatio-temporal bayesian modelling using r," Journal of Statistical Software, vol. 63, no. 15, 2015, pp. 1–32.

[25] J.-M. Marin, K. Mengersen, and C. P. Robert, "Bayesian modelling and inference on mixtures of distributions," Handbook of statistics, vol. 25, 2005, pp. 459–507.

[26] C. Fernández and M. F. Steel, "On bayesian modeling of fat tails and skewness," Journal of the American Statistical Association, vol. 93, no. 441, 1998, pp. 359–371.

[27] A. O. Finley, S. Banerjee, and A. E. Gelfand, "spBayes for large univariate and multivariate point-referenced spatio-temporal data models," ArXiv e-prints, Oct. 2013.

[28] N. Cressie and H.-C. Huang, "Classes of nonseparable, spatio-temporal stationary covariance functions," Journal of the American Statistical Association, vol. 94, no. 448, 1999, pp. 1330–1339.

[29] J. R. Stroud, P. Müller, and B. Sansó, "Dynamic models for spatiotemporal data," Journal of the Royal Statistical Society: Series B (Statistical Methodology), vol. 63, no. 4, 2001, pp. 673–689.

[30] A. Arab, M. B. Hooten, and C. K. Wikle, "Hierarchical spatial models," in Encyclopedia of GIS. Springer, 2008, pp. 425–431.

[31] B. Huang, B. Wu, and M. Barry, "Geographically and temporally weighted regression for modeling spatio-temporal variation in house prices," International Journal of Geographical Information Science, vol. 24, no. 3, 2010, pp. 383–401.

[32] K. Bakar, "Bayesian analysis of daily maximum ozone levels," Ph.D. dissertation, University of Southampton, June 2012. [Online]. Available: https://eprints.soton.ac.uk/340039/

[33] H. R. Moon and M. Weidner, "Dynamic linear panel regression models with interactive fixed effects," Econometric Theory, vol. 33, no. 1, 2017, pp. 158–195.

[34] B. Craven and S. M. Islam, Ordinary least squares regression. Sage Publications, 2011.

[35] L. Anselin, "Local indicators of spatial associationlisa," Geographical analysis, vol. 27, no. 2, 1995, pp. 93–115.

GeoCubes Finland – A Unified Approach for Managing Multi-resolution Raster Geodata in a National Geospatial Research Infrastructure

Lassi Lehto, Jaakko Kähkönen, Juha Oksanen and Tapani Sarjakoski
Finnish Geospatial Research Institute (FGI)
National Land Survey of Finland
Finland
e-mail: lassi.lehto@nls.fi, jaakko.kahkonen@nls.fi, juha.oksanen@nls.fi, tapani.sarjakoski@nls.fi

Abstract—**Providers of geospatial data are facing the challenge of diverse user needs when delivering their products to different user groups. Academic researchers represent a user group with quite specific requirements, like good support for analysis and high-performance computing. A national infrastructure providing both geospatial data and powerful geocomputing facilities for research use is being developed in Finland. The part of the infrastructure described in this paper focuses on the management, storage and efficient delivery of raster-formatted geospatial data by applying the concept of datacube.**

Keywords-research infrastructure; raster data; datacube; GeoTIFF; GDAL.

I. Introduction

National Spatial Data Infrastructures (SDIs) are mostly developed as general-purpose data delivery platforms. The main driving force is usually the availability of various data sets that providers have initially built for their own use. As data sharing principles gain momentum in society, existing data sets are being made available without any specific adaptation. An example of development aiming at a customised, user-oriented SDI is the Finnish Open Geospatial Information Infrastructure for Research (oGIIR) initiative [1]. The oGIIR is a part of a major national programme developing research infrastructures (Finnish Research Infrastructure [FIRI]). The building phase of oGIIR is funded by the Academy of Finland in the context of Finland's Roadmap for Research Infrastructures [2].

The oGIIR is an open-access virtual infrastructure supporting the broad multidisciplinary scientific research community by offering geospatial data services, scalable geocomputing services and a knowledge-sharing network. The oGIIR is jointly developed by the Finnish Geospatial Research Institute (FGI) in the National Land Survey of Finland (NLS), the University of Turku, Aalto University, the University of Eastern Finland, the Finnish Environment Institute (SYKE), the Geological Survey of Finland (GTK), the Natural Resources Institute Finland (LUKE) and CSC – IT Center for Science (the provider of high-performance computing facilities for Finnish universities). The oGIIR will make the Finnish geospatial research infrastructure internationally unique in two ways: 1) by providing a strong network of cooperation, open access infrastructure and researcher knowledge sharing in order to support scientific research with geospatial information and 2) by facilitating access to high-performance geocomputing resources for research organisations.

An initiative called GeoCubes Finland (hereafter also referred to as 'GeoCubes') has been launched in the context of the oGIIR to develop a cached storage of geospatial data for supporting the needs of the Finnish research community. GeoCubes is a unified, multi-resolution repository of raster-formatted geospatial data. The main use case for this data storage is a research task involving spatial components and requiring geospatial raster source data sets. The substantial effort involved in acquiring and combining disparate spatial data sets is often seen as a major impediment for wider utilization of spatial methods in research. GeoCubes aims at facilitating spatial analysis processes by providing interoperable data sets that have been pre-processed for easy access and integration.

GeoCubes Finland contains a representative selection of Finnish geospatial data sets with national coverage. The contained data sets are transformed into a common two-dimensional grid and into a unified set of resolution levels. Standardised mechanisms are applied for the storage and provision of essential metadata. A wide set of access protocols are supported for accessing the contents of GeoCubes in order to facilitate utilisation in various client applications. In particular, mechanisms are provided for easy access to GeoCubes data sets from the high-performance geocomputing platform of CSC. The GeoCubes Finland platform is currently in its early stages of development. Thus, detailed information on performance, adaptability for a particular purpose, or user acceptance of the platform, is not yet available.

The rest of the paper is organised as follows. Section II describes the concept of a datacube and its application in the geospatial domain. Section III describes the main aspects of the GeoCubes Finland data repository. Section IV deals with the implementation details of GeoCubes Finland. Section V contains discussion and Section VI presents conclusions and possible future developments of the platform.

II. Datacubes for Geodata

In general computing technology, a *datacube* is understood as a multi-dimensional array of data (the term *OLAP cube* is also used; OLAP: Online Analytical Processing). The dimensions of a datacube represent the points of view from which a certain value (called a *measure*) is looked at. If a datacube contains more than three dimensions, the term *hypercube* is also used [3]. The concept of a datacube has recently raised interest also in the geospatial domain. In this context, datacubes are defined as multi-dimensional arrays containing spatially referenced data. Examples of datacubes include one-dimensional arrays of geolocated sensor observation time series, two-dimensional arrays containing range values of geospatial coverage, three-dimensional arrays of volumetric data sets (like voxel representations of data sets in geoscience) and four-dimensional arrays representing the time series of volumetric data sets [4].

In particular, satellite images can be seen as a promising application area for datacube-based storage and data management [5]. Earth observation (EO) missions have been carried out regularly since the sixties, and the images captured thus form an extensive time series. This allows for natural treatment of EO data as a three-dimensional datacube [6].

Open Data Cube (ODC) is a large international initiative aimed at improving access to EO imagery through a unified pre-processing, harmonisation and indexing procedure [7]. An open source Python-based implementation is available to help communities in organising and analysing vast amounts of EO data and in creating useful end-user applications based on those data resources [8].

An important example of an operational national-level ODC implementation is the Australian Geoscience Data Cube (AGDC) [9]. The main three components of the AGDC include a) data preparation for improved comparability and better time-series analysis, b) a software platform that supports better data access and management, and c) the provision of a high-performance computing platform for data analysis tasks. In the data ingestion process, source imagery is processed in order to achieve comparable spatial, spectral and quality properties, and then it is tiled and stored as netCDF files. The AGDC can also deal with data sets that are only indexed and processed into the common form in an on-the-fly manner, when needed.

In standardisation, the concept of a datacube has also been raised as a possible organising principle for storing massive amounts of raster-formatted geodata. A working group, called Datacube Domain Working Group (Datacube.DWG), is planned to start working on this topic in the Open Geospatial Consortium (OGC) [10].

Recently, Baumann has made an attempt to formalise the properties of a geospatial datacube in the Datacube Manifesto [11]. According to Baumann, geospatial datacubes are supposed to express the following properties: a) they must support at least one through to four dimensions, b) datacubes must treat all axes equally, in particular they must yield good performance in selecting subsets along all axes c) datacubes must support adaptive partitioning to improve query and processing efficiency, d) datacube service implementations must support a well-defined query language for accomplishing various tasks (like data extraction, filtering, processing and integration).

The most important existing specifications unifying datacube access methods include the following OGC standards: Coverage Implementation Schema (CIS) [12], Web Coverage Service (WCS) [13] and Web Coverage Processing Service (WCPS) [14].

III. GeoCubes Finland's specifications

A. Content

The contents of GeoCubes Finland include a representative selection of spatial data sets maintained by governmental research organisations in Finland (like SYKE, LUKE and GTK). As reference data, some general-purpose data sets provided by the NLS are also included. Data sets are organised as individual layers of information with common representational properties for easy integration and analysis.

Examples of data sets to be stored in GeoCubes in the first phase include high-resolution elevation models and surface models (from the NLS), land-use layers (from the SYKE), soil map layers (from the GTK) and national forest inventory layers (from the LUKE).

B. Metadata

Metadata concerning the data sets stored in GeoCubes Finland are provided as a centralised resource. Because of the particular nature of the data sets, special attention is put on providing descriptive information about the classifications applied in raster layers. This information will be made available either as Raster Attribute Tables (RATs), as internal metadata fields of the raster data file or as online code list files. As GeoCubes provides multi-resolution data storage, the applied nomenclature in most cases form hierarchical classification structures.

C. Encoding

The encoding of GeoCubes Finland cell values depends on the nature of the data set being represented. Both classified data sets (like land use or soil maps) and data sets with continuous value ranges (like Digital Elevation Models (DEMs) or orthophotos) are included. No-data areas are represented as zero-valued cells in classified data sets and by a separate mask channel in data sets with continuous value ranges. Where practicable, the data capture date is presented as a separate time layer.

D. Grid

The standardised grid applied in GeoCubes is based on the Finnish national Coordinate Reference System (CRS) ETRS-TM35FIN (EPSG code 3067). This projected CRS is compatible with the pan-European ETRS89 system. ETRS-TM35FIN covers the whole country in one projection zone and has the false easting value of 500 000 m on its central meridian at 27°E longitude. The origin of the GeoCubes Finland's grid (top-left corner) is located at the coordinate point (0, 7800000). The easting value of the origin is selected to avoid negative coordinates. The northing coordinate value is selected as a round 100 km value, allowing for good coverage of the country.

E. Resolution Levels

GeoCubes Finland applies the following resolution levels: 1, 2, 5, 10, 20, 50, 100, 200, 500, and 1000 m. The resolution levels applicable for a given source data essentially depend on the properties, like spatial accuracy, of the data set. Round resolution values, rather than the traditionally used exponents of two in image pyramids, are selected to facilitate integration with external sources (like statistical data sets) and to follow the values commonly used in spatial analysis reporting.

F. Spatial Subdivision

For easy transfer and processing of the GeoCubes Finland data sets, the content is subdivided in 100 km * 100 km blocks with a round 100 km origin (top-left corner) coordinate values. The territory of Finland can be covered with 60 such blocks (see Figure 1). The so-called virtual raster mechanism is used to treat the 60 individual files as a one continuous data set.

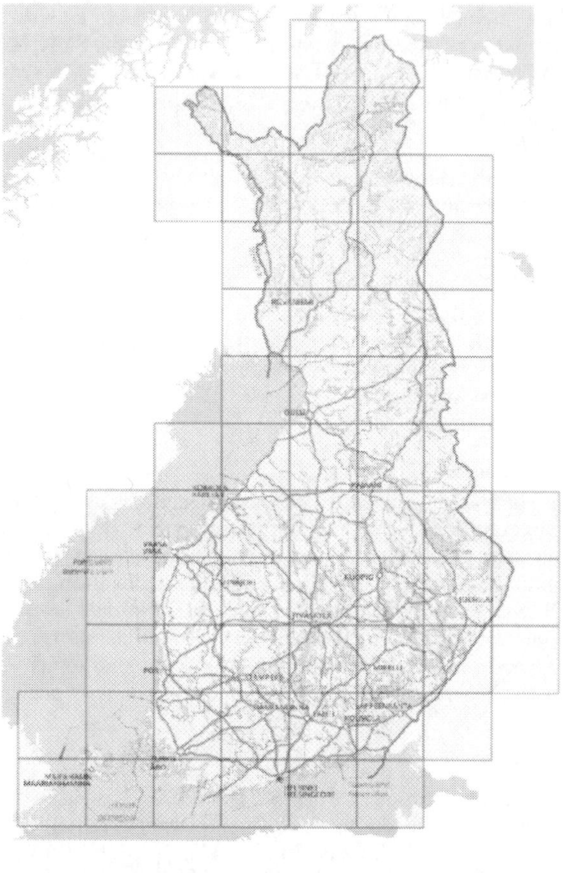

Figure 1. The block-wise spatial subdivision of GeoCubes Finland's data storage.

G. Access Methods

Several access methods are supported in GeoCubes Finland in order to enable smooth usage in various user environments. Block-wise raster files are available for easy http access. A custom-made download service supports the selection of an arbitrary bounding box at a given resolution level. The efficient partial downloading of an individual block-wise raster file is also supported using an http 'GET range' request. A Web Coverage Service (WCS) interface is available for downloading GeoCubes content, supporting the definition of spatial extents both in ground and raster coordinates.

Visualisation of the GeoCubes content is provided via a Web Map Service (WMS) instance (MapServer) that can use the virtual raster representation of an individual GeoCubes data theme as its source data.

IV. IMPLEMENTATION

A. Platform

GeoCubes Finland – like most of the other research infrastructure components being developed in the oGIIR project – will be running on the high-performance cloud computing platform provided by the IT services provider CSC. The platform consists of two different computing environments: supercluster Taito, which is destined for massive parallel computing tasks, and cPouta, a traditional Infrastructure as a Service (IaaS) cloud computing platform. Large-scale geocomputing tasks will be run on the Taito platform, whereas interactive applications and the open data access interfaces of GeoCubes will be located in the cPouta environment. Data storage will be organised in the CSC's fast storage units. Investigation into the best possible manner to share the data storage between Taito and cPouta usage is underway.

B. Processing

Data sets available in raster form are transformed into the standardised grid and into all applicable resolution levels. Vector-formatted source data sets are rasterised with selected attribute values and added to the raster storage. The needed generalisation processes are carried out in order to fill in the required resolution levels. If source data sets are available in generalised forms, those layers are used as input data.

C. Storage format

In the first implementation, GeoCubes Finland data sets are stored as GeoTIFF files [15]. Each file covers one block. The different resolution levels are maintained as internal GeoTIFF overview layers. The internal structure of the GeoTIFF file is organised in the so-called cloud-optimised form for efficient extraction of the various overview levels using standard http transmission mechanisms. The BigTIFF mode is used to support vast spatial raster files. Raster content is organised into internal 256*256 cell GeoTIFF tiles to facilitate the fast extraction of sub-regions. The architecture of the initial GeoCubes implementation is illustrated in Figure 2.

D. Tools

Processing of GeoCubes Finland data sets is mainly performed by the open source spatial data processing platform called the Geospatial Data Abstraction Library (GDAL) [16]. Automated processes for importing different data sources into the GeoCubes are based on the use of GDAL functionalities via Python scripting.

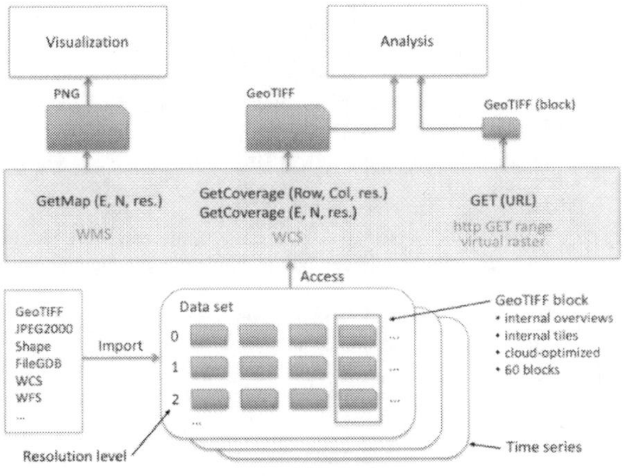

Figure 2. The system architecture of GeoCubes Finland and planned data access mechanisms.

V. Discussion

The development of GeoCubes Finland arose from the need to have a unified approach for handling raster geodata in a multi-resolution fashion, without direct relation to the advancement of datacube approaches in the geospatial domain that we reviewed in Section II. Referring to Section III, the very central aspects of GeoCubes specifications are the following:

1. It supports handling of raster geodata sets that are mutually heterogeneous with respect to their content.
2. It uses a single coordinate reference system and one specified location for the origin of the raster data sets.
3. It uses multiple resolutions to store and represent geodata, like image pyramids are used in remote sensing imagery.
4. It uses unified principles to encode the data in raster cells.

Northing and *Easting* are the only natural dimensions of our datacube. Height and time could be considered to be other natural dimensions in the datacube. Looking at the datasets that are to be primarily used in the oGIIR infrastructure, there seems to be little (if any) need for voxel data with height as the third dimension. For time to be a natural dimension in a datacube, we should have data representing a phenomenon at rather regular intervals, thus forming time series data over longer periods of time. In our case we have data representing current phenomena, or only some snapshots representing the phenomenon at certain specified time instances. To summarise, on a logical level our way of modelling the data is, in many aspects, the traditional layer- and raster-based approach. Related to datacubes, GeoCubes Finland seems to mainly resemble the AGDC and ODC. However, it is useful to analyse how GeoCubes Finland fits with a datacube as defined by Baumann in his manifesto [11].

First of all, it is rather natural to consider each resolution level to form its own datacube. That is why the approach is named in the plural form – GeoCubes Finland. Secondly, the enumeration of the layers or themes can be considered to form the first dimension within each of these datacubes. Thirdly, Northing and Easting would form the second and the third dimension. GeoCubes Finland's formalism can be extended to handle volumetric and/or time series data by replacing a layer with three- or four-dimensional datacubes. Baumann's Datacube Manifesto assumes that the data values within a cube are of the same data type. This is not the case in our approach; the data type is only constrained to be the same within each layer.

Baumann's Datacube Manifesto implicitly defines or describes a datacube as a database management system and data processing environment for multi-dimensional raster data. In GeoCubes Finland, on the contrary, the focus is on representation (i.e., how the data is modelled and represented on a logical level). On the implementation level, GeoCubes uses a file-based approach and utilises the features available in the GDAL library, for example virtual rasters and overviews. As such GeoCubes' implementation is not restricted to GDAL – other realisations may be made using any software that suits the purpose. GeoCubes is not a processing and analysis environment for geodata; processing is assumed to take place in GIS or other software that has the capability to process raster geodata. The plan is to use WCS as the primary mechanism for accessing selected parts of the data. These observations make it evident that all the issues related to optimisation and performance will remain highly dependent on the specific solutions made in each implementation.

VI. Conclusions and Outlook

The oGIIR project aims at improving access to geospatial data sets and geocomputing resources for academic and governmental research organisations. One of the aims of the project is to set up a datacube, called GeoCubes Finland, to facilitate researchers' work in cases where spatial data in raster form can contribute to the problem resolution.

GeoCubes Finland is currently in its early development phase. The first version of the specification has been developed, and the first tests with real data sets are ongoing. The future work includes further testing to refine the specifications, develop the service modules and user interfaces, and better integrate the data storage with high-performance computing facilities for spatial analysis.

Acknowledgment

The work described in this paper has been carried out in the context of the project 'Open Geospatial Information Infrastructure for Research' (oGIIR, urn:nbn:fi:research-infras-2016072513), a part of Finland's Roadmap for Research Infrastructures. The project is funded by the Academy of Finland, grant number 306536. The computing infrastructure used in the work is funded by the Academy of Finland through 'Finnish Grid and Cloud Infrastructure', urn:nbn:fi:research-infras-2016072533, grant number 283818.

REFERENCES

[1] oGIIR, Open Geospatial Information Infrastructure. http://ogiir.fi [retrieved: Jan, 2018]

[2] Academy of Finland, "Finland's Strategy and Roadmap for Research Infrastructures 2014-2020". http://www.aka.fi/globalassets/awanhat/documents/firi/tutkimusinfrastruktuurien_strategia_ja_tiekartta_2014_en.pdf [retrieved: Jan, 2018]

[3] Wikipedia, Data cube. https://en.wikipedia.org/wiki/Data_cube [retrieved: Jan, 2018]

[4] U. Pyysalo and T. Sarjakoski, "Voxel approach to landscape modelling". *The International Archives of the Photogrammetry and Remote Sensing*, July 2–11, 2008, Beijing, China, XXXVII(B4/1), pp. 563–568

[5] A. Lewis et al., "Rapid, high-resolution detection of environmental change over continental scales from satellite data – the Earth Observation Data Cube". *International Journal of Digital Earth*, Vol. 9 , Iss. 1, 2016, pp: 106-111

[6] ESA, Earth Observation Datacube. https://eodatacube.eu/ [retrieved: Jan, 2018]

[7] CEOS, Open Data Cube. https://www.opendatacube.org [retrieved: Jan, 2018]

[8] ODC, Open Data Cube Source Code Repository. https://github.com/opendatacube [retrieved: Jan, 2018]

[9] A. Lewis et al., "The Australian Geoscience Data Cube – Foundations and lessons learned". *Remote Sensing of Environment*, 2017, ISSN 0034-4257, https://doi.org/10.1016/j.rse.2017.03.015, pp. 276-292

[10] OGC, Datacube Domain Working Group Charter. https://external.opengeospatial.org/twiki_public/pub/CoveragesDWG/Datacubes/17-071_Datacube-DWG_Charter.pdf [retrieved: Jan, 2018]

[11] P. Baumann, The Datacube Manifesto. http://earthserver.eu/sites/default/files/upload_by_users/The-Datacube-Manifesto.pdf [retrieved: Jan, 2018]

[12] OGC, Coverage Implementation Schema. http://docs.opengeospatial.org/is/09-146r6/09-146r6.html [retrieved: Jan, 2018]

[13] OGC, Web Coverage Service. http://www.opengeospatial.org/standards/wcs [retrieved: Jan, 2018]

[14] OGC, Web Coverage Processing Service (WCPS) Standard. http://www.opengeospatial.org/standards/ wcps [retrieved: Jan, 2018]

[15] GeoTIFF, GeoTIFF home page. http://trac.osgeo.org/geotiff/ [retrieved: Jan, 2018]

[16] GDAL, Geospatial Data Abstraction Library. http://gdal.org [retrieved: Jan, 2018]

Coupling an Unstructured NoSQL Database with a Geographic Information System

Amandine Holemans, Jean-Paul Kasprzyk, Jean-Paul Donnay

Geomatics Unit
University of Liege
Liege, Belgium
email: holemans.a@gmail.com, jp.kasprzyk@uliege.be, jp.donnay@uliege.be

Abstract—**The management of unstructured NoSQL (Not only Structured Query Language) databases has undergone a great development in the last years mainly thanks to Big Data. Nevertheless, the specificity of spatial information is not purposely taken into account. To overcome this difficulty, we propose to couple a NoSQL database with a spatial Relational Data Base Management System (RDBMS). Exchanges of information between these two systems are illustrated with relevant examples involving spatial queries. The spatial data stored in MongoDB consists of field surveys (points, photos, etc.) and scanned plans, while reference data (cadastre) is recorded in PostGIS. The extensions required to allow this coupling are written in Python.**

Keyword- Document-Oriented Database; MongoDB; Spatial RDBMS; PostGIS; Spatial Queries, Python.

I. INTRODUCTION

Like any Information System (IS), a Geographic Information System (GIS) uses a relational-type (RDBMS) or object-relational (O-RDBMS) database management system to store and manage spatial entities and their attributes. The database is based on a conceptual data model, written in UML (Unified Modelling Language) for example, where spatial entities are modelled by particular classes. In the physical database model, these classes are converted into spatial tables. According to the standards, the spatial footprint of entities is recorded in a dedicated field (GEOMETRY) in any spatialized table. This structure, relatively rigid, is suitable for any collection of entities always having the same fixed properties.

However, it appears in many projects that this inflexible structure does not lend itself to a large amount of heterogeneous information while remaining likely to be geo-located (Google, Facebook, etc.). This unstructured information, which can be described as documentation, can take the form of printed plans and diagrams, written reports, photographs, and so on. Whatever the origin, the documentation can always be scanned but in the form of a variable number of files in various formats.

Non-structured database management, known as NoSQL, has undergone a great development in recent years, particularly with the raise of voluminous and heterogeneous digital data (Big Data) [1]. Several recent systems have been designed for the management of documentation in its most various forms, even if the specificity of spatial information is not clearly addressed.

It is therefore possible to implement a GIS, based on an RDBMS, in parallel to a NoSQL system for the relevant documentation. The concern for many users is to choose between these two management systems to store and manage all the information [2]. However, it would be beneficial to couple these two systems in order to coherently associate and exploit the common spatial characteristics of these two types of information.

Our research objective consists precisely in proposing a coupling protocol between these systems as part of a pipe network management application.

In Section II, we describe the context of application that led us to propose this solution. Then, Section III takes stock of the specificities of NoSQL - particularly MongoDB software - compared to the standard RDBMS. Several scenarios are then presented in Section IV to illustrate the possibilities of exchanging information between a NoSQL system and a RDBMS, both in vector and in raster modes, while limiting data redundancy. Finally, we conclude in Section V with a discussion of the current capabilities and limitations of this type of coupling.

II. ABOUT THE APPLICATION

The issue of combining the management of a vector GIS and a documentation relating to this geographical information was posed to the AIDE company (*Association Intercommunale pour le Démergement et l'Epuration*: protection against floods caused by mining subsidence and management of the network of water sanitation, Liege Province, Belgium).

The company's geographical objects (pipes, manholes, zones of intervention, etc.) are defined by vector geometries collected on the field by surveying techniques. In parallel, the GIS manages various reference data, such as cadastral objects and other administrative boundaries imported from institutional data providers.

The documentation includes survey blueprints and plans at different scales, geo-located digital photos and written reports that may include geo-located or geo-localizable information. This data – analogue or digital - is classified by projects. The projects are defined in time and space but the volume and the nature of the data constituting the documentation of a project vary very significantly, making a rigid data model unsuitable. Moreover, the projects are likely to interact or to merge in a planned way (e.g., renovation projects) or not (e.g., failures and various incidents on the network). Due to all these considerations, the documentation associated with the projects appears as an unstructured set of data that must be related to reference data which, conversely, is structured according to an invariable scheme.

As part of a reengineering of the AIDE's GIS, it was considered desirable to integrate the documentation into the database. It was at this point that the company asked us to examine the feasibility to couple NoSQL with a standard GIS solution.

III. STATE OF THE ART

A. *RDBMS versus NoSQL*

Among the open source DBMSs that can handle spatial data, PostgreSQL and its PostGIS geospatial extension have great advantages. They give efficient functions, both in vector and in raster models, as well as a community offering a significant support [3]. In accordance with the OpenGIS Standard for "Simple Features for SQL", vector geometries are stored in the GEOMETRY field of spatialized tables. Since version 2.0, PostGIS can use two ways to store and process raster data: "in-db" or "out-db". In the first case, the raster data is stored in the RASTER field of spatialized tables, according to a principle similar to vector data storage. In the second case, only the metadata is stored in the database, the actual raster data being retrieved from the file system.

It is on PostgreSQL and PostGIS that the GIS of our application rests (version PostGIS 2.3.2 - PostgreSQL 9.6.3 at the time of application). Like all RDBMSs, however, it is not designed to handle large amounts of data for transactional processing. Indeed, SQL vertical scalability is limited with hardware improvement of the server (contrary to NoSQL horizontal scalability) [4]. In addition, the unstructured data leads to a considerable drop in performance (e.g., introduction of null values) or outrights practical impossibility. It is worth noting that RDBMSs remain effective in decision-making on large data warehouses [5].

First, NoSQL has developed to cope with large amounts of data [6]. Then, the need for simpler and less rigid models has strengthened the development of unstructured database models [7]. The term NoSQL groups various unstructured database families that can be characterized by their schema type. There are currently 4 families: key-value, column, graph and document-oriented databases [8]:

- Key-value-oriented: They constitute the simplest schema where a key refers to a particular type of value. This type of schema offers quite limited query capabilities.
- Column-oriented: This is an extension of the key-value schema by allowing a key to return multiple values.
- Graph-oriented: The diagram is here in the form of a graph composed of edges and nodes.
- Document-oriented: These databases are composed of keys that refer to a document, which can itself contain multiple embedded documents. Collections thus gather several documents from the same family, but their internal structure may vary. They do not require schemas beforehand and have a structure able to evolve over time without excessive costs. In addition, the contents of the document can be scrutinized by queries.

B. *MongoDB*

In the AIDE application briefly described above (II) the problem comes from the management of a variable documentation in quantity and content, essentially attached to the point objects (manholes). The network aspect is not explicitly exploited so that the solution chosen for our analysis is based on a document-oriented and not a graph-oriented database as one might have imagined at first glance with a pipe network management company. The choice of the document-oriented DBMS focused on MongoDB (version 3.4; [9]). This DBMS is easy to handle thanks to the various drivers available and its installation facilities. It does not have its own query language, but adapts to the chosen driver. MongoDB also uses standard formats (JavaScript Object Notation – e.g., JSON), which can be interesting for the expected manipulations. Currently, this NoSQL DBMS is the most popular one in the NoSQL category. It offers a large community making its use easier [10].

Presently, the geospatial domain is not a priority in the design of a NoSQL DBMS. Systems sometimes have an extension to manage geographic data while in other systems these features are natively included [11]. MongoDB is able to natively manage geospatial data, but dedicated processing is quite limited as soon as non-point geometries are concerned [12]. These limits come from the lack of maturity of this type of DBMS, but it is obviously constantly evolving.

MongoDB can spatially index and process vector geometries in 2 coordinate systems, labelled 2D and 2DSphere. In 2D, the coordinates (x, y) are local (not attached to a spatial reference system) and are described as legacy coordinate pairs in JSON. In 2DSphere, the coordinates are expressed in the geodetic system WGS84 (EPSG: 4326) and are described in GeoJSON. Elementary spatial predicates (within, near) are applicable to both domains, but the intersection is only possible in 2DSphere.

Raster geospatial data is not explicitly recognized by MongoDB. However, images can be manipulated in many ways by this software [13]. The image file can either (1) be managed by the file system, out of the database, or (2) be embedded in binary form in a MongoDB document if it is not too large (16 Mb maximum, and it is even recommended not to exceed 1 Mb), or (3) be incorporated into a document managed by the GridFS method.

With GridFS, the files, written in BSON (Binary JSON) format, can be much bigger, and a larger number of files can be managed in one directory [13]. The files are actually divided into several chunks, gathered in one "fs.chunk" collection, while the document metadata, notably allowing grouping the chunks, are the subject of a separate "fs.files" collection [14]. GridFS processes files and their metadata at the same time [15]. The facilities offered by GridFS are implemented in all official MongoDB drivers and a GridFS management tool, called Mongofile, is also available [16]. It should be noted in passing that the document management method via GridFS is particularly well suited to the classification of project-based documentation as carried out by the company AIDE.

It should be noted further that any image in MongoDB can be geo-located by a point in WGS84 coordinates (e.g., a geo-located photograph). But except for this location point, the image geospatial data are not necessarily geo-referenced in the WGS84 datum.

C. *Drivers and Interfaces*

Several extensions exist to interface MongoDB but they are not yet fully satisfactory. For a quick check, Compass for example, can be handy. But for maximum interactivity, it is desirable to work directly with a server language. C++, Java, Python, Perl or PHP, for example, may be perfectly suitable.

For visualizing geospatial data from MongoDB, an Open Source GIS application should be a good solution. For instance, QGIS has a long history of extensions to PostGIS and is currently offering four extensions dedicated to MongoDB. But they do not seem to be perfect yet [17].

In this application, we have retained Python language. It is enough to import the drivers PyMongo and Psycopg2 in the same routine to provide a common interface to the couple of databases. Note that it is also in Python that the QGIS extensions can be written.

IV. EXAMPLES OF SPATIAL INTERACTIONS

In order to illustrate the coupling of the two systems, MongoDB and PostGIS, we have selected some types of data contained in the application of the AIDE company. The spatial data likely to feed MongoDB is either scanned plans, georeferenced (Geo-TIFF format) or not, and field data: manholes in point form (vector format) and photographs (image/raster format) geo-located on a point. The spatial data stored in PostGIS are reference data, from which we have selected the cadastral data [18] in vector form. It should be mentioned that the cadastre does not cover the public domain and that, consequently, the vector entities surveyed by the AIDE (manholes and pipes) are not located on the cadastral territory.

A. *Vector interactions*

The interactions will be done in both directions: from MongoDB to PostGIS and vice versa.

1) From MongoDB to PostGIS:

A simple query example consists in identifying the cadastral parcels (preserved in PostGIS) that are located in

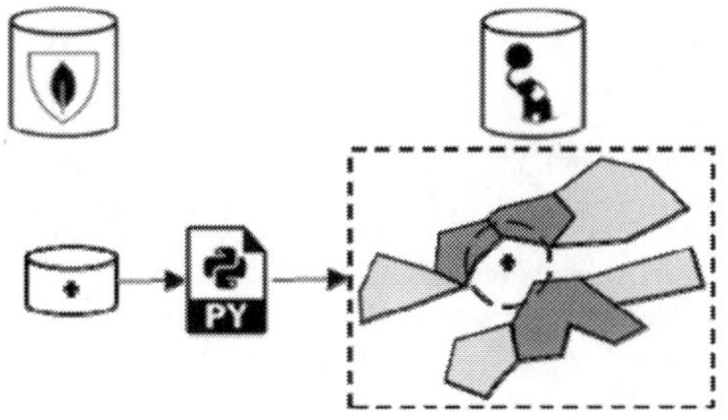

Figure 1. Selection of parcels in PostGIS in the vicinity of a selected point from MongoDB (search radius provided by the Python routine).

the vicinity of a point (e.g., manhole) whose coordinates are stored in MongoDB (Figure 1).

The Python routine first selects the point using a MongoDB request. Its WGS84 coordinates are received in GeoJSON format and are associated to a PostGIS point after conversion in the user's reference system (recorded in the parcel metadata). Python interrogates the user on the search radius and launches the PostGIS request to select the parcels (to reduce the listing size (Table I), the interactive data entry is replaced by predefined constants).

TABLE I. PYTHON SCRIPT LOOKING FOR PARCELS IN POSTGIS WITHIN A CERTAIN DISTANCE OF A POINT RECORDED IN MONGODB.

```
############################ INIT
import json
import pymongo
from pymongo import MongoClient
import psycopg2                                  #PostGIS connection
import sys
############################ MONGODB
client = MongoClient()                           #User Data Entry
db=client.geoprocess
collection=db.manholes                           #Define source collection
collection_2=db.manholes_array                   #Define target collection
id="64056-02CA007430"                            #Define id source
distance="10"                                    #Define search radius
point_rech=collection.find_one({"_id":id},{"geometry":1,"_id":0})
                                                 #Display corresponding
                                                 document
geom=point_rech['geometry']                      #Geometry extraction
coord=geom['coordinates']                        #Point coordinates
                                                 extraction
############################ POSTGIS
connection =
psycopg2.connect(database="geoprocessing",user="postgres",
password="***")
cursor = connection.cursor()
lat=str(coord[1])
lon=str(coord[0])
query="select cadasterparcelkey from b_cadasterparcel
where st_distance(geom,
st_transform(st_setsrid(st_makepoint("+lon+","+lat+"), 4326),
st_srid(geom))) <"+distance
cursor.execute(query)
results = cursor.fetchall()
for line in results:
        cadasterparcelkey=line[0]
        print(cadasterparcelkey)
cursor.close()
connection.close()
```

2) From PostGIS to MongoDB:

The reverse query should identify the point(s) (MongoDB) located near a cadastral parcel (PostGIS).

The notion of proximity is easily translated by the definition of a buffer around the cadastral parcel. However, this simple operation cannot be achieved in MongoDB. It is then entrusted to a POSTGIS request and the coordinates of the obtained polygon are converted into WGS84 in GeoJSON format to query MongoDB. In this example, the MongoDB request (within operator) will have to identify the geo-location points of the photographs taken within the buffer polygon (Figure 2).

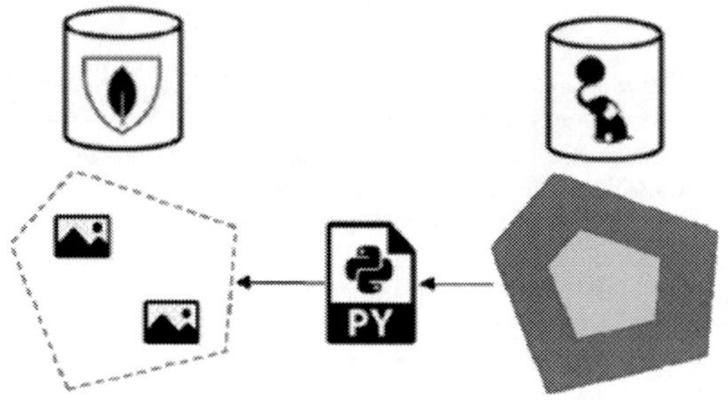

Figure 2. Selections of photographs (point georeferenced in MongoDB) falling in a buffered parcel in PostGIS.

B. Raster interactions

The documentation of AIDE company is essentially composed of scanned plans and it is essentially around these that the interaction is sought. However, it must be remembered that scanned plans are available at multiple scales: small-scale assembly plans, large-scale detail plans. This multi-scale cover can be organized as embedded documents in MongoDB. In addition, the plans cover areas of interest that are not necessarily rectangular, so the scanned images likely incorporate portions without data (No-Data). Finally, the plans are not systematically georeferenced after scanning. As a result, the edges of the image are generally not parallel to the axes of the reference coordinate system.

1) Raster / Vector interactions:

A priori, for general queries concerning the presence of geographical objects within the plan, in one way or the other, it suffices to define the neatline (according to the OGC encoding best practices [19]) defining the border of the raster file and to confront it with the geometry of the vector objects preserved in PostGIS. The neatline is made of a series of point coordinates in clockwise order. The minimum of two points is considered as the diagonal of the minimum bounding rectangle (MBR), which assumes that the sides of the raster are parallel to the axes of the projected coordinate system. The coordinates of the neatline and the user's Spatial Reference Identifier (SRID), are provided to PostGIS to build a polygon in the GEOMETRY field of a spatial table (Figure 3). It is then possible to easily check the occurrence of vector objects within the polygon via a general purpose 2D clipping algorithm, such as the Weiler's algorithm [20] in the PostGIS environment.

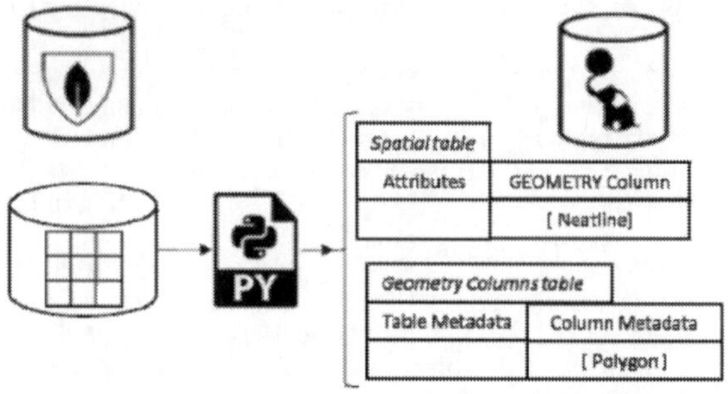

Figure 3. Preservation of the neatline (polygon) of a scanned plan (MongoDB) in the GEOMETRY column of a spatial table (PostGIS).

On the other hand, if the query involves the value of the pixels of the scanned plan (to avoid the No-Data values for example), it is necessary to make the georeferenced scanned plan accessible to PostGIS or to replicate it in a RASTER field of a raster table. These cases are discussed below and because the image neatline can be obtained by the raster function "st_enveloppe" in PostGIS, it will be no longer necessary to store the neatline in a vector spatial table.

2) Georeferenced scanned plan:

The scanned plan can be georeferenced and available e.g., in Geo-TIFF format. If it is managed by the MongoDB file system, it allows an immediate sharing solution with the PostGIS environment because of its ability to access, from the RASTER field, to external files (out-db alternative – Figure 4). If the image file is managed by GridFS in MongoDB, it is desirable to export it from the database in order to share it with PostGIS. This is achieved by a Python script listed below (Table II).

TABLE II. PYTHON SCRIPT EXTERNALIZING AN IMAGE MANAGED BY GRIDFS AS A TIFF FILE.

```
############################## INIT
import pymongo
from pymongo import MongoClient
from bson import objectid
import gridfs
from os.path import basename
import os
from bson.objectid import ObjectId
from io import BytesIO
############################## EXPORT
conn = MongoClient()            #Connection to MongoDB & GridFS
db = conn.geoprocess
fs = gridfs.GridFS(db, "plan")  #Connection to image file in DB
gridout = fs.get(ObjectId("5a1ee153a9e79f1934cdf3a1"))
                                #Read file with objectId
fout = open('plan_mongo.tiff', 'wb')
                                #Open TIFF file
fout.write(gridout.read()       #Write TIFF file
fout.close()
```

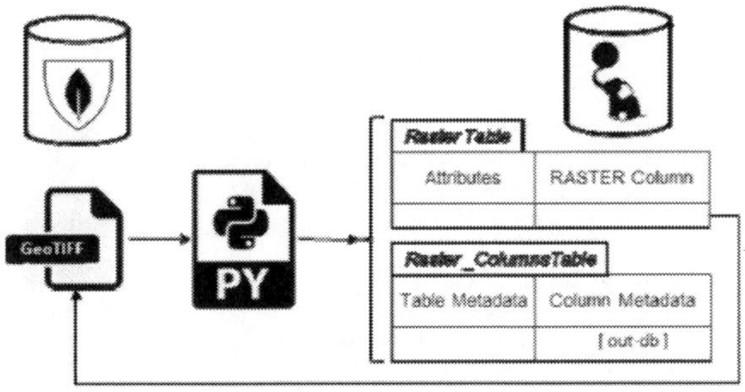

Figure 4. MongoDB and PostGIS share an external GeoTIFF File.

3) Un-referenced scanned plans and World File:

If the scanned plan is not georeferenced, it is necessary to proceed to this geo-registration under PostGIS. This involves, on the one hand, communicating to PostGIS the necessary parameters and, on the other hand, transmitting the image file itself, exported from MongoDB.

Regarding the registration parameters, the proposed solution is to enrich the metadata of the plan with the corresponding World File resuming the 6 parameters of the affine transformation between the image-coordinates and the user's projected coordinates [21] (Table III).

TABLE III. WORLD FILE PARAMETERS.

# Line	Parameter	Meaning
1	*A*	*x*-scale
2	*D*	*y*-skew
3	*B*	*x*-skew
4	*E*	*y*-scale
5	*C*	*x*-translation
6	*F*	*y*-translation
Parameters used in equations : $x' = Ax + By + C$ $y' = Dx + Ey + F$		

At the choice of the user, the World File parameters can be computed from the neatline coordinates by the Python script (the neatline is generally easier for the user to specify than the 6 parameters of the transformation matrix). In addition, the destination SRID must be specified to PostGIS.

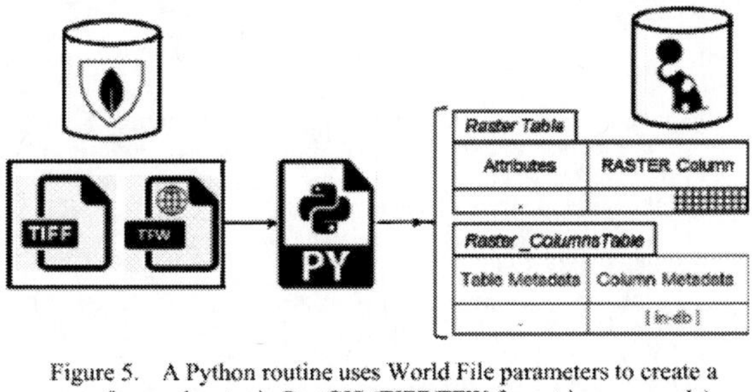

Figure 5. A Python routine uses World File parameters to create a georeferenced raster in PostGIS (TIFF/TFW format is an example).

As in the previous example, the image in MongoDB can be managed as an external file or more likely, to meet the company's project-based management, managed by the GridFS method. In the latter case, it is still necessary to reconstitute the image in a file which is external to the database. The Python script transmits it to PostGIS which

TABLE IV. PYTHON SCRIPT TAKING A TIFF FILE FROM MONGODB AND USING WORLD FILE PARAMETERS TO GEO-REFERENCE A RASTER IN POSTGIS.

```
############################ INIT
import psycopg2
import os
import subprocess
import pymongo
from pymongo import MongoClient
from bson import objectid
import gridfs
from os.path import basename
import os
from bson.objectid import ObjectId
from io import BytesIO
############################ MONGODB
conn = MongoClient()            #Connection to MongoDB &
                                GridFS
db = conn.geoprocess
fs = gridfs.GridFS(db, "plan")
gridout = fs.get(ObjectId("5a1ee153a9e79f1934cdf3a1"))
filelist=fs.list()              #List all files in the collection
print (filelist)
fout = open('plan_mongo.tiff', 'wb')  #Open TIFF file
fout.write(gridout.read())      #Write TIFF file
fout.close()
world= open("C:/Projets/geoprocessing/donnees/plans/world/02014-
01-I003_01_ech1000-V1(1).wld",'r')  #Open World File
read_data=world.read()          #Read World File
world_list=read_data.split("\n")  #Create parameters list
############################ POSTGIS
xscale=world_list[0] #A         # Read georegistration parameters
yskew=world_list[1] #D
xskew=world_list[2] #B
yscale=world_list[3] #E
xtranslate=world_list[4] #C
ytranslate=world_list[5] #F
srid="31370"
db_name = 'geoprocessing'       # Connection to PostGIS
db_host = 'localhost'
db_user = 'postgres'
db_password = '***'
connection = psycopg2.connect(database=db_name,user=db_user,
password=db_password)
cursor = connection.cursor()
query="drop table if exists public.test"  #Delete previous test table
cursor.execute(query)
connection.commit()
                                #Import raster in test table
os.environ['PGPASSWORD'] = db_password   # Set pg password
environment variable
cmd = 'raster2pgsql plan_mongo.tiff public.test | psql -U {} -d {} -h
{} -p 5432'.format(db_user,db_name,db_host)
subprocess.call(cmd, shell=True)
                                # Georegistration of the test table
query="update test set rast=st_SetGeoReference(rast,'"+xscale+"
"+yskew+" "+xskew+" "+yscale+" "+xtranslate+" "+ytranslate+"',
'GDAL') where rid=1"
cursor.execute(query)
                                #Assign SRID to the test table
query="update test set rast=st_setsrid(rast, "+srid+") where rid=1"
cursor.execute(query)
cursor.close()
connection.commit()
```

stores the temporary image in a raster table. Then the script invokes the PostGIS function "st_setgeoreference" with the World File parameters to update a georeferenced version of the image with its proper metadata (Figure 5). The process is detailed in the last listing (Table IV).

V. CONCLUSION

As soon as a language offers drivers for PostGIS and MongoDB, which is the case of Python used here, it is technically easy to couple the two databases with a single interface. However, the sharing of geospatial data is not immediate because MongoDB introduces some limitations.

In vector mode, the 2DSphere coordinate system implies the use of geodetic coordinates WGS84, which is impractical and confusing in calculations on non-point geometries. It is likely a corollary that the facilities offered for geometries other than points are so undeveloped. However, the combined functionalities offered by MongoDB and PostGIS are enough to obtain a fast and satisfactory result for simple queries on points. But if objects with complex geometries are included in the MongoDB database, it is clear that currently, their replication in PostGIS is the best or the only solution to allow serious spatial processing.

MongoDB does not explicitly recognize geographic raster data. The proposed solution is to manage a georeferenced file (e.g., GeoTIFF) by the MongoDB file management system. If it is managed by GridFS, it is first necessary to reconstitute an external image file through MongoDB commands. Then, the file can be shared without replication by PostGIS which will take care of all the required spatial processing. On the other hand, if the raster data is stored in a non-georeferenced image file in MongoDB it will be necessary to entrust this geo-registration to PostGIS using enriched metadata, which significantly increases the operations and creates unnecessary redundancy.

Geo-visualization is also problematic in MongoDB. Our proposal is to assimilate the Python interface common to both databases, to an extension of QGIS. However, the investment in the development of a general extension is jeopardized by the rapid evolution of the NoSQL systems in general, and MongoDB in particular. But the fast and multiple updates experienced by these systems are in themselves a good thing that should progressively remove the locks registered today on geospatial information.

ACKNOWLEDGEMENT

AIDE is thanked for allowing us to carry out this study and for providing the necessary data and documents. The digitized cadastral plans (version 01/01/2016) were provided for educational purposes by the General Administration of Heritage Documentation (AGDP) as a manager of the authentic source.

REFERENCES

[1] A. B. M. Moniruzzaman and S. A. Hossain, "NoSQL Database: New Era of Databases for Big data Analytics – Classification, Characteristics and Comparison", International Journal of Database Theory and Application, Vol. 6, No. 4, 2013.

[2] S. Agarwal, and K. S. Rajan, "Performance analysis of MongoDB versus PostGIS/PostGreSQL databases for line intersection and point containment spatial queries," Spatial Information Research, 24 pp. 671-677, 2016.

[3] Postgis-users – PostGIS Users Discussion. [Online]. http://lists.osgeo.org/mailman/listinfo/postgis-users [retrieved 01, 2018].

[4] C. Birgen, H. Preisig and J. Morud, "SQL vs. NoSQL". Norwegian University of Science and Technology, Scholar article, 42 p., 2014.

[5] R. Kimball, and M. Ross, "The Data Warehouse Toolkit: The Definitive Guide to Dimensional Modeling," New York: John Wiley & Sons, 3d ed., 2013.

[6] A. Oussous, F.-Z. Benjelloun, A. Ait Lahcen, and S. Belfkih, "Comparison and Classification of NoSQL Databases," International conference on Big Data, Cloud and Applications (Tetouan, Morocco), pp. 1-6, May 2015.

[7] S. Gupta, and G. Narsimha, "Efficient Query Analysis and Performance Evaluation of the Nosql Data Store for BigData," Proceedings of the First International Conference on Computational Intelligence and Informatics (Singapore), S. C. Satapathy *et al.* (eds.), pp. 549-558, 2017.

[8] P. Amirian, A. Basiri, and A. Winstanley, "Evaluation of Data Management Systems for Geospatial Big Data," Computational Science and Its Applications (ICCSA), Springer International Publishing, pp. 678-690, 2014

[9] MongoDB, "MongoDB Documentation". [Online]. https://docs.mongodb.com/ [retrieved 01, 2018]

[10] L. Bonnet, A. Laurent, M. Sala, B. Laurent, and N. Sicard, "Reduce, You Say: What NoSQL Can Do for Data Aggregation and BI in Large Repositories", Proceedings of 22nd International Workshop on Database and Expert Systems Applications (DEXA), IEEE, pp. 483-488, 2011.

[11] C. de Souza Baptista, C. E. Santos Pires, D. Farias Batista Leite, M. Guimares de Oliveira, and O. F. de Lima Junior, "NoSQL Geographic Databases: An Overview," E. Pourabbas (ed.), Geographical Information: Trends and Technologies, CRC Press, pp. 73-103, 2014.

[12] MongoDB, "Migration Guide from RDBMS to MongoDB (Guide de migration d'un système RDBMS vers MongoDB)." 2015. [Online]. https://www.mongodb.com/collateral/rdbms-mongodb-migration-guide/ [retrieved 01, 2018].

[13] K. Banker, P. Bakkum, S. Verch, and T. Hawkins, "MongoDB in action," Manning Publications Co, 2016.

[14] W. Xin, "Design and Implementation of CNEOST," Chinese Astronomy and Astrophysics, 38, pp. 211-221, 2014.

[15] G. Kloss, "MataNui – A Distributed Storage Infrastructure for Scientific Data," Procedia Computer Science, 18, 2607-2610, 2013.

[16] C. Dasadia, and A. Nayak, "MongoDB Cookbook," 2d edition, Packt Publishing, 2016.

[17] QGIS, QGIS Python Plugins Repository [Online]. https://plugins.qgis.org/ [retrieved 01, 2018].

[18] Service Public Fédéral Finance, "CadGIS". [Online]. http://ccff02.minfin.fgov.be/cadgisweb/ [retrieved 01, 2018].

[19] Open Geospatial Consortium, "PDF Georegistration Encoding Best Practice Version 2.2, OGC 08139r3," G. Demmy, and C. Reed, (eds), 2011.

[20] J. D. Fooley, A. van Dam, S. K. Feiner and J. F. Hughes, "Computer Graphics. Principles and practice," Addison-Wesley, 2d ed., 1992.

[21] Library of Congress, "ESRI World File," Sustainability of Digital Formats: Planning for Library of Congress Collections," 2015. [Online]. https://www.loc.gov/preservation/digitalformats/fdd/fdd000287.shtml [retrieved 01, 2018].

ClusterWIS

A Decentralized Forest Information and Management System for the Cluster Forestry and Wood

Jürgen Roßmann, Michael Schluse, Martin Hoppen
Institute for Man-Machine Interaction
RWTH Aachen University
Aachen, Germany
email: {rossmann,schluse,hoppen}@mmi.rwth-aachen.de

Gregor Nägele, Tobias Marquardt
Department Robot Technology
RIF Institute for Research and Transfer e.V.
Dortmund, Germany
email: {gregor.naegele,tobias.marquardt}@rt.rif-ev.de

Christoph Averdung
CPA ReDev GmbH
Siegburg, Germany
email: averdung@supportgis.de

Werner Poschenrieder, Fabian Schwaiger
Chair of Forest Growth and Yield Science
Technical University of Munich
Freising, Germany
email:
{werner.poschenrieder,fabian.schwaiger}@lrz.tum.de

***Abstract*—The cluster forestry and wood's major challenges are its structural complexity and heterogeneity, its many stakeholders, and its decentralized processes. The aim of the ClusterWIS approach is to overcome these challenges. Its core idea is the development of a novel forest information system based on a decentralized infrastructure integrating new planning and consulting methods and interconnecting existing decentralized work processes. It provides end-to-end encrypted communication to run the various processes and to supply them with data while using international standards throughout the system and keeping participation requirements low.**

Keywords-forest information system; sustainable feedstock management; wood and biomass mobilization; decentralized data management.

I. INTRODUCTION

The cluster forestry and wood is the economic sector comprising all stakeholders from forest owners to forestal service providers and the woodworking industry. Its major challenges are its structural complexity and heterogeneity, a huge number of stakeholders with often contrary objectives, and decentralized processes. In the federal state of North Rhine-Westphalia (Germany) alone, 150,000 private forest owners own two-thirds of the forest (90% of which own less than 5 ha), and many small service providers (for planning, tending, logging, etc.) exist [1]. Furthermore, the "production plant" forest provides not only wood as its main product (used for building, paper or as a fuel) but also serves as a long-term CO2 reservoir or as a recreation area. Altogether, this renders process optimization far more complex than in classical manufacturing industry.

Thus, for a sustainable feedstock management and an efficient wood and biomass mobilization throughout the cluster, the increasing demand for wood from sustainably cultivated forests need to be aligned with the requirements of climate change and resilience, environmental protection and society in general. This is the aim of the research project ClusterWIS (WIS for German "Waldinformationssystem" – Forest Information System). For that purpose, new planning and consulting methods need to be introduced and existing decentralized work processes need to be refined and interconnected.

Often, centralized approaches are used to resolve this structural weakness of the cluster. However, this contradicts its highly decentralized organization. Furthermore, many conservative forest owners do not accept an obligatory centralized data management for reasons of data privacy (especially in Germany). For this reason, the foundation of the ClusterWIS approach is a novel, decentralized infrastructure based on standards for data modeling and data exchange. It provides end-to-end encrypted communication to run the various processes and to supply them with highly topical inventory and process data. To provide for the cluster's heterogeneity, it keeps the participation requirements for third party systems low. Furthermore, international standards are used throughout the system like Open Geospatial Consortium (OGC) Web service standards, Geography Markup Language (GML) for data exchange in general, ForestGML [2] for *n*D temporal inventory data, ELDAT [3] for timber logistics data, StanForD [4] for forest machine data, or papiNet [5] for communication with the paper industry. However, the approach is open to other formats and standards.

A ClusterWIS network (Figure 1) comprises applications and services as its nodes, connected by means of the secure communication infrastructure. In the context of the research project, stakeholders will use specialized desktop and mobile applications (e.g., for forest information, forest inventory, production planning, etc.) or Web applications (e.g., for forest owners, service providers, etc.) to access this network. Specialized services, e.g., for processing remote sensing data or forest growth simulations, perform computationally expensive and data intensive tasks for a broad user group even on thin clients like mobile devices. Finally, services for administrative tasks like communication, cloud storage or registration build the network's backbone.

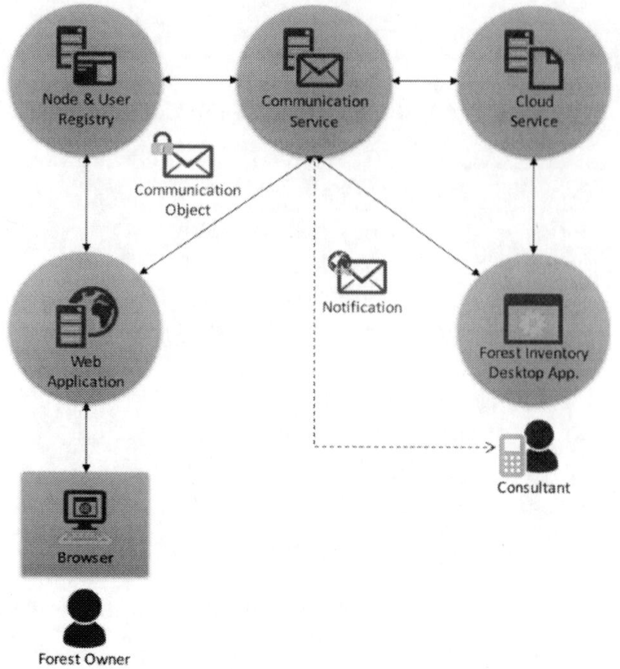

Figure 1. A ClusterWIS network consists of service and application nodes.

For the first time, this decentralized network allows for process optimization across the cluster. In the research project, eight interdependent reference processes (like forest information, planning, consulting, timber trade and production) are analyzed in detail.

The rest of this paper is structured as follows: Section II presents work related to our own and motivates the development of the ClusterWIS approach. Sections III and IV give more details on the ClusterWIS infrastructure and its communication approach. Sections V and VI introduce the ClusterWIS applications (desktop, mobile, Web) and specialized services while Section VII gives an overview of the reference processes analyzed in the research project. Finally, Section VIII concludes this paper.

II. Related Work

ClusterWIS is built on its project partners' preliminary work. Important results come from the research project series Virtual Forest in general, its commercial spin-offs, the underlying SupportGIS technology, and the forest growth simulator SILVA [26]. ClusterWIS aims at making these results available to the whole cluster. Besides summarizing this work, this section introduces similar approaches developed by others.

A. *The Virtual Forest*

The ClusterWIS approach is built on the methods of the "*n*D Forest Management System Virtual Forest" [6], developed in the research project series "Virtual Forest". It provides the necessary technological framework as well as the basis for data modeling, management and distribution.

The idea of the Virtual Forest is a central database that manages all forestal data. It provides various applications for remote sensing data processing (tree species classification [7], stand attributes evaluation [8], or single tree delineation and attribution [9]), forest inventory, planning in biological and technical production, forest machine simulation for training, and support of the logging process.

The technological basis of the central database is the SupportGIS technology [10]. It is widely used for GIS related applications, is based on the standards of OGC and ISO, and powered by object-relational databases. It efficiently manages large amounts of data and supports exchange by standard OGC Web services. Furthermore, data can be managed in *n* spatiotemporal dimensions [2], allowing to track and analyze forestal data over time.

The Virtual Forest uses ForestGML [2], a GML-based modeling language, to model forestal data on a consistent, OGC compliant basis. This facilitates its widespread usage and allows for the usage of OGC Web services.

Central parts of the system are currently implemented in two German state enterprises. While the Virtual Forest focuses on the usage in such large, homogenous enterprises, ClusterWIS aims at making these results available to the whole cluster by decentralizing the approach.

B. *Forest Growth Simulator SILVA*

Silviculture today has to consider a wide range of ecosystem services (ES) that earlier were considered a by-product of traditional forestry. Moreover, on the background of climate change, forest management has to maintain climatic resilience and stability through provision of an adequate forest structure. Thus, forest consulting increasingly applies forest simulation models to estimate the effect of various silvicultural pathways on productivity, quality and further ES [11] [12]. Such ES are carbon sequestration, biodiversity, recreation, and groundwater recharge. As yet, they typically stand within the focus of state forestry. However, private forest stakeholders today also advocate to foster the adaptation of such services by private forestry based on financial incentives [13]. The forest ecosystem model [10] is a preferential tool to take into account ES synergies and tradeoffs and to optimize among various silvicultural objectives. It enables to compare scenarios that adhere to a sensible preselection of silvicultural pathways and to direct forest management towards the most effective subset of them. Such simulation models, as yet, are primarily available for state forestry, as state institutions maintain the necessary IT infrastructure.

The forest growth simulator SILVA provides such a simulation model and is already integrated into the aforementioned Virtual Forest system. SILVA implements the paradigm of a service oriented architecture (SOA). Its kernel is an independent application that does not expose any specific tasks but rather a wide collection of services that may be coupled and assembled to provide specific simulations or evaluations. Moreover, it provides its services through various types of interfaces, e.g., Simple Object Access Protocol (SOAP)-based. Thus, it integrates well into a distributed environment as well as a strictly local one.

Within the Virtual Forest project, several scenarios that integrate SILVA both locally and as a remote service into the larger environment were envisaged and tested.

C. *Similar Approaches*

Until now, others developed approaches similar to ClusterWIS. Some proprietary solutions are available, e.g., online platforms like "IHB Holzbörse" for timber trade [14] or the "Branchenbuch Wald und Forst" as a business directory for consultants [15]. The internet marketplace "CoSeDat" offers the possibility to exchange data and electronically signed PDF documents [16]. In Finland, UPM Paper offers "UPM Customer Online" [17], a digital service channel for customers. In summary, these approaches focus on specific aspects of the complex process chain, only. Hence, a permeability of shared data between the different processes is not given. Often, the idea was to develop centralized systems such as "virtual enterprises" [18] or the "FOCUS-Platform" [19]. As mentioned in the introduction, usually, this is not accepted by cluster actors.

Software solutions like "WaldPlaner" [20] already deliver functionality for planning and decision-making regarding sustainable forest management, but on their own they lack the necessary communication infrastructure and integration into larger processes. Approaches like the "Scottish Forest and Timber Technologies initiative", supported by enterprises and industry, promote knowledge exchange and cooperation between enterprises in the sector [21]. They are successfully able to connect regional actors, but the know-how remains in small and medium sized enterprises of the region. The Web portals "Wald in Österreich" [22] in Austria and "WaldSchweiz" [23] in Switzerland serve the exchange of information in the sector.

Thus, existing approaches do not fulfill all the requirements of the complex and decentralized cluster forestry and wood. This motivates the development of the ClusterWIS approach as introduced in Section I.

III. INFRASTRUCTURE

The cluster's achievable efficiency is strongly related to the way its actors communicate. This requires a framework that does not unnecessarily restrict an actor's professional view or its organization's structure. The ClusterWIS infrastructure is based on secure networking of so-called ClusterWIS nodes. These nodes can either be applications (Section V), specialized Web services (Section VI) or services for administrative tasks.

To use its services and applications, any actor can register and participate in the ClusterWIS network. Well-established methods of IT security are employed to guarantee the safety of connections and exchanged data between actors, applications and Web services. Client-side Hypertext Transfer Protocol Secure (HTTPS) is used for authentication and secure connections. It is integrated into a public key infrastructure (PKI) that allows for end-to-end data encryption. Finally, authorization is based on GeoXACML (Geospatial eXtensible Access Control Markup Language) providing user rights on data and methods.

The administration of the ClusterWIS network is reduced to few central services:

- A node and user registry for all participating actors and nodes (applications and Web services) accessed via Lightweight Directory Access Protocol (LDAP).
- A communication service as a mediator between sender and receiver of so-called communication objects.
- A cloud service used to buffer communication objects, as a general data storage for the network, and as a platform to initialize and run OGC compliant Web services (Web Feature Service (WFS), Web Map Service (WMS) and Web Map Tile Service (WMTS)) on its stored data.

This lean infrastructure (combined with its communication approach presented in the next section) also keeps the participation requirements for third party systems low.

IV. COMMUNICATION

Three basic rules apply to communication within a ClusterWIS network: Data and (service) requests are always transferred by secure connections and encrypted by the public key of the recipient. Furthermore, recipients account for conformant data usage inside their domain. Finally, it has to be assumed that many communication partners and systems are regularly offline (e.g., when being in the forest with bad reception).

A. *Communication Object*

The aforementioned communication objects are used to transfer data and corresponding requests (Figure 2). The structure comprises information on the type of data, the sender, the receiver and the tasks the data is intended for. Data comprises embedded files, links to files on cloud services, metadata describing files, or simple parameters for service calls. The complete communication object is realized as a ZIP archive containing the XML encoded data structure and additional embedded files. These files as well as the parts of the communication object in the dashed box are encrypted by the receiver's public key. Thus, only its id, the sender and the receiver are visible.

B. *Communication Service*

The transfer of communication objects is operated by the communication service. The use of HTTPS and encryption of the data ensures that neither unauthorized third parties nor the cloud service or the communication service itself get access to the data.

A dispatch method for communication objects is specified for every receiving user (or node, as well) within the registry. This comprises:

- Notification by mail or smartphone push message that contains a download link to the communication object.
- Direct delivery using a SOAP interface of the recipient.
- Actively pulling the list of new communication objects from the communication service.

The communication service provides a SOAP interface to send a new communication object and to request a list of receivable communication objects.

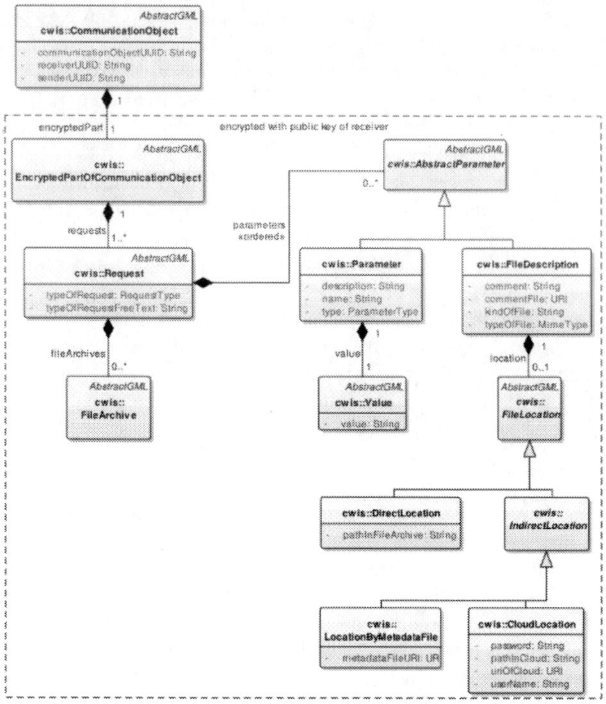

Figure 2. Structure of the ClusterWIS communication object.

A communication example is shown in Figure 1. A forest owner uses a browser to access the Web application (Section V.B) and create a communication object with a request for forest inventory. It is encrypted (public key of the consultant) and sent to the communication service, which buffers it into the cloud service and sends a notification to the recipient (consultant). The latter starts its Forest Inventory application (Section V.A.2), which asks the communication service for new communication objects that are subsequently downloaded from the cloud service. Finally, the consultant decrypts the communication object with his private key and processes the message. Note that all connections between nodes are additionally secured by client-side HTTPS, which is also used for authentication.

C. *OPC UA*

The decentralized ClusterWIS approach is similar to those approaches subsumed as "Industry 4.0" in the manufacturing industry. Furthermore, ClusterWIS communication not only takes place between actors but also from and to forest machinery. This motivates the integration of standard Industry 4.0 protocols into the network. As a well-established standard, Open Platform Communications – Unified Architecture (OPC UA) [25] is advisable for this purpose. Especially, as it provides a decentralized client server architecture without the need for central servers, it integrates well into the ClusterWIS PKI, it is an open and vendor-independent standard, it is robust, and it supports participants being temporarily offline.

Thus, to complement the aforementioned SOAP-based approach, ClusterWIS nodes may also be equipped with an OPC UA client and server component allowing the exchange of communication objects.

V. APPLICATIONS

An important part of the ClusterWIS approach are the user and scenario specific portals the actors can use to access the network. These comprise desktop, mobile and Web applications.

A. *Desktop and Mobile Applications*

Desktop and mobile end-user applications provide online as well as offline access to ClusterWIS features. They can be used by actors like forest owners, service providers, or contractors to view, gather, modify, and exchange forestal data. In the context of the research project, applications are based on the Virtual Forest prototypes. They use the VEROSIM framework [24] that combines an integrated runtime database with subject-specific modules to create adapted applications for diverse scenarios.

Four different applications are being developed and refined to meet the requirements of the project's reference processes as described in Section VII:

1) Forest Information

The Forest Information application acts as an information portal to the data managed by ClusterWIS. Its primary functions are visualization, combination and analysis of geographic and business data, e.g., orthophotos, satellite imagery, Lidar, cadaster, inventory, or regulatory data. This data may be available locally via files and databases or provided by OGC-compliant Web services (WMS, WMTS, WFS) within the ClusterWIS network.

2) Forest Inventory

This application supports the forest inventory process. It allows a service provider to work with data made available by the commissioning forest owner and provides tools to record relevant stand attributes and single tree information. As this data is typically gathered on-site, the software also offers assistance for spatial localization during the process.

3) Forest Planning

The Forest Planning application provides a user-friendly and efficient interface to forest growth simulation. This comprises input parameterization as well as result analysis and visualization. The computationally intensive simulation itself is sourced out to a service (see Section VI.B).

4) Technical Production

This application supports the technical production process in its different phases, namely preparation of work assignments, assistance of forest workers and machine operators with instructions, and practical guidance as well as documentation of the harvesting operations and its results.

B. *Web Applications*

Web applications are ideally suited to provide a low-threshold access to the ClusterWIS network. They do not need client-side installation and can be used on both desktop and mobile devices alike. Capacity and performance scaling is easy and new features can be provided to users with no effort. Finally, Web applications easily support operation in secure networks.

The browser-based GIS SGJ GeoHornet is one example of such a Web application that is used in ClusterWIS. It has already successfully been employed in the Virtual Forest project as well as its commercial spin-offs. Various data sources like ForestGML databases or Web services can be accessed and embedded. This way, e.g., a registered forest owner can get an overview of his or her entire property. GeoHornet also provides methods to plot maps and enhance these plots with own graphical and textual annotations. It can create, send and receive communication objects, e.g., to send a request to another actor in the ClusterWIS network. GeoHornet can be customized for the user's demands.

VI. Specialized Services

As mentioned in Section I, besides backbone services (Sections III-IV), the ClusterWIS network comprises specialized services, e.g., to process remote sensing data or simulate forest growth.

A. *Remote Sensing Data Processing*

Often, the data necessary for a sustainable feedstock management can only be made available using remote sensing methods like tree species classification [7], stand attributes evaluation [8], or single tree delineation and attribution [9]. However, such methods usually need to access, process and store vast amounts of raw geo data, unfeasible, e.g., for mobile apps. Furthermore, existing methods need to be enhanced to easily incorporate stakeholders to refine the data with their expert knowledge (e.g., provide tree samples to optimize local tree species classification results). Thus, a goal of the ClusterWIS project is to make these methods available as services to allow the usage of suitable hardware on server side and to provide service interfaces for user provided calibration data.

B. *Forest Growth Simulation*

Forest growth simulators - beyond scenarios of stand development - provide further services that are closely connected to a simulator's core function. Such services are virtual tree generation based on stand structure attributes and computation of assortments using individual tree data. Hence, one relevant task within ClusterWIS is to extend existing data formats, such as ForestGML, to comply with the time-related data content that is specific to simulation models.

SILVA provides stand development as a result of rule-based management plans. That way, the simulator may provide scenarios that put emphasis on a specific subset of ecosystem services or that promote the development of specific stand structures and species mixtures. The seamless and manifold integration of SILVA [26] into the ClusterWIS infrastructure enables to couple to any other service that might receive data from the simulator or provide essential basic data to it. That objective is particularly important on the background of eocsystem service provision. Ecosystem services are typically linked by mutual synergies and tradeoffs. Therefore, one relevant coupling scenario is the linkage between SILVA and vegetation distribution models. Such specialized land surface models [12] represent processes of vegetation growth, seed dissemination and disturbance. Thus, they may provide valuable results about the establishment of regeneration trees and individual young trees to forest growth simulators. Moreover, as vegetation models often use a simplified representation of main stand development, they might straightforwardly integrate individual tree data provided by the growth simulator.

VII. Reference Processes

ClusterWIS not only provides an infrastructure, protocols and applications. It also specifies processes for a sustainable feedstock management realized on this foundation, which will be tested and demonstrated in actual forest stands. An important aspect of ClusterWIS is that these processes do no longer take place in a parallel and unrelated manner but start to interact with each other. A selection of practically relevant reference processes is considered within the project and briefly introduced below:

A. *Forestal data provision*

Sustainable natural resource management requires information and planning. For that purpose, up-to-date, highly qualitative, and detailed (geo) data is needed. Data is usually compiled of various data sources (ForestGML-structured data, third party spatial base data and business specific data). Currently, the comprehensive provision of such data to the cluster is an unresolved problem. Thus, this process describes the provision within the ClusterWIS network.

B. *Forest information*

This process describes an actor's access to the provisioned forestal data of a specific area in the right time at the right place, comprising visualization, analysis, and editing.

C. *Forest inventory*

Forest inventory is the acquisition and management of environmental data in forestry. Thus, the purpose of this process is to provide the cluster with always up-to-date, detailed and high-quality data. An important aspect in this context is to automatically and logically connect different data sources and, if applicable, different timestamps (for trend analysis) within the *n*D forest information system.

D. *Planning and consulting*

The comprehensive data provided by the ClusterWIS network enables consultants to give forest owners efficient and goal-orientated advice on how to manage their forests. In particular, they can use simulation tools to demonstrate how different management alternatives result in different future outcomes.

E. Timber trade

The ClusterWIS network opens new ways for getting in contact. By providing all relevant information to all actors involved in the process, a more efficient communication between sellers and buyers can be established. Thus, ClusterWIS provides the framework for a more efficient timber trade and contributes to a more efficient wood and biomass mobilization.

F. Sustainable Harvesting

Integrated into the aforementioned processes within the ClusterWIS network, the technical production process can access a vast number of relevant data. This allows for the planning of more sustainable harvesting measures. It comprises the (simulated) determination and visualization of wood assortments, harvesting costs, accessibility and harvesting routes, average skidding distances, as well as aspects of nature conservation. Besides planning, this process also comprises the execution of planned measures and their documentation, where the latter can again be used in downstream processes.

VIII. CONCLUSION

The cluster forestry and wood is an important economic sector. Yet, its major challenges (structural complexity and heterogeneity, huge number of stakeholders, and decentralized processes) are insufficiently addressed in current IT solutions. The ClusterWIS approach can resolve these problems by providing a decentralized, secure, and lean infrastructure for communication and data management. Based on this infrastructure, services and applications are orchestrated to realize novel, interconnected, and sustainable processes for feedstock management among the cluster's actors.

In the current phase of the ClusterWIS research project, the infrastructure and all reference processes are analyzed and specified in detail. The next step is the realization and implementation of the infrastructure (services, applications, etc.) and the execution of a first communication demo scenario.

ACKNOWLEDGMENT

The research project ClusterWIS is co-financed by the European Union and the German federal state of North Rhine-Westphalia: European Union - Investing in our Future - European Regional Development Fund (EFRE-0800088).

REFERENCES

[1] Waldbauernverband NRW e.V. (English: Wood owner association of North Rhine-Westphalia), "Waldbauernverband NRW e.V.," URL: http://www.waldbauernverband.de/2016/ [accessed: 2018-03-05].

[2] M. Hoppen, M. Schluse, J. Rossmann, and C. Averdung, "A New nD Temporal Geodata Management Approach using GML," in GEOProcessing 2015 - The Seventh International Conference on Advanced Geographic Information Systems, Applications, and Services, Lisbon, Portugal, 2015, pp. 110–116. ISBN 978-1-61208-383-4, Permalink https://www.thinkmind.org/index.php?view=article&articleid=geoprocessing_2015_6_20_30086 [accessed: 2018-02-02]

[3] Kuratorium für Waldarbeit und Forsttechnik e.V. (KWF, English: German Center for Forest Work and Technology), "ELDAT," URL: http://www.eldatstandard.de [accessed: 2017-12-04].

[4] Skogforsk, "StanForD," URL: http://www.skogforsk.se/english/projects/stanford [accessed: 2017-12-04].

[5] papiNet Europe/NA, "The intelligent choice.....papiNet," URL: http://www.papinet.org [accessed: 2017-12-04].

[6] J. Rossmann, M. Hoppen, and A. Buecken, "Semantic World Modelling and Data Management in a 4D Forest Simulation and Information System," in *ISPRS 8th 3DGeoInfo Conference & WG II/2 Workshop, International Archives of the Photogrammetry, Remote Sensing and Spatial Information Sciences*, Istanbul, 2013, vol. XL-2/W2, pp. 65–72.

[7] P. Krahwinkler, "Machine learning based classification for semantic world modeling : support vector machine based decision tree for single tree level forest species mapping," PhD thesis, RWTH Aachen, 2013.

[8] A. Buecken and J. Rossmann, "Mining for the Timber-Volume for a State-Wide Forest Information System," Intl. LiDAR Mapping Forum 2017, Denver, pp. 1-4, 2017

[9] A. Buecken and J. Rossmann, "Modelling of Forest Landscapes from Remote Sensing LiDAR Data and Aerial Photos," in *Capturing Reality - 3D, Laser Scanning and LiDAR Technologies Forum 2015, 23-25 November, 2015, Salzburg, Austria, pp. 1-6*, 2016.

[10] CPA, "CPA ReDev GmbH," URL: http://www.cpa-redev.de/index.php?lang=e [accessed: 2017-12-04].

[11] P. Biber et al., "How Sensitive are Ecosystem Services in European Forest Landscapes to Silvicultural Treatment?," Forests, 6(5), 1666–1695, 2015. doi: 10.3390/f6051666

[12] S. Hudjetz et al., "Modeling Wood Encroachment in Abandoned Grasslands in the Eifel National Park – Model Description and Testing," PLoS One 9:e113827, 2014. doi: 10.1371/journal.pone.0113827, 2014.

[13] I. Prokofieva, "Payments for Ecosystem Services—the Case of Forests," Current Forestry Reports, 2(2), pp. 130–142, 2014. doi: 10.1007/s40725-016-0037-9

[14] Fordaq, "IHB," URL: http://www.ihb.de [accessed: 2017-12-04].

[15] Wald-wird-mobil.de gGmbH, "Branchenbuch Wald und Forst (English: Yellow Pages Wood and Forest," URL: http://www.waldhilfe.de [accessed: 2017-12-04].

[16] EGGER, "Der Internet-Marktplatz CoSeDat (English: The internet marketplace CoSeDat)," URL: http://www.cosedat.com [accessed: 2017-12-04].

[17] The Biofore Company UPM, "UPM Customer Online" URL: http://www.upmpaper.com [accessed: 2017-12-04].

[18] H. Jacke, "Abschlussbericht zur Pre-Feasibility-Study "Holztransport und Logistik / Virtueller Betrieb Forst und Holz NRW (English: Final report of the pre feasibility study "wood transport and logistics / virtual enterprise forest and wood NRW")"," Göttingen, 2001.

[19] "Vision, FOCUS - The Project,“ [Online]. Available: http://focusnet.eu/about-focus/project-vision.

[20] Nordwestdeutsche Forstliche Versuchsanstalt (NW-FVA, English: Northwest German Forest Research Institute), "Softwareprogramme und Webapplikationen der NW-FVA (English: Software programs and web applications of NW-FVA),“ URL: http://www.nw-fva.de/index.php?id=3 [accessed: 2017-12-04].

[21] Scottish Forest & Timber Technologies, "The Scottish Forest and Timber Technologies initiative" URL: http://www.forestryscotland.com [accessed: 2017-12-04].

[22] Wald in Österreich (English: Forest in Austria), "Das Portal zu Wald und Holz (English: Portal to forest and wood)" URL: http://www.wald-in-oesterreich.at [accessed: 2017-12-04].

[23] WaldSchweiz, Verband der Waldeigentümer (English: Suisse wood owner association), "WaldSchweiz" URL: http://www.waldschweiz.ch [accessed: 2017-12-04].

[24] J. Rossmann, M. Schluse, C. Schlette and R. Waspe, "A New Approach to 3D Simulation Technology as Enabling Technology for eROBOTICS," in 1st International Simulation Tools Conference & EXPO 2013 (SIMEX'2013), 2013, pp. 39-46.

[25] J. Lange, F. Iwanitz, and T. Burke, "OPC From Data Access to Unified Architecture," 2010. ISBN 978-3-8007-3242-5

[26] M. Kahn and H. Pretzsch, "Parametrisierung und Validierung des Wuchsmodells SILVA 2.2 für Rein- und Mischbestände aus Fichte, Tanne, Kiefer, Buche, Eiche und Erle (English: Parameterisation and validation of the growth model SILVA 2.2. for pure and mixed stands of spruce, fir, pine, beech, oak and alder)," in *Jahrestagung der DVFFA Sektion Ertragskunde*, Kevelaer , 1998.

Assessing and Evaluating Standard Compliance with a State and Local Government GIS Metadata Profile in Large Geospatial Databases

Timothy Mulrooney
Dept. of Environmental, Earth and Geospatial Sciences
North Carolina Central University
Durham, NC, USA
e-mail: tmulroon@nccu.edu

Abstract— **Under the supervision of the North Carolina Geographic Information Coordinating Council (NCGICC) and Statewide Mapping Advisory Committee (SMAC), a committee defined and developed a State and Local Government Metadata profile intended for use in North Carolina. This profile is based on the International Organization for Standardization (ISO) 191** standards. In addition to dictating best practices and conventions for existing metadata entries such as the Title, Publication Date and Use Constraints, this standard accounts for evolving technologies that did not exist when original metadata standards were first developed. While the rate at which geoinformation is created has exponentially increased, the time dedicated to cataloging and subsequently assessing and evaluating this metadata information remains nearly the same. In addition to educating the North Carolina Geographic Information Systems (GIS) community on this new standard, the research team is currently developing tools so GIS managers can gauge standard compliance more efficiently and proactively than in the past. In this short paper, the research team has begun using programming methods in which metadata entries from multiple layers in large geospatial databases can be assessed and evaluated. These methods will be tested using various quantitative methods, including the Technology Acceptance Model (TAM). This can provide insight into the various accuracies (horizontal, vertical, temporal, etc.) of layers which in turn can dictate future efforts. It can also be used to identify inconsistencies in metadata entries with an end goal of understanding misinterpretation of the profile so it can be improved in future incarnations.**

Keywords-GIS Metadata; Metadata; Metadata Profile; North Carolina State and Local Government Profile.

I. RATIONALE

A GIS serves as the tangible and intangible means by which information about spatially related phenomena can be created, stored, analyzed and rendered in the digital environment. In the North Carolina GIS community, GIS is used to represent transportation routes, elevation, delineate land ownership parcels, highlight patterns of crime and help make zoning decisions. The manner in which geospatial data is captured varies. Some methods include using a Global Positioning System (GPS) unit, extracting or improving existing GIS data, the use of an Unmanned Aerial Vehicle (UAV) or some other remote sensing platform, or creating data from an analog format via digitization. Regardless of the method, the resources (e.g., the computers, time and people dedicated to the process of collecting and creating geospatial data) are the most time-consuming portion of a GIS-related project [1]. As a result, the GIS community needs to ensure the quality of geospatial data created from these methods is captured and assessed in a systematic way.

Geospatial metadata serves as the formal framework to catalog descriptive, administrative and structural information about geospatial data. Geospatial metadata is inherently different from other forms of electronic metadata because each metadata file can be applied a spatial component that is not implicit with other forms of metadata. Given the capricious rate at which all forms of geo-information can be created, formal metadata serves as a lifeline between the tacit knowledge of the data creator and current and future generations of geospatial data consumers.

In the United States, the Federal Geographic Data Committee (FGDC) metadata standard, commonly referred to as the Content Standard for Digital Geospatial Metadata (CSDGM) allows for more than 400 individual metadata elements. The North Carolina GIS community has been proactive about understanding the importance of metadata. Under the supervision of the NCGICC and SMAC, a committee was tasked to develop a State and Local Government Metadata profile for geospatial data intended for use in North Carolina. This standard is based on the ISO 191** format and is an improvement over prior metadata standards to account for evolving technologies such as remotely sensed imagery, online services and ontologies. These were not considered when original metadata standards such as the CSDGM (formally known as *FGDC-STD-001-1998)* were first published. At this time, assessing and evaluating adherence to this standard for large spatial databases is an exhaustive process, as users must toggle through multiple levels of metadata records among multiple features a using a metadata editor. The goal of this paper is to propose a programmatic and faster assessment and evaluation alternative that can be used by GIS management to facilitate decision-making.

The rest of this paper is organized as follows. Section II describes the evolution of metadata. Section III describes the specific use and application of the North Carolina State metadata profile. Section IV addresses the how standard compliance is addressed. Section V discussed preliminary results. The acknowledgement and conclusions close the article.

II. THE EVOLUTION OF METADATA SCIENCE AND ASSESSMENT

Although metadata's original use was simply as a means to catalog data, its storage and assessment has become a science in itself. The role of metadata assessment can be seen in a variety of different fields. An Electronic Metadata Record (EMR), for example, is a technology that is produced and edited when an electronic document is edited or created, such as a patient record or digital x-ray. Thus, the ease of storing, accessing and retrieving electronic metadata and files for medical data can help prevent litigation against malpractice lawsuits [2]. A complex statistical analysis was to retrieve biomedical articles from more than 4,800 journals to help support decision-making processes [3]. If properly maintained, metadata serves as a capable surrogate when querying scanned imagery or hard-copy information is not feasible and further validates in-situ decisions as they are reinforced by easily accessible support literature.

Early research and commentary on the concept of geospatial metadata has touted its value as an effective decision-making tool, regardless of its native format [4]. These formats include Hyper Text Markup Language (HTML), Extensible Markup Language (XML) along with its various ISO standards (19115, 19139), TXT (Text File), Geography Markup Language (GML) and Standard Generalized Markup Language (SGML), as well as proprietary formats. Methodology has explored the ability to integrate spatial metadata to a stand-alone database long before metadata was stored in a standardized format, as well as compiling statistics about metadata elements within the confines of specific software [5] [6].

The population of geospatial metadata is a monotonous process and subject to error, although research has explored the large-scale production of standards-based metadata in order to alleviate these issues [7][8]. Because of this, research maintains that human nature alone undermines the immediate and long-term goals of metadata for an organization and the GIS user community [9]. While the omission of one minor element would not degrade a layer's metadata or invalidate the geospatial data on which it is based, it may compromise quantitative data quality measures captured from which decisions can be made. More recently, feature level metadata has been able to capture data quality information, but is typically limited to quantitative measures of positional accuracy and qualitative information related to data lineage within eight of the more than 400 entries that comprise a complete FGDC-compliant metadata file [10] [11]. Even now, the population of these metadata elements is not fully automated and some entries must be done by a GIS data steward.

III. THE NORTH CAROLINA STATE AND LOCAL GOVERNMENT PROFILE

Geospatial metadata standards serve as a cohesive means by which organizations can define, store and more importantly share information about geospatial data. It defines the categories of information that needs to be stored, individual entries, or tags, of individual elements within these categories and the types of data (text, date, number) and their lengths that can be stored while expressing these tags. FGDC metadata is divided into 7 sections or divisions that transcend descriptive, administrative and structural components. They are: Identification Information, Data Quality Information, Spatial Data Organization Information, Spatial Reference Information, Entity and Attribute Information, Distribution Information, and Metadata Reference Information [12]

Within these high-level divisions, subdivisions and eventually individual metadata tags can be populated to catalog various forms of information about the GIS data layer. The hierarchy of these divisions and subdivisions are consistent with a standard. In addition to providing this structure, the FGDC also creates guidelines by dictating which metadata elements are to be populated. The FGDC requires seven metadata elements be populated for all GIS data. The FGDC also suggests that fifteen metadata elements be populated. These suggested and required elements are included in Table I below.

TABLE 1: REQUIRED AND SUGGESTED FGDC ELEMENTS

FGDC -Required Elements	*FGDC- Suggested Elements*	
Title Reference Date Language Topic Category Abstract Point of Contact Metadata Date	Dataset Responsible Party Geography Locations by Coordinates (X and Y) Data Character Set Spatial Resolution Distribution Format Spatial Representation Type Reference System Metadata Character Set	Lineage Statement Online Resource Metadata File Identifier Metadata Standard Name Metadata Standard Version Metadata Language

Organizations actively create content standards for new technologies and manners in which geospatial data are collected and stored. One such example is the FGDC content standard for Remotely Sensed Data. This includes two divisions germane to the equipment and methods such as platform name, sensor information and algorithm information used to capture the imagery, in addition to the seven existing aforementioned divisions [13]. Standards such as these and others must be increasingly flexible and updatable to account for the evolving technologies in which geospatial data can now be captured (crowdsourcing, Unmanned Aerial Vehicle, large scale geocoding), processed (new geostatistical and interpolation algorithms) and ultimately delivered (web map service, web feature service) to the GIS user community.

In recent years, the North Carolina SMAC has recognized most GIS data managers lack the time and resources necessary to learn and apply a metadata standard. To address the problem of missing or incomplete metadata records among state and local data publishers, the SMAC chartered an ad-hoc Metadata Committee in October 2012 to "recommend ways to expand and improve geospatial metadata in North Carolina that are efficient for the data producer and benefit data users in the discovery and application of geospatial data." The Metadata Committee submitted a draft of this profile, based on the ISO 19115 (for Geographic Information – Metadata: 2003), ISO 19115-1 (for Geographic Information – Metadata – Part 1: Fundamentals: 2014) and ISO 19119 (Geographic Information – Services: 2016) standards. After review and modification by SMAC and its standing committees, the most current version of this standard has been in effect since December 30, 2016 and is available through the NCOneMap portal [14].

Given seven required and fifteen recommended metadata elements are fairly ambiguous and less than ideal for many organizations whose data is integrated into the NCOneMap [15], the North Carolina state geospatial data portal, this profile provides explicit guidance on required/suggested metadata elements, wording for these elements, standardization of naming/date conventions and domain fields for topic categories for more than 75 metadata tags. A few examples of the rules for geospatial metadata include:

1. Publication Date is required and the format for Publication Date is YYYY-MM-DD or YYYYMMDD. If day is not known, use YYYY-MM and use YYYY if month is not known.
2. Abstract is required as a free text entry.
3. Status is required and only possible values are 'historicalArchive', 'required', 'planned', 'onGoing' 'completed', 'underDevelopment' and 'obsolete'.
4. Topic Category is required and can be one of 23 possible values from domain table.
5. Online linkage is required to an URL address that provides access, preferably direct access, to the data

The following are additional examples of rules for Geospatial Services:

1. Metadata Scope code must be 'service'.
2. Online Function code is required from domain of one of five possible values.

This richer metadata enables content consistency and improves the search and discovery of data through NCOneMap.

IV. ASSESSING STANDARD COMPLIANCE

Given the ever-increasing size of GIS data sets and the metadata requirements for each data layer, there needs to be a mechanism to assess the quality of these metadata not seen in previous generations or documented in existing literature. There also needs to be a means by which individual metadata entries adhere to predefined profiles and standards. Programming techniques and software packages have allowed users to assess information that would take a human days or perhaps weeks to do.

Open source solutions using Perl and R have been used to assess and evaluate metadata by traversing geospatial metadata stored in XML format as per FGDC requirements [16], resulting in quantitative metrics, graphs and reports regarding metadata compliance, as shown in Figure 1.

As applied to the NC State and Local Government Profile, one major challenge exists. Primarily, geospatial data and metadata is typically software specific. While optimal open source solutions could be used to gleam information from metadata stored in XML using an appropriate xPath, these software-agnostic solutions are typically loosely-coupled and not intuitive to the average user. As a result of reliance on Esri products throughout the state, the Python programming language is being used to run this iteration of an assessment and evaluation tool before open source solutions are explored.

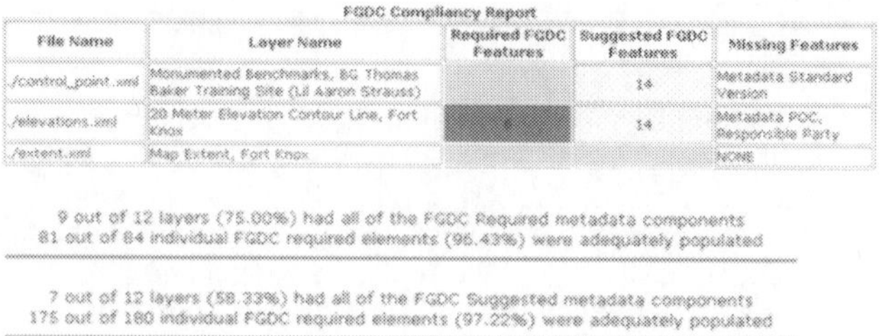
FGDC Compliancy Report

File Name	Layer Name	Required FGDC Features	Suggested FGDC Features	Missing Features
./control_point.xml	Monumented Benchmarks, BG Thomas Baker Training Site (Lil Aaron Strauss)		14	Metadata Standard Version
./elevations.xml	20 Meter Elevation Contour Line, Fort Knox	[illegible]	14	Metadata POC, Responsible Party
./extent.xml	Map Extent, Fort Knox			NONE

9 out of 12 layers (75.00%) had all of the FGDC Required metadata components
81 out of 84 individual FGDC required elements (96.43%) were adequately populated

7 out of 12 layers (58.33%) had all of the FGDC Suggested metadata components
175 out of 180 individual FGDC required elements (97.22%) were adequately populated

Figure 1: Sample of Metadata Compliance Report Generated Using Open Source Assessment Tool

Using the NC State and Local Government Profile as a guideline, the research team has been developing tools for data managers to access and evaluate metadata entries. At the current time, metadata entries are written to CSV (Comma Separated Values). While doing this, string operations are run to ensure that required entries are populated, date entries comply with required conventions and domain entries match those in the domain table, all while agglomerating results and statistics at the database, layer (record) and tag (attribute) level. They can provide GIS managers with insight on non-compliant metadata entries to determine relationships between non-compliant entries and data steward or particular attributes that are continually non-compliant. The current working application of this code takes less than one minute to assess and evaluate 75 metadata elements for a GIS database containing 70 individual layers.

V. PRELIMINARY RESULTS

The TAM (Technology Acceptance Model) was used to assess and quantify the effectiveness of the open source metadata assessment tool. The TAM that we know of today was originally created as a means to universally quantify the effectiveness of technology by exploring relationships between the technology's Perceived Ease of Use, Perceived Usefulness, Attitude Towards Using and the Intention to Further Use the technology [17]. Using Chronbach's Alpha, Principal Components Analysis and Simple Linear Regression, associations can be found between these various components, as shown in Figure 2.

In this case, TAM has shown the potential effectiveness of this tool. However, H5 (Attitude Towards Using has a significant effect on Intention to Use) is not supported with 95% confidence. Possible reasons why this model is not supported is not a disconnect between these two concepts, but the actual implementation of technology given the role of the respondents. This survey used 50 respondents whose roles ranged from GIS technicians to GIS managers. GIS technicians working on few GIS data layers have little to no need for metadata assessment and therefore no intention to further use it. When enough GIS Managers have completed the assessment on which TAM is based, it will be run once again on this new tool to assess its effectiveness for a more germane usership.

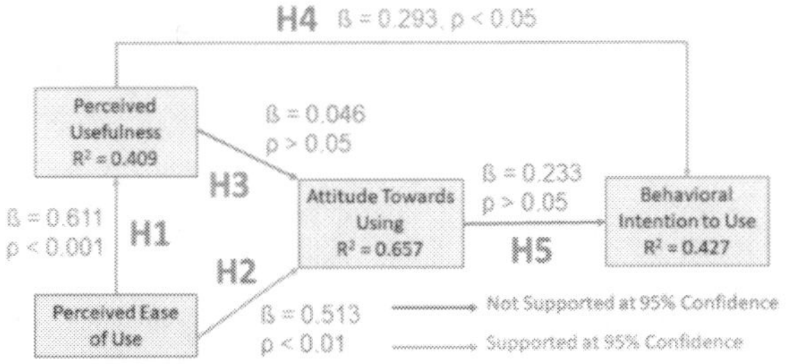

Figure 2: Regression Used to Test Research Hypotheses

VI. DISCUSSION

While a powerful and efficient tool, the programmatic assessment and evaluation of metadata entries still cannot altogether replace the human component. While these technologies can traverse metadata schema and extract tags to deem if they are complete, compliant or belong to a particular domain, it does not necessarily mean they are correct. QA/QC (Quality Assurance/Quality Control) techniques should be used to determine metadata quality across the entire dataset via ANSI (American National Standards Institute), ANSQ (American Society of Quality Control) or other institution-wide QA/QC procedures that best fit needs, resources and limitations.

VII. CONCLUSION

The increasing schism between the rate at which data are created and the efficiency at which the metadata are assessed serves as the impetus of this preliminary research. This paper looked to explore solutions to measure adherence to a state-level profile. Thus far, a programmatic solution using the Python programming language has been implemented. However, it is too early to tell how well these can be integrated into business processes at organizations such as the NCGICC. This ongoing research highlights the importance and need of programmatic approaches to the assessment and evaluation of metadata for large spatial datasets. This information can provide GIS Managers with already limited resources with the tools to make informed decisions that are not feasible with visual inspection or a qualitative knowledge of these increasingly large datasets.

ACKNOWLEDGMENT

The author wishes to thank the North Carolina Department of Transportation (NCDOT) for their generous support of this ongoing research.

REFERENCES

[1] K. Leiden, K. Laughery, J. Keller, J. French, J., W. Warwick and S. Wood, "A Review of Human Performance Models for the Prediction of Human Error," Moffett Field, CA : National Aeronautics and Space Administration, 2001.

[2] T. McLean, L. Burton, C. Haller and P. McLean, "Electronic Medical Record Metadata: Uses and Liability," Journal of the American College of Surgeons, vol. 206(3), pp. 405 – 411, 2008.

[3] T. Theodosiou, L. Angelis and A. Vakali, "Non-Linear Correlation of Content and Metadata Information Extracted From Biomedical Article Datasets," Journal of Biomedical Informatics, vol. 41(1), pp. 202 – 216, 2008.

[4] D. Wong and C. Wu, "Spatial Metadata and GIS for Decision Support," Proceedings of the Twenty-Ninth Hawaii International Conference, vol. 3 (3 – 6), pp. 557 – 566, 2006.

[5] D. Lanter, "A Lineage Meta-Database Approach Towards Spatial Analytic Database Optimization," Cartography and Geographic Information Systems, vol. 20(2), pp. 112-121, 1993.

[6] D. Lanter, "The Contribution of ARC/INFO's Log File to Metadata Analysis of GIS Data Processing," Proceedings of the Fourteenth Annual ESRI User Conference, Palm Springs, California, 1994.

[7] G. Giuliani, Y. Guigoz, P. Lacroix, N. Ray and A. Lehmann, "Facilitating the production of ISO-compliant metadata of geospaital datasets," International Journal of Applied Earth Observation and Geoinformation, vol. 44, 23-243.

[8] S. Trilles, L. Diaz and J. Huerta, "Approach to facilitating a geospatial data and metadata publication using a standard geoservice," International Journal of Geo-Information, vol. 6(5), pp 126.

[9] C. Doctorow. *Metacrap: Putting the Torch to Seven Straw-Men of the Meta-Utopia.* [online]. Available from http://www.well.com/~doctorow/metacrap.htm. [retrieved February 2018].

[10] L. Qiu, G. Lingling, H. Feng and T. Yong, "A unified metadata information management framework for the digital city," Proceedings of IEEE's Geoscience and Remote Sensing Symposium, pp. 4422–4424, 2004

[11] R. Devillers, Y. Bédard, and R. Jeansoulin, "Multidimensional management of geospatial data quality information for its dynamic use within Geographical Information Systems," Photogrammetric Engineering and Remote Sensing, vol. 71(2), pp. 205–215, 2005.

[12] Federal Geographic Data Committee (FGDC), "Content Standard for Digital Geospatial Metadata Workbook," Washington D.C.: Federal Geographic Data Committee, 2000.

[13] Federal Geographic Data Committee (FGDC), "Content Standard for Digital Metadata: Extensions for Remote Sensing Data," Washington D.C.: Federal Geographic Data Committee, 2002.

[14] North Carolina Geographic Information Coordinating Council (NCGICC), *North Carolina State and Local Government Metadata Profile for Geospatial Data and Services* [online]. Available from http://www.nconemap.gov/DiscoverGetData/Metadata.aspx#iso. [retrieved February 2018]

[15] North Carolina Geographic Information Coordinating Council (NCGICC). *North Carolina OneMap* [online]. Available from http://www.nconemap.gov. [retrieved February 2018].

[16] T. Mulrooney, "Turning Data into Information: Assessing and Reporting GIS Metadata Integrity Using Integrated Computing Technologies," Greensboro, North Carolina: University of North Carolina, Greensboro, 2009.

[17] F. Davis, "Perceived Usefulness, Perceived Ease of Use and User Acceptance of Information Technology," MIS Quarterly, vol. 13(3), pp. 319-340, 1989.

Methodology of Knowledge Mapping for Arbitrary Objects and Entities: Knowledge Mining and Spatial Representations – Objects in Multi-dimensional Context

Claus-Peter Rückemann
Westfälische Wilhelms-Universität Münster (WWU),
Leibniz Universität Hannover,
North-German Supercomputing Alliance (HLRN), Germany
Email: ruckema@uni-muenster.de

Abstract—**The research presented in this paper focusses on a new methodology for knowledge based mapping of objects and entities for creating new multi-dimensional context. The mapping to new context can improve complex knowledge mining, discovery, and decision making results. The new context increases the potential for creating new insights. The paper introduces the new methodology used with advanced knowledge mining and provides the results of the present research. Examples from an implementation and a case study on knowledge mining and spatial representations are given. The case study utilises commonly available unstructured data and creates new multi-disciplinary context, especially spatial mapping of entities and integration with data and advanced tools, which can be used for further analysis, e.g., automated and visual analysis. The methodology can employ integrated knowledge resources and services for mapping support and can be applied to any content from arbitrary disciplines. The results of the mapping to new context can be used for knowledge mining workflows, for gaining new insight, and for creating and further improving long-term knowledge resources. The methodology also supports automated learning processes. This research aims on creating required bases for these goals and for new practical mining procedures and algorithms.**

Keywords–Data-centric Knowledge Mining; Mapping Objects and Entities; Spatial Mapping and Visualisation; Knowledge Resources; Advanced Computing.

I. Introduction

It is a truth universally acknowledged, that any knowledge, e.g., based on unstructured and structured data, can contain parts, which may refer to other knowledge but which are not explicitely linked. Further, existing methods promising to deal with lexical and term mapping or ontologies showed deficient and inadequate for coping with challenges of arbitrary knowledge mapping and multi-dimensional context. Methods [1] and implementations for automated mapping [2] are not sufficient, the more as approaches do not span disciplines [3]. Term identification [4] is not suitable for mapping beyond simple context like bibliographic data, too. Available mapping approaches are very limited to non-general knowledge related tasks [5], even when dealing with context [6].

The methodology presented here was developed in order to identify entities inside of or referenced with data and create new context for knowledge objects and entities. Knowledge is an excellent integrator as it can complement, e.g., from factual, conceptual, procedural, and metacognitive knowledge.

Knowledge mapping is the process of creating mappings between two data objects. In that way knowledge mapping contributes significantly to data integration and data sciences methods [7]. The means of referring objects and sub-objects, "entities", with a new context is considered as "knowledge mapping". Objects, e.g., a document, a part of a text, or an image may be associated with other objects, by its knowledge, e.g., its factual or conceptual knowledge. For example, creating new spatial context for textual entities in knowledge objects requires to build non-fixed associations, apply a fuzzy spatial locate, and implement a text location to map-mapping.

The procedure enables to automatically create a spatial mapping for possible locations in a document, e.g., Points Of Interest (POI) or other places in a data set or file.

The rest of this paper is organised as follows. Section II introduces the new methodology applied for knowledge mapping. Section III discusses previous work, components, and used resources. Section IV presents the implementation and case study based on the methodology. Section V presents generated interactive dynamical context examples. Section VI summarises the lessons learned, conclusions, and future work.

II. Methodology

The methodology can be used for creating new object and entity context environments, e.g., in knowledge mining context. The following steps describe the methodology.

1) Start is an arbitrary object.
2) Object / entity analysis.
3) Object / entity mapping.
4) Context creation.
5) Result is an object and / or entity with a new context environment.

Objects can be arbitrary objects, unstructured or structured, unreferenced or referenced, e.g., containing different entities of content. The methodology is not limited to any possibly restricted implementation or platform. In case of textual objects and entities, the object can, e.g., be a text document. In case the mapping targets on geo-referencing otherwise non geo-referenced objects or entities, then the mapping can be considered a spatial mapping. With the latter target the context creation can be considered a spatial visualisation.

The methodology of knowledge mapping for arbitrary objects and entities can be schematically summarised (Figure 1).

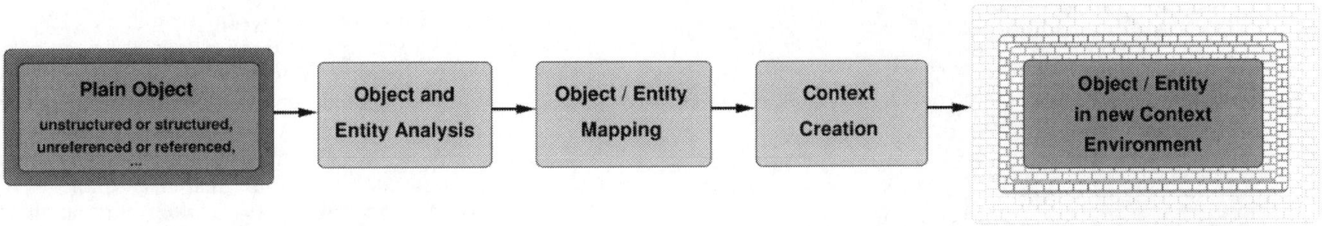

Figure 1. Methodology mapping arbitrary objects and entities for creating new context environments. The methodology requires the major complementary steps of object/entity analysis, mapping, and context creation. Depending of the object, the steps can be implemented using different tools.

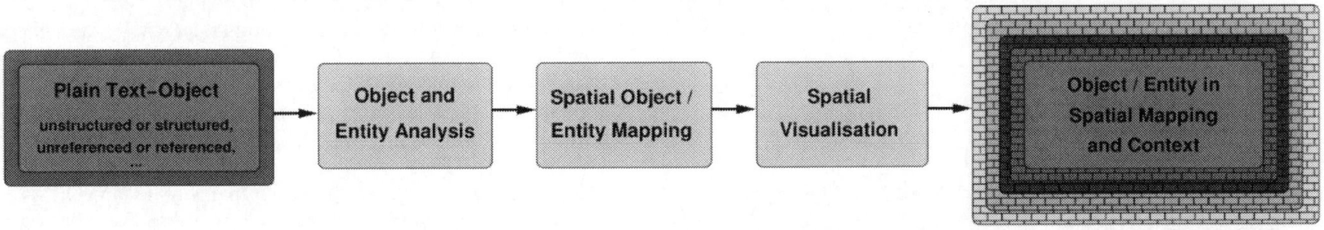

Figure 2. Plain text to spatial mapping context: Mapping arbitrary text objects and entities to new spatial mapping and context. In this case the object is plain text, analysis is conducted with knowledge-mining-in-text algorithms, mapping is spatial mapping, and context creation is spatial visualisation context.

For example (Figure 2): When the object is a plain text-object and creating spatial visual context is the target, then the steps can be implemented with object and entity analysis, spatial object / entity mapping, and spatial visualisation for creating an object / entity spatial mapping in a new context.

The targets for the case study are spatial visualisation and context. The implementation architecture of mapping arbitrary objects and entities to a new object context environment is shown in Figure 3. Data and modules are provided by Knowledge Resources. The originary resources deliver the data objects and entities, which can be unstructured or structured. The application resources and components contain appropriate modules for the required steps. The object is retrieved, possible object entities are extracted, object data resources are being analysed, objects are being compared, a conceptual mapping is performed on objects, spatial mapping is performed on objects, appropriate spatial media is generated, including media formats and colourisation, and a spatial visualisation is performed. The result is an object / entity instance in a new context environment. The modules and filters perform the analysis and handle the objects and entities, e.g.,

- entities in different context inside an object,
- transcriptions,
- transliterations,
- translations,
- abbreviations,
- acronyms, . . .

In many cases, additional handling of data will be desired, even if not essential for the procedure of a method or the operation of a service. For example, in case of textual objects and entities a number of aspects exist, which contribute to the attainment of a certain quality:

- Differently organised or structured entities per object.
- Sub-entities, multiple entities in a pseudo-entity.
- Inconsistencies in data.
- Errors in data.
- Typographic differences.
- Ambiguous or plurivalent entities.
- Multi-lingual entities.
- Different diction.
- Different syntax.
- Different element ordering in entities.
- Different structures.
- Time dependencies of aspects, mapping, and meaning.
- Different character sets.
- Different formatting.

Any of these and comparable aspects are handled by the modules and appropriate pre- and post-filters. With the case study, for the above aspects respective research was conducted gathering various data and developing suitable methods over several years, data which can be deployed to create filters, which were used for holding the results presented here.

It is required to abstract certain information in many application scenarios, e.g., for generalisation or privacy. Besides any kind of filter, the method also allows to implement fuzziness in a flexible and wide range of ways. For example, on the one hand a precise location can be reduced to city, region, or country. Comparable but different locations can be unified to one different location representing a larger area. On the other hand, location coordinates can be automatically or manually reduced in precision and/or equipped with an offset. With these means, workflows can deliver kind of "Fuzzy Context", e.g., a fuzzy location, providing a precision level of a public region instead of showing a certain building in a result.

III. Previous Work, Components, and Resources

For the implementation of case studies, the modules are built by support of a number of major components and resources, which can be used for a wide range of applications, e.g., creation of resources and extraction of entities.

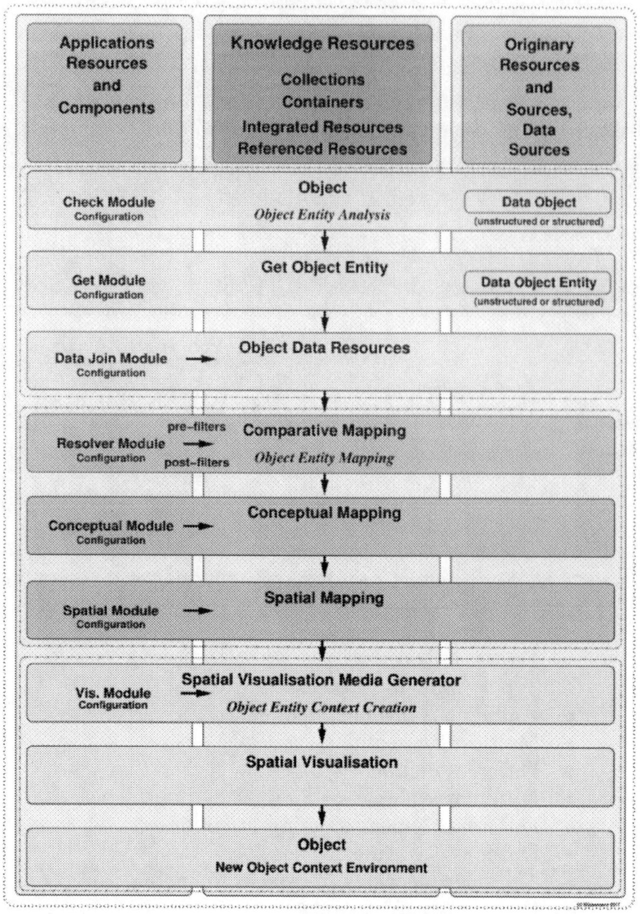

Figure 3. Architecture for implementation of mapping arbitrary objects and entities to new context environments, e.g., spatial visualisation and context. Data and modules are provided by Knowledge Resources, originary resources, and application resources and components.

The facility for consistently describing knowledge is a valuable quality, especially conceptual knowledge, e.g., using the Universal Decimal Classification (UDC). The knowledge resources objects can refer to main UDC-based classes, which for this publication are taken from the Multilingual Universal Decimal Classification Summary (UDCC Publication No. 088) [8] released by the UDC Consortium under the Creative Commons Attribution Share Alike 3.0 license [9] (first release 2009, subsequent update 2012).

Data and objects result from public, commonly available, and specialised Knowledge Resources. The Knowledge Resources are containing factual and conceptual knowledge as well as documentation and instances of procedural and metacognitive knowledge. These resources contain multi-disciplinary and multi-lingual data and context.

Context data for calculations and visualisation also requires cartographic thematic context data. The knowledge resources were integrated with data based on the gridded ETOPO1 1-arc-minute global relief model data [10]. Data can be composed from various sources, e.g., adding Shuttle Radar Topography Mission (SRTM) data [11].

The Network Common Data Form (NetCDF) [12] developed by the University Corporation for Atmospheric Research (UCAR/Unidata), National Center for Atmospheric Research (NCAR) is used for spatial context data. NetCDF is an array based data structure for storing multi-dimensional data. A NetCDF file is written with an ASCII header and stores the data in a binary format, e.g., with a mapping suite.

The Generic Mapping Tools (GMT) [13] suite application components are used for handling the spatial data, applying the related criteria, and for the visualisation.

The visualisation files generated from the mapping results are using the Keyhole Markup Language (KML), an eXtended Markup Language (XML) based format for specifying spatial data and content. KML is considered an official standard of the Open Geospatial Consortium (OGC). The KML description can be used with many spatial components and purposes, e.g., with a Google Earth or Google Maps presentation [14], with a Marble representation [15], using OpenStreetMap (OSM) [16].

Modules are employing Perl Compatible Regular Expressions (PCRE) for specifying common string patterns and Perl [17] for component wrapping purposes with this case study.

IV. Implementation Case Study: Spatial Context

The following sections provide information regarding implemented components (`lxloccoord`, module for location coordinates) and a practical case study, which was done for demonstrating the methodology of mapping objects and entities, creating new context environments. The case study shows components, which were built for mapping scenarios creating spatial context (Figure 3) and illustrates new insights and relevance for knowledge creation and advanced mining.

A. The components

All the components and modules required for the architecture (Figure 3) were implemented. The following components were created for the practical implementation of the three major central modules, object / entity analysis, mapping, and context creation, demonstrating all steps of the methodology.

- The object / entity analysis modules process objects for entities, which can be fed into a mapping mechanism.
- The pre-filters change, mark, and remove entities before the mapping modules try to create entity mappings.
- The mapping modules do have the task to deliver spatial coordinates for appropriate entities.
- The post-filters change, mark or remove entities after the resolver worked on entities for a spatial mapping.
- The context creation modules deliver the geo-referencing for a spatial application.

The modules can be centralised or distributed, e.g., implemented as a local directory of comparable and resolved entities or an online service. Appropriate directories can be provided by knowledge resources as well as by spatial mapping services.

Change processes in pre- and post-filters can include unification, improvements for resolvability, mapping and so on.

Different application components with different features can be deployed for dynamical and interactive use and visualisation, e.g., GMT, Marble, and Google Maps.

B. Case study: From plain text to spatially linked context

The following passages show some major steps for creating spatially linked context from plain text, which were used in the workflows required for the case studies.

The single data object in Figure 4 contains mostly unstructured text [18], markup, and formatting instructions.

```
<!DOCTYPE html PUBLIC "-//W3C//DTD␣XHTML␣1.0␣Transitional//EN" ... <title>
 GEOProcessing 2018 ...</title>
..., Leibniz Universit&auml;t Hannover / Westf&auml;lische
 Wilhelms-Universit&auml;t M&uuml;nster / North-German Supercomputing Alliance
     (HLRN), Germany ...
..., Technion - Israel Institute of Technology, Haifa,      Israel<br />
..., Consiglio Nazionale delle Ricerche - Genova,      Italy <br />
..., Centre for Research in Geomatics - Laval University,      Quebec, Canada <
 br />
..., Curtin University, Australia <br />
..., Lomonosov Moscow State University, Russia  <br />
..., FH Aachen, Germany</p> ...
        <p>..., Universiti Tun Hussein Onn Malaysia, Malaysia<br />
          ..., Cardiff University, Wales, UK<br />
          ..., Universidade  Federal do Rio Grande, Brazil<br />
          ..., GIS unit Kuwait Oil  Company, Kuwait<br />
          ..., Middle East Technical  University, Turkey<br />
          ..., University of  Sharjah, UAE<br />
          ..., Georgia State University, USA<br />
          ..., Centre for Research  in Geomatics - Laval University, Quebec,
           Canada<br />
          ..., Environmental Systems  Research Institute (ESRI), USA<br />
          ..., ORT University -  Montevideo, Uruguay<br /> ...
```

Figure 4. Mapping target: Single object, unstructured text (excerpt).

Passages not relevant for demonstration were shortened to ellipses. Figure 5 shows the object content after automatically integrated with the Knowledge Resources via a join module.

```
GEOProcessing 2018 [...]: ...
  ..., Leibniz Universität Hannover / Westfälische Wilhelms-Universität Münster
   / North-German Supercomputing Alliance (HLRN), Germany ...
  ..., Technion - Israel Institute of Technology, Haifa, Israel
  ..., Consiglio Nazionale delle Ricerche - Genova, Italy
  ..., Centre for Research in Geomatics - Laval University, Quebec, Canada
  ..., Curtin University, Australia
  ..., Lomonosov Moscow State University, Russia
  ..., FH Aachen, Germany ...
  ..., Universiti Tun Hussein Onn Malaysia, Malaysia
  ..., Cardiff University, Wales, UK
  ..., Universidade  Federal do Rio Grande, Brazil
  ..., GIS unit Kuwait Oil  Company, Kuwait
  ..., Middle East Technical  University, Turkey
  ..., University of  Sharjah, UAE
  ..., Georgia State University, USA
  ..., Centre for Research  in Geomatics - Laval University, Quebec, Canada
  ..., Environmental Systems  Research Institute (ESRI), USA
  ..., ORT University -  Montevideo, Uruguay ...
```

Figure 5. Object instance representation after integration (excerpt).

The Object Entity Mapping can associate relevant objects, e.g., via conceptual knowledge and comparative methods. Table I shows an excerpt of the conceptual data (UDC) used for characteristics and place classification, creating spatial context.

TABLE I. CLASSIFICATION REFERENCES, OBJECT/ENTITY ANALYSIS AND MAPPING: CHARACTERISTICS & PLACE (LX [19]).

UDC Code	*Description (English, excerpt)*
UDC:(1)	Place and space in general. Localization. Orientation
UDC:(100)	Universal as to place. International. All countries in general
UDC:-05	Common auxiliaries of persons and personal characteristics
UDC:-057.4	Professional or academic workers
UDC:378	Higher education. Universities. Academic study

The codes especially reflect the common auxiliaries of general characteristics and place with the analysis of the object and entities, e.g., affiliation and spatial location.

Figure 6 shows an excerpt with possible entities of locations after an object entity analysis and mapping.

```
...
Centre for Research in Geomatics, Laval University, Quebec, Canada
Curtin University, Australia
Lomonosov Moscow State University, Russia ...
Universiti Tun Hussein Onn Malaysia, Malaysia ...
Environmental Systems Research Institute (ESRI), USA ...
```

Figure 6. Possible place entities after object / entity analysis (excerpt).

After object entity analysis, filters, and mapping, a resolver module can equip the entities with geo-references (Figure 7).

```
...
-71.2747424,46.7817463,Centre for Research in Geomatics, Laval University,
 Quebec, Canada
115.8944182,-32.0061951,Curtin University, Australia
37.5286696,55.7039349,Moscow State University, Russia ...
103.0855782,1.858626,Universiti Tun Hussein Onn Malaysia, Malaysia ...
-117.195686,34.056077,Environmental Systems Research Institute (ESRI), USA ...
```

Figure 7. Resolver module result: Resulting entities equipped with geo-references after object entity analysis, filters, and mapping (excerpt).

For this result, the pre- and post filters handled all issues as described. The entries are shown in a special 3 column Comma Separated Value (CSV) format. The GMT format for the geo-referenced CSV is straight forward (Figure 8).

```
...
-71.2747424 46.7817463 Centre for Research in Geomatics, Laval University,
 Quebec, Canada
115.8944182 -32.0061951 Curtin University, Australia
37.5286696 55.7039349 Moscow State University, Russia ...
103.0855782 1.858626 Universiti Tun Hussein Onn Malaysia, Malaysia ...
-117.195686 34.056077 Environmental Systems Research Institute (ESRI), USA ...
```

Figure 8. Geo-references object entity in GMT format (excerpt).

The context creation includes the media generation. Figure 9 excerpts a KML representation of the above geo-referenced entities, resulting from the original mapping.

```
<?xml version="1.0" encoding="UTF-8"?>
<kml xmlns="http://www.opengis.net/kml/2.2">
<Document>
<name>Locations</name>
<Folder><name>Conferences</name><Style id="locationsconferences"><BalloonStyle>
<text><![CDATA[<b><font color="#0000CC" size="+2">$[name]</font></b><br/><br/><
 font face="Courier">$[description]</font><br/><br/>$[address]
$[id]
$[Snippet]
$[geDirections]
]]></text></BalloonStyle>
<IconStyle><Icon><href>http://maps.google.com/mapfiles/kml/pushpin/grn-pushpin.
 png</href></Icon></IconStyle></Style> ...
<Placemark><name>Centre for Research in Geomatics</name>
<description>Centre for Research in Geomatics, Laval University Quebec Canada</
 description>
<styleUrl>#locationsconferences</styleUrl>
<Point><coordinates>-71.2747424,46.7817463,0</coordinates></Point></Placemark>
 ...
</Folder></Document></kml>
```

Figure 9. Media representation (KML) of geo-referenced object entities, resulting from original mapping (excerpt).

A global view of all resulting entities automatically analysed and mapped from the single object [18] is shown in Figure 10. The single-object-view integrates the new spatial context of the object entities with a high precision topographic-oceanographic thematic view. The bullets are very much oversized for this illustration. The respective components are provided by GMT suite applications, especially `pscoast` and `gmtselect` [19], which allow a multitude of spatial operations and criteria in context with the entities. Further, KML can be used with many spatial applications, e.g., with Marble and Google Maps. Generators can be configured to mark different types of locations with different markers. It is also possible to automatically mark locations with thumbnail photos being associated with the respective location and so on.

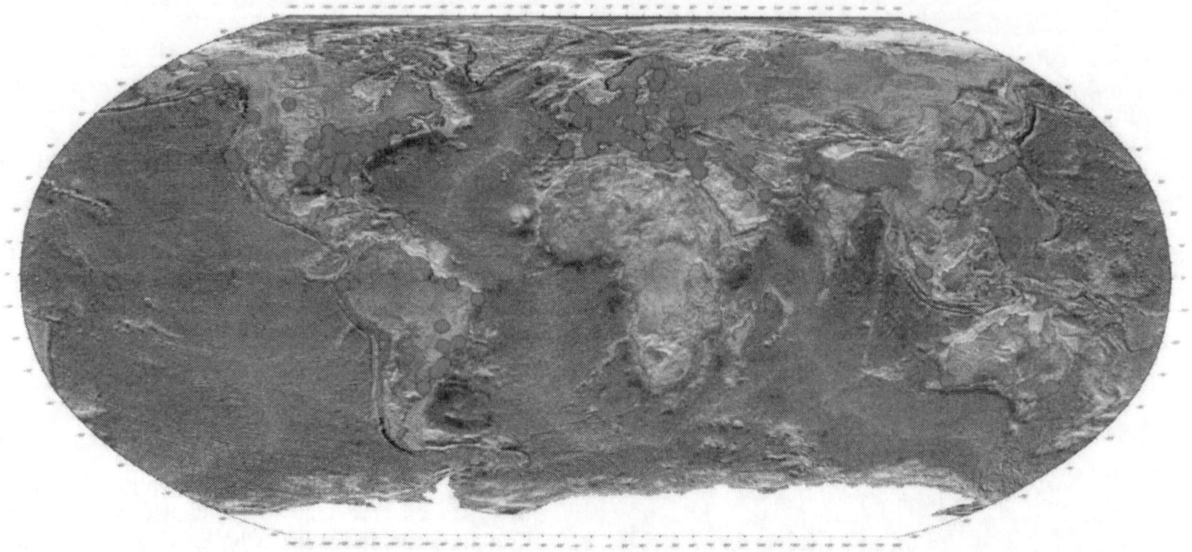

Figure 10. Spatial visualisation result for mapping entities in the text of a single object to a new spatial context and topographic-oceanographic thematic view: Entities resulting from automated analysis and affiliation mapping (red bullets). Sample object: Committee page [18], GEOProcessing 2018 conference, Rome.

V. Further Dynamical Context Examples

Figure 11 is a screenshot of an dynamical, interactive view (Marble), a political map context for above created context.

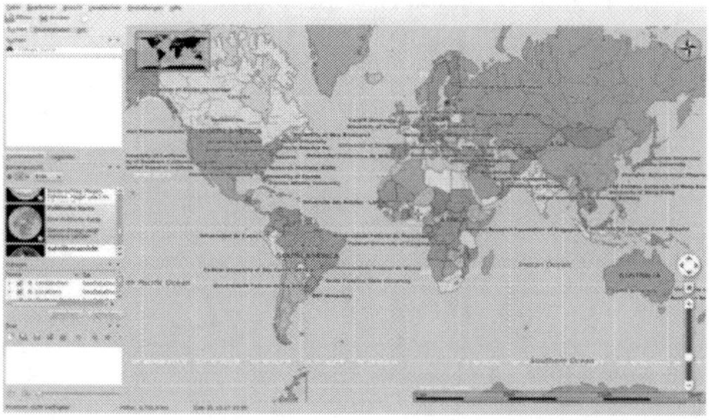

Figure 11. New context for automatically created analysis and mapping of resulting entities of a single object: Political context for labeled entities.

A consecutive mapping allows to analyse the entities in completely new context. For example, parts of an unstructured document can be put into context with any type of n-dimensional information, e.g., historical and climatological context by using spatial information [20] and mapping for finding links. In this case, data entities can be spatially mapped and associated with multi-dimensional data from many disciplines, and data entities can not only be associated in space but also in time. The data allows to do detailed knowledge mining analysis as well as visual analysis. For the created context, Figures 12 and 13 show screenshots of an interactive globe-view (Marble) with climate zone context and an interactive view (Google Earth) with Earth view context.

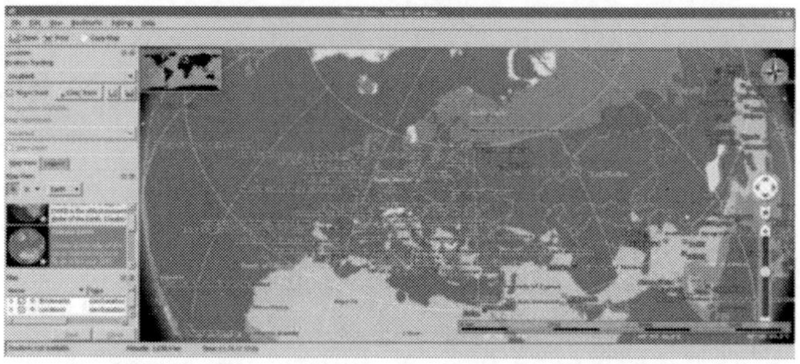

Figure 12. New context for automatically created analysis and mapping of resulting entities of a single object: Climate zones context in 3D.

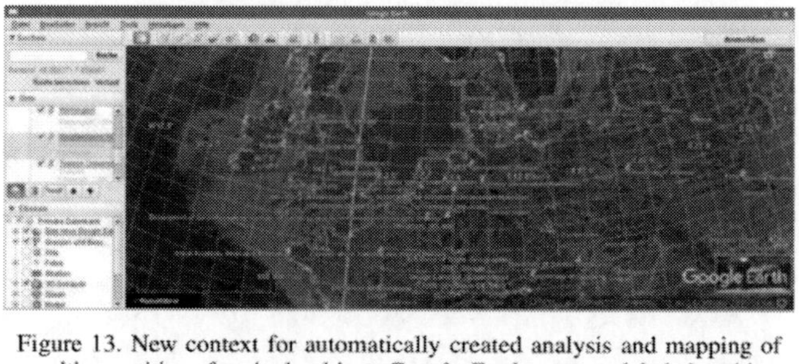

Figure 13. New context for automatically created analysis and mapping of resulting entities of a single object: Google Earth context, labeled entities.

Besides the new context of spatial distribution and according algorithms and math, the new context environments build links in order to associate entities with knowledge from arbitrary disciplines and proceed with further analysis.

Due to conceptual attributes of knowledge mapping and spatial algorithms, the implementation allows high grades of scalability and fuzziness. New context can also be kept and used in learning systems components. This, e.g., can provide conditional object / entity aggregation and time sequences.

VI. Conclusion

This paper introduces a new methodology for knowledge based mapping of arbitrary objects and entities and creating new multi-dimensional context. The research presented the theoretical background, a successful implementation based on the methodology and a case study. The methodology fulfills the goals of successfully creating new context, knowledge mapping can improve complex knowledge mining and associated tasks as well as it can be beneficial for the development of knowledge resources. A practical case study, evaluated by groups of independent researchers, showed that applying the methodology can create relevant new context for entities in commonly available unstructured data. Mapping to a spatial context is just one of an arbitrary number of possible mappings, which can be created with the methodology. The quality of results can significantly benefit from a training and learning phase, depending on context. Here, with resolving nearly all possible place entities with the used new resources, the creation and learning phase of the modules accumulates to several years. The methodology allowed to implement a data-centric checkpointing, which corresponds to associated learning processes. As shown, in most cases it may be advisable for flexibility to create modular architectures of components instead of monolithic applications. It can further be convenient to consider robustness and reliability of service modules, depending on the architecture of an overall implementation. One means of dealing with infrastructure can be a failure correction, e.g., multiple task runs and check modules.

Analysis and case studies are on the way implementing advanced context generation, e.g., with spatial visualisation, 2D, 3D, route mapping, public transport, animation, and fly-over tours as well as analysing computational requirements, which are widely scalable, depending on implementation of components and computing architectures.

In addition, future work concentrates on further developing and improving the mapping modules and features for closer integration with the multi-disciplinary knowledge resources.

Acknowledgements

We are grateful to the "Knowledge in Motion" (KiM) long-term project, Unabhängiges Deutsches Institut für Multi-disziplinäre Forschung (DIMF), for partially funding this research, implementation, case study, and publication under grants D2017F1P04708 and D2017F1P04812 and to its senior scientific members, especially to Dr. Friedrich Hülsmann, Gottfried Wilhelm Leibniz Bibliothek (GWLB) Hannover, to Dipl.-Biol. Birgit Gersbeck-Schierholz, Leibniz Universität Hannover, to Dipl.-Ing. Martin Hofmeister, Hannover, and to Olaf Lau, Hannover, Germany, for fruitful discussion, inspiration, practical multi-disciplinary case studies, and the analysis of advanced concepts. We are grateful to Dipl.-Ing. Hans-Günther Müller, Cray, Germany, for his work and assistance providing practical private cloud and storage solutions and excellent technical support. We are grateful to all national and international partners in the Geo Exploration and Information cooperations for their constructive and trans-disciplinary support. We thank the Science and High Performance Supercomputing Centre (SHPSC) for long-term support.

References

[1] Y. Sun, "Methods for automated concept mapping between medical databases," Journal of Biomedical Informatics, vol. 37, 2004, pp. 162–178, DOI: https://doi.org/10.1016/j.jbi.2004.03.003 [acc.: 2017-11-04].

[2] J. Y. Sun and Y. Sun, "A System for Automated Lexical Mapping," Journal of the American Medical Informatics Association, vol. 13, no. 3, 2006, pp. 334–343, DOI: 10.1197/jamia.M1823.

[3] "Automatic Term Mapping," 2017, PubMed Tutorial - Building the Search - How It Works, URL: https://www.nlm.nih.gov/bsd/disted/pubmedtutorial/020_040.html [accessed: 2017-11-04] .

[4] N. J. van Eck, L. Waltman, E. C. M. Noyons, and R. K. Buter, "Automatic term identification for bibliometric mapping," Scientometrics, vol. 82, no. 3, 2010, pp. 581–596, URL: https://link.springer.com/article/10.1007/s11192-010-0173-0 [accessed: 2017-11-04].

[5] "Automated Mapping Applications," 2017, interpret Geospatial Solutions, URL: http://www.interpret.co.nz/projects/automated-mapping-applications/ [accessed: 2017-11-04].

[6] R. Haga and K. Feigh, "Context maps-classifying contextual influence for decision support system design," in Proceedings of the Digital Avionics Systems Conference (DASC 2015), Sep. 13–17, 2015, Prague, Czech Republic. IEEE CPS, 2015, ISBN: 978-1-4799-8940-9 (Electronic Proceedings), DOI: 10.1109/DASC.2015.7311576.

[7] C.-P. Rückemann, O. O. Iakushkin, B. Gersbeck-Schierholz, F. Hülsmann, L. Schubert, and O. Lau, "Best Practice and Definitions of Data Sciences – Beyond Statistics," 2017, Delegates' Summit, The 7th Symp. on Adv. Comp. & Inf. in Nat. & Appl. Sci. (SACINAS), The 15th Int. Conf. of Num. Analysis & Appl. Math. (ICNAAM), Sep. 25–30, 2017, Thessaloniki, Greece, URL: http://www.user.uni-hannover.de/cpr/x/publ/2017/delegatessummit2017/rueckemann_icnaam2017_summit_summary.pdf [accessed: 2017-11-04].

[8] "Multilingual Universal Decimal Classification Summary," 2012, UDC Consortium, 2012, Web resource, v. 1.1. The Hague: UDC Consortium (UDCC Publication No. 088), URL: http://www.udcc.org/udcsummary/php/index.php [accessed: 2016-01-01].

[9] "Creative Commons Attribution Share Alike 3.0 license," 2012, URL: http://creativecommons.org/licenses/by-sa/3.0/ [accessed: 2016-01-01].

[10] C. Amante and B. W. Eakins, "ETOPO1 1 Arc-Minute Global Relief Model: Procedures, Data Sources and Analysis," 2009, NOAA Technical Memorandum NESDIS NGDC-24. National Geophysical Data Center, NOAA. DOI: 10.7289/V5C8276M .

[11] "Consultative Group on International Agricultural Research (CGIAR)," 2017, URL: http://www.cgiar.org [accessed: 2017-11-04].

[12] "NetCDF – Network Common Data Form," 2017, DOI: http://doi.org/10.5065/D6H70CW6 [accessed: 2017-11-04] URL: http://www.unidata.ucar.edu/software/netcdf/ [accessed: 2017-11-04].

[13] "GMT - Generic Mapping Tools," 2017, URL: http://gmt.soest.hawaii.edu/ [accessed: 2017-11-04].

[14] "Google Maps," 2017, URL: http://www.google.com/maps [accessed: 2017-02-12].

[15] "Marble," 2017, URL: https://marble.kde.org/ [accessed: 2017-11-04].

[16] "OpenStreetMap (OSM)," 2017, URL: http://www.openstreetmap.org [accessed: 2017-02-12].

[17] "The Perl Programming Language," 2017, URL: https://www.perl.org/ [accessed: 2017-11-04].

[18] "GEOProcessing 2018: Committees," 2017, the Tenth International Conference on Advanced Geographic Information Systems, Applications, and Services (GEOProcessing 2018) March 25–29, 2018 – Rome, Italy, URL: https://www.iaria.org/conferences2018/ComGEOProcessing18.html [accessed: 2017-11-04].

[19] C.-P. Rückemann, "Methodology and Integrated Knowledge for Complex Knowledge Mining: Natural Sciences and Archaeology Case Study Results," in Proc. of The 9th Int. Conf. on Adv. Geo. Inf. Syst., Appl., and Serv. (GEOProcessing 2017), Mar. 19 – 23, 2017, Nice, France. XPS, 2017, pages 103–109, ISSN: 2308-393X, ISBN: 978-1-61208-539-5, URL: http://www.thinkmind.org/index.php?view=article&articleid=geoprocessing_2017_7_10_30036 [acc.: 2017-06-05].

[20] "Marble Maps," 2017, URL: https://marble.kde.org/maps.php [accessed: 2017-11-04].

Using Smart A* Algorithm to Solve TSP Navigation Problem

Hatem F. Halaoui
Computer Science
Haigazian University
Beirut, Lebanon
Email: hhalaoui@haigazian.edu.lb

Abstract—**Navigation queries are very common among travelers. Moreover, traveling to multiple destinations in one trip is very common as well. The Traveling Salesman Problem (TSP) is one of the most famous multi-destination path problems. Solving TSP efficiently with real-time factors (traffic, distance, real-time delays) is very useful for multiple navigation queries. Google maps, Yahoo maps, and many others are examples of such online navigation applications. Calculating the best driving path between multiple addresses is subject to many factors including distance, road situation, road traffic, speed limitations and others. This paper presents the use of smart heuristic functions, intelligent algorithm A*, traditional graph algorithms like Hamilton circuit, as well as efficient data structures in finding an efficient cycle path between multiple addresses.**

Keywords— Traveling Salesman Problem; Intelligent Navigation Algorithms; Smart Navigation; Hamilton circuit; A* Algorithm.

I. INTRODUCTION

Traveling between places (destinations) is a common task for many people like tourists, sales people, and others. Most of these would like to visit multiple destinations in one trip. This paper proposes a solution for such queries.

This section introduces the main topics behind the proposed approach: the Travelling Salesman Problem (TSP), Spatial Databases (presented as the main data warehouse of our approach), Geographical Information Systems (GIS), and heuristics. We also present an overview of the adopted approach.

A. Traveling Salesman Problem (TSP)

The Travelling Salesman Problem (TSP) [11], which was defined in the 1800s by the Irish mathematician W. R. Hamilton and by the British mathematician T. Kirkman, describes a salesman who needs to travel between a certain numbers of cities. The order in which the cities are to be visited is not important, as long as they are all visited in one trip which ends back at the start city. Cities are connected to each other by roads, railways, airplane paths, or any other means of transportation. Each one of the links between the cities has one or more weights that could represent distance, time, or cost. The main problem is to find the shortest path starting at a source, traveling to all needed destinations, and ending at the source. The TSP is typical of a large class of "hard" optimization problems that have intrigued mathematicians and computer scientists for years.

An optimal solution for the TSP with high number of vertices using traditional algorithms is very time consuming and does not match with real-time problems. Traditional algorithms work well when the number of vertices in low, below 10, so they are better used after decreasing the number of map (graph) vertices. For this reason, our approach will adopt a solution that uses heuristics to decrease the number of graph vertices.

B. Spatial Databases

Spatial databases are the main data warehouses used by Geographical Information Systems. Spatial databases are databases used to store information about geography such as geometry, positions, coordinates, and others [4] [9]. Also, they might include operations to be applied on such data.

C. Geographical Information Systems and Driving Path Applications

A Geographic Information System (GIS) is a collection of computer hardware and software for capturing, managing, analyzing, and displaying all forms of geographical information [6] [7]. Finding the Directions (driving/walking) path is one of the most asked queries in GIS applications. The most important factors that influence the response to such queries include: distance, road situation, road traffic, speed limitations, and others.

D. Heuristic

As an adjective, heuristic pertains to the process of gaining knowledge by making anintelligent guess rather than by following some pre-established formula [2] [3]. Most of what people do in their daily lives involves heuristic solutions. In map problems, when moving from one point to another to reach a certain destination, there are two options. In the first option, the algorithm tries all possible paths from all possible neighbours (next address on the way to destination). It keeps doing this until the destination is reached. Finally, it chooses the best path among all possibilities. In the second option, at each location, the algorithm chooses the next move using some smart evaluation function (called the heuristic function).

E. Navigating Using Heuristic Functions and Hamilton Circuit

This paper addresses the issue of navigating to multiple destinations in any order. The main problem is to find the fastest path starting at a given source and passing over all given destinations, in any order. The importance of the proposed approach is that existing solutions, such as Google

Maps [8], let users select the order of destinations rather than suggesting the fastest path. Moreover, calculating the fastest path using the traditional mathematical algorithms like Hamilton path [1] has a high time complexity for real-time large graphs representing real cities. As a result, the use heuristic algorithms like A*, substantially minimize the graph size and hence minimize the Hamilton algorithm running time for such navigation real-time solutions. The Hamilton circuit definition, algorithm, and examples are presented in Section II.

The paper is organized as follows: Section II presents some related work, including widely used applications. Section III presents the main solution of this paper. Section IV discusses our results and, finally, Section V presents conclusions and future work.

II. BACKGROUND AND RELATED WORK

This section presents the relevant background, including definitions, notations, and algorithms, used in the proposed approach. Some terms used, such as graph, vertex, edge and others assume prior knowledge of these data structures.

*A. Artificial Intelligent Heuristic Algorithm A**

A* [2] is an Artificial Intelligent graph algorithm proposed by Pearl. The main goal of A* is to find a cheap cost (time) graph path between two vertices in a graph using a heuristic function. The goal of the heuristic function is to minimize the selection list at each step. In the graph example, finding the shortest path from a node to another has to be done by getting all possible paths and choosing the best, which is very expensive when having a huge number of nodes. On the other hand, using an evaluation function (heuristic) to minimize the problem choices according to an intelligent criterion would be much faster. In case of A* algorithm, the heuristic function H (S, D) is defined as follows:

Input: a source vertex S and a destination D.
Task: evaluate S based on the destination D using the following heuristic function:
Distance_So_Far + Stright_Line_Distance (S, D)
where:
Distance_So_Far = Distance traveled so far to reach vertex S.
Stright_Line_Distance (S, D) = Straight line distance from source S to destination D calculated by using their coordinates.

A* Algorithm
A*(Graph, Source, Destination)
Task: takes a Graph (Vertices and Edges), Source and Destination (Vertices) and returns the Best path solution (stack of vertices) from Source to Destination.

- If Source = Destination then return solution (stack)
- Else expand all neighbours Ni of Source
- Mark Source as Unvisited
- For each Neighbour Ni
    - Get Vi = H(Ni, Destination)
    - Add all (Ni, Vi) to the Fringe (list of all expanded Vertices)
    - From the Fringe, Choose an Unvisited Vertex V with Least Vi
    - If no more Unvisited return Failure
    - Else Apply A*(V, Destination)

The time complexity of A* is $O(n^2)$ [2].

Figure 1 is an example of the A* algorithm behavior to find a path starting from "Arad" to "Bucharest", cities in Romania [2]. First of all, start at Arad and go to the next neighbor with the best heuristic function (Sibiu). Second, explore all neighbors of Sibiu for the best heuristic function. The algorithm continues choosing the best next step (with the least value of the heuristic function) until it reaches Bucharest. All vertices with values (heuristic function) are kept in the fringe in order to be considered at each step.

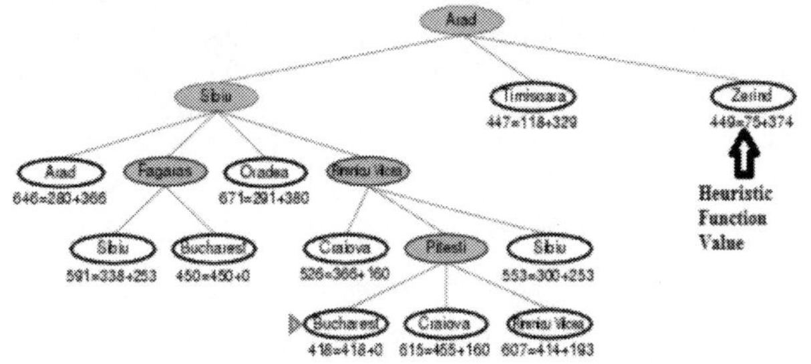

Figure 1. Calculating the path from Arad to Bucharest

B. Graph Definitions and Notations

This sub-section presents the graph definitions and algorithms used in the proposed approach. The time-complexities of these algorithms is briefly stated.

Definition 1. Graph G (V,E): where V is the set of vertices and E is the set of edges. Figure 2 illustrates a graph with vertices: 2,3,5,8,9, and 11 and edges: (5,11), (11,2), (11,9), (7,11), (8,9), (3,8).

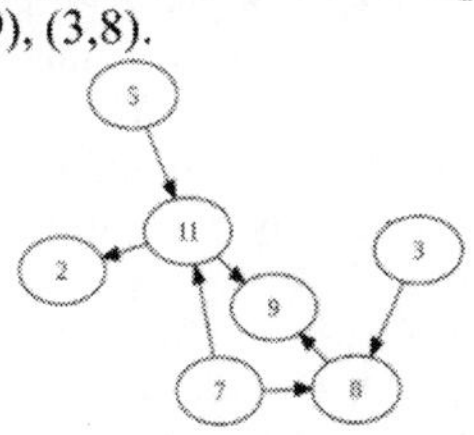

Figure 2. A sample graph

Definition 2. Complete graph: a graph without loops or multiple edges and every vertex is connected to every other vertex. See Figure 3.

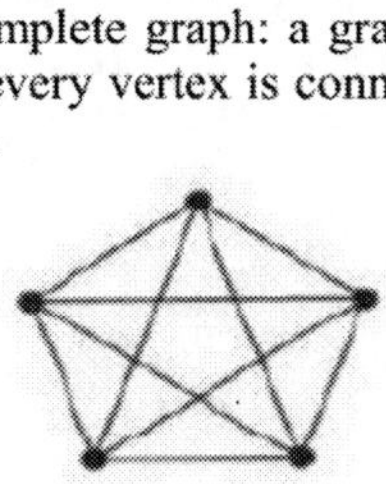

Figure 3. A complete graph

Definition 3. Hamilton circuit [1]: A path in the graph that passes over all vertices once and gets back to the source node where it started. Only the source vertex is visited twice. See Figure 4.

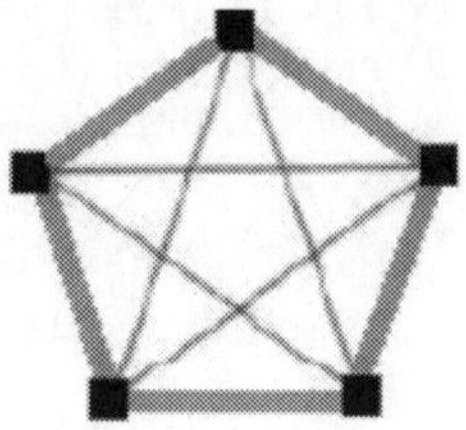

Figure 4. Hamilton Circuit

Definition 4. All permutations: It represents how many ways there are to arrange n different objects out of k objects. The mathematical formula is:

$$^{n}P_{k}=\frac{n!}{(n-k)!} = n\,(n-1)\,(n-2)\ldots(n-k+1).$$

Example: How many ways can 4 students from a group of 15 be lined up for a photograph? Answer: There are $^{15}P_4$ possible permutations of 4 students from a group of 15.

$$^{15}P_4=\frac{15!}{11!} = 15.\ 14.\ 13.\ 12 = 32760.$$

Hence, the permutation of n objects out of n objects (how many different ways to arrange n objects) will be = $\frac{n!}{(n-n)!} = n!$.

C. Related Work: Multi-Destinations Using Google Maps

This subsection presents two existing solutions: Google maps [8], and a previous work A*Multiple [10].

(1) Google Maps

Google Maps [8] is a Web-based service that provides detailed information about geographical regions and sites around the world. In addition to conventional road maps, Google Maps offers aerial and satellite views of many places. Figure 5 shows an example a driving directions query using Google Maps [8]. The query is to get driving directions, over multiple destinations in Rome: Termini station, Vatican City, Coliseum, and Basilica di San Pietro. It also offers real-time traffic information. However, Google Maps [8] does not suggest any order of visiting these sites. The user has to provide Google Maps with the order and the user has to perform multiple trials and look for the best sequence of destinations to be visited. In order to make it a cycle, the user has to provide a path from the last destination to the source (Termini station).

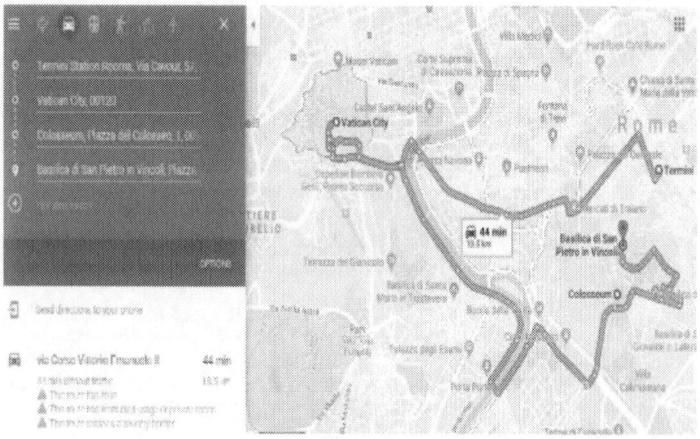

Figure 5. A multi-destination Path by Google Maps where order is chosen by the user

(2) A*Multiple

The main idea behind A*Multiple [10] is to find the best path (shortest in time) to visit multiple destinations in one tour. The algorithm uses a heuristic function to find the next destination.

Algorithm 1. A*Multiple (Source, Destinations)

Task: find an efficient path from source passing over all members in the destinations array.

Returns: 2 lists, namely

1) VSL: Vertices Solution List which is an ordered list vertices that the path follows in the trip.
2) PSL: Path Solution List, which is the list of paths to take each time to each destination (vertex) from a vertex in the VSL list to another in the same list.

Pseudo code

```
If the Destination is Empty return "done".
For all Vertices Vi in Destinations
  Di=H(source, Vi)
  Get the Vs with the Minimum Di
  Remove Vs from Destinations
  Add Vs to the Vertices Solution List VSL
  Add A*Traffic (Source, Vs) to the Path Solution List PSL
 If A*Traffic fails return Failure.
A*Multiple (Vs, Destinations).
```

How does A*Multiple Work?

Next, we present the execution of A*Multiple. To present the proposed approach better, we consider the following problem: suppose the user is at Termini station, Rome and wants to visit the following destinations in Rome: Vatican City, Coliseum and Basilica di San Pietro. If the only priority is time, it means that one can visit them in any order with efficient time. In this case, one has to choose the next destination (at each step) in a smart way.

After creating the Time-Weighted graph (subset of the vertices shown in black in Figure 6) over the map of Rome (from Google Maps), the A*Multiple will return the following:
VSL: Termini station, Vatican City, Coliseum, and Basilica di San Pietro.
PSL: Path1, Path2, Path3.
where VSL is the ordered list of destinations to be visited, PSL is the list of paths from each destination in VSL to the next one, Path1 is Termini station-Vatican City, Path2 is Vatican City- Coliseum, and Path3 is Coliseum, - Basilica di San Pietro. Figure 6 shows these solutions in different colors: orange (Path1), blue (Path2) and pink (Path3). It also gives an estimated time for each path according to current (at time of calculation) traffic situation. However this is not a cycle.

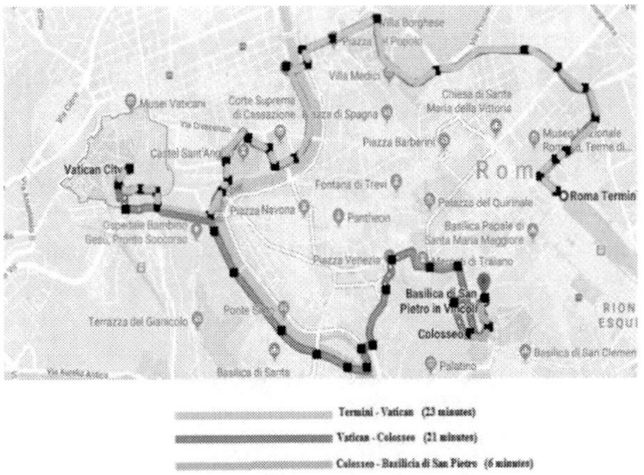

Figure 6. Paths for Multiple destinations (Termini, Vatican City, Coliseum, Basilica di San Pietro)

III. PROPOSED APPROACH: A* HAMILTON CIRCUIT

This section presents the approach to navigate a multi-destination path starting and ending from/to a certain source. The main idea behind this approach is the following:

- Given: graph G representing the map, destination list L repressing the destinations, and source S the start point.
- Create a new virtual complete graph G1 with vertices V1=L+S and edges E1={(ai,bi),..} where edge (ai,bi) is a path calculated using A* algorithm.
- Find all Hamilton circuits in G1 starting and ending at S
- Choose the shortest

The idea behind building the virtual graph is to dramatically minimize the number of vertices of the graph where Hamilton path algorithm is to be applied. In order to present a formal pseudo-code algorithm of the proposed approach, A*HamiltonCircuit, the following algorithms are presented:

Algorithm 2. Hamilton circuit (G (V, E), S): Finds the shortest Hamilton circuit (see Figure 4) in graph G starting and ending at source S.
G: Graph with vertices V and Edges E.
S: Starting node $S \in V$
Returns L: Ordered List of vertices that form the Hamilton Circuit starting and ending at S.
Algorithm:

1. List all permutations (LSP_i) of n vertices.
2. Choose permutations that start with S.
3. Add S to the end of each LSP_i: it becomes S,….,S
4. Choose the valid permutation from LSP_i where $\forall$ i (vi,vi+1) $\in$ E
5. Choose the shortest

The time complexity of Algorithm 2 is as follows:
Step1: n! where n is the number of vertices
Step2: n!
Step3: (n-1)!
Step4: n^2 * (n-1)!
Step5: n

The total time complexity is (n^2+4) n! which is exponential-time algorithm O(n!) and, hence, time consuming for high values of n. Figure 7 shows one result out of many (24 in this case) executions of the Hamilton circuit algorithm starting from vertex v1 all the way back to v1. Later, the shortest path is chosen.

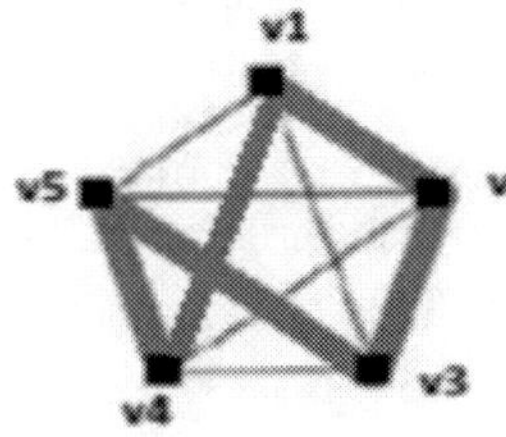

Figure 7. Hamilton circuit starting and ending at v1

Algorithm 3. BuildA*Graph (G(V, E), L): Build a complete virtual graph using the smart A* algorithm

G: graph with vertices V and edges E
L: List of destinations ($L \in V$)
Returns G1(V1, E1): a virtual complete graph with the list of vertices V1 (equal to L) and set of virtual edges E1 where each edge in E1 refer to a path (list of real edges from E) computed using A*.

1. For each vertex Vi in L.
2. Using A*, find all paths from Vi to all other destinations and then to E1.
3. Using these paths, build the Virtual Complete Graph G1(V1,E1).

The time complexity of Algorithm 3 is as follows:
Step1: O ($m*n^2$), where m is the number of vertices in the destinations list L and n^2 is A* time complexity.

Step2: O (m^2) (since G1 has m vertices and maximum of m^2 edges.

Step3 is constant.

As a result, the total time complexity will be O (n^2) since m will be considered a constant compared to n (<=10).

Figure 8 shows the actual graph. Figure 10 presents the extraction (using BuildA*Graph) of the virtual graph. The edges in Figure 9 are built using A*. Each one of the edges represents a path with multiple vertices. Each of these paths will be used as a single edge when applying the Hamilton path algorithm on the virtual graph. For example, the path from v1 to v5 is p1, the path from v5 to v2 is p2, and so on. Figure 10 is an example of the virtual graph. For example, the edge (v1, v5) with weight 45 in Figure 10 represents a real path p1 in Figure 9 calculated using A* algorithm. The weights of these edges are the weights of the calculated path. Hence 45, the edge weight of (v1, v5) is the weight of p1 calculated using A*. Note that, for simplicity of examples, the graph in Figure 8 is used as un-directed graph.

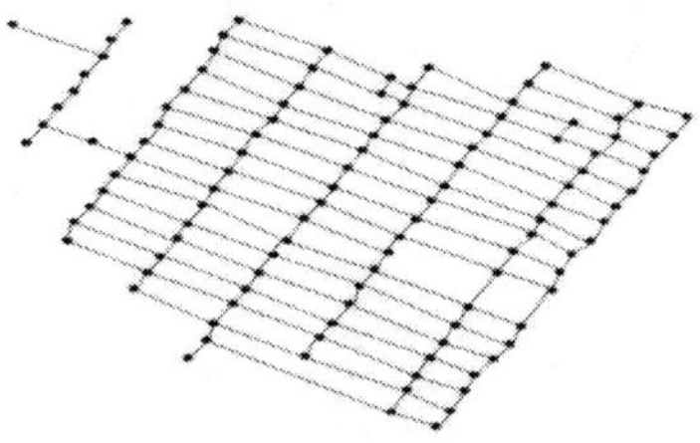

Figure 8. Initial actual graph

Looking at Figure 10, examples of paths starting from v1 (using StartHamilton algorithm) are:

Path1= v1, v2, v3, v4, v5 with weight = 120 +124 +112+ 135 = 491

Path2= v1, v3, v4, v5, v2 with weight = 114+ 112+ 134+221= 581

There will be other 24 options. The option with the lowest weight (shortest) will be chosen.

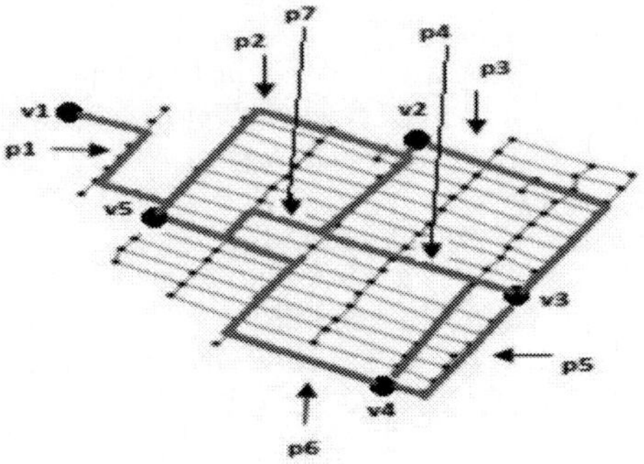

Figure 9. Paths calculated using A*

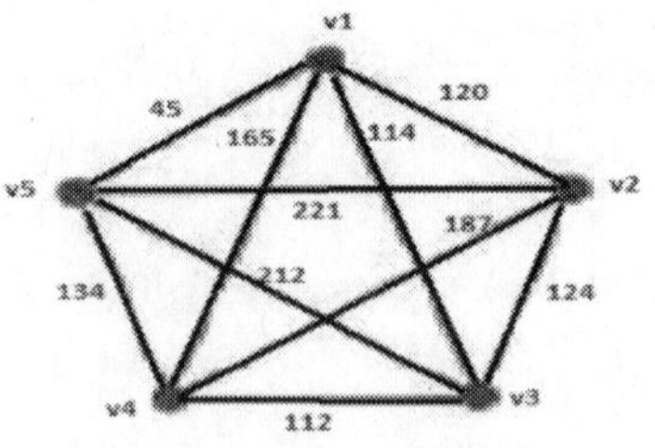

Figure 10. The complete virtual graph extracted from graph is figure 9

Algorithm 4. A*HamiltonCircuit (Graph G (V,E), L, S): Finds the shortest path from a source passing all desired destinations. It uses algorithms 2 and 3 to build a new virtual graph and applies the Hamilton circuit algorithm on it.

G: Graph with vertices V and Edges E

S: Start Vertex that belong to V#

L: List of destinations (L∈ V)

1- G1(V1,E1) = BuildA*Graph (G, L)

2- HP = HamiltonCircuit (G1, S) (Find the shortest Hamilton Circuit in G1 that start with S∈V1)

The time complexity of Algorithm 4 is as follows:

Step1: O (n^2), where n is the number of vertices in the destinations list

Step2: O (m!), finding all permutations (possible paths) of m vertices out of m vertices.

The total time complexity will be in O (n^2 + m!). If m is a relatively small number (<= 10), its maximum time will be around 3 seconds. Example: 10! = 3,628,800 steps (around 3 seconds to compute), then A*Hamilton will be acceptable.

IV. RESULTS

In this section, we discuss the results of some sample executions using our proposed approach.

A testing tool is developed where 120 samples using 6142 vertices were tested in 2 groups: Group 1 (between 10 and 15 destinations), Group 2 (less than 8 destinations).

Results shown in Table I where:

- Optimal solution represents the absolute best solution.
- Good solution takes maximum of 20% more time than the optimal solution.
- Bad solution takes more than 20% more time than the optimal solution.

TABLE I. PERCENTAGES OF QUALITY OF SOLUTIONS

Number of Destinations	Optimal solution	Good Solution	Bad Solution
Between 10 & 15 destinations Over 6142 vertices	81.6 %	14.3%	4.1%
Less than 8 destinations Over 6142 vertices	97.8%	2.1%	0.1%

Comparing these results to the previous results (81% average) [10] shows a very good progress. Note that existing online solutions do not offer such options and hence comparison with those solutions is not applicable.

V. CONCLUSION AND FUTURE WORK

The approach proposed in this paper offers a TSP solution (full cycle path) with an order of destinations claiming an efficient time. To find a solution the following was done:

- Build a real graph G (V,E) that represents the map.
- Build a complete virtual graph G1 (V1, E1) where V1 is the set of destinations and E1 is the set of edges between these destinations. E1 represents a paths intelligently calculated with the smart algorithm A*[2].
- Calculate the shortest cycle path from the selected source (vertex) using HamiltonCircuit Algorithm (Algorithm 3).

The following are the two main concerns:

1. Knowing that HamiltonCircuit Algorithm's time complexity is exponential, its effect is null when applied on a small number of destinations.
2. The weights of edges are not guaranteed to be the best as A* does not guarantee that.

For future work, finding good heuristic functions is a challenge. This is an open research question and highly dependent on the geography of the surface in the query.

REFERENCES

[1] K. Ross and C. Wright, *"Discrete Mathematics"*. Prentice Hall, Upper Saddle River, New Jersey, 2003.

[2] S. Russell and P. Norving, *"Artificial Intelligence a Modern Approach"*. Prentice Hall, Upper Saddle River, New Jersey, 2003.

[3] J. Pearl, *"Heuristics: Intelligent Search Strategies for computer Problem Solving"*. Addison Wesley, Reading, Massachusetts, 1984.

[4] H. Halaoui, "Smart Traffic Online System (STOS): Presenting Road Networks with time-Weighted Graphs". IEEE International Conference on Information Society (i-Society 2010) London, UK. June 2010, pp. 349-356.

[5] Google Earth Blog Google Earth Data Size, Live Local, New languages coming. Available: http://whatis.techtarget.com/definition/Google-Maps. Retrieved: September, 2015.

[6] H. Halaoui, "Smart Traffic Systems: Dynamic A*Traffic in GIS Driving Paths Applications". Proceeding of IEEE CSIE09, IEEE, Los Angeles, USA. March, 2009, pp. 626-630.

[7] H. Halaoui," *Intelligent Traffic System:* Road Networks with Time-Weighted Graphs". International Journal for Infonomics (IJI), Volume 3, Issue 4, December 2010, pp. 350-359.

[8] Google Maps. Available: https:// Maps.google.com. Retrieved: September, 2015.

[9] H. Halaoui, "Spatial and Spatio-Temporal Databases Modeling: *Approaches for Modeling and Indexing Spatial and Spatio-Temporal Databases"*. VDM Verlag, 2009.

[10] Hatem Halaoui, "SMART NAVIGATION: Using Artificial Intelligent Heuristics in Navigating Multiple Destinations". Proceedings of SOTICS 2015 (The Fifth International Conference on Social Media Technologies, Communication, and Informatics). Barcelona, Spain. November, 2015.

[11] E. L. Lawler, J. K. Lenstra, A. H. G. Rinooy Kan, & D. B. Shmoys (Eds.), *"The traveling salesman problem"* (pp. 145–180). Chichester: John Wile, 1985.

A Spatial Decision Support System for Waste Management in Municipal Society of Lahore City

Muhammad Haris
GIS Centre, PUCIT
University of the Punjab
Lahore, Pakistan
e-mail: haris@pucit.edu.pk

Beenish Fatima
Department of Electrical Engineering
NUCES
Lahore, Pakistan
e-mail: beenish.fatima@nu.edu.pk

Abstract— **The paper discusses waste management issues in urban regions, which is an area of concern in highly populated cities of developing countries. Lahore, being the second most populated city of Pakistan, is also facing waste management issues, with both private and public organizations struggling to cater to it. A government operated housing society in Lahore named WAPDA (Water and Power Development Authority) Town is facing this issue due to improper waste dumping by residents. To resolve this problem, a door-to-door survey was conducted in the G5 block of the housing society. The survey results showed that most of the residents were not satisfied with waste management services and reported that absence of waste bins was a major reason for inappropriate waste dumping. Identifying the best possible location for placement of new waste bins made this a spatial decision-making problem. The required spatial data was collected using physical street surveys and mapping in ArcGIS 10.2 software. The existing waste dumping locations were taken as alternatives. Additionally, multiple criteria were chosen for evaluation which were given weights using pairwise comparison method, while various geo-processing tools were used to evaluate the criteria. Finally, alternatives were scored in terms of their appropriateness using Analytical Hierarchical Process (AHP), a multi-criteria decision-making technique. The proposed solution will help in minimizing improper waste dumping, leading to a positive environmental impact on the housing society.**

Keywords- GIS; Multi-criteria Decision Making; Waste Management; Spatial Modeling.

I. INTRODUCTION

Massive population rise, unmanaged urbanization and uplift of living standards have greatly contributed to the increasing rate of solid waste generation in developing countries [1]. For urban planners, waste management in municipal areas has become a major problem. Its severity is manifold in developing countries because of inadequate urban planning and scarcity of resources [2].

This is the case in Pakistan as well, where poor planning in cities and high rate of urbanization have led to many problems [3]. One of the major issues in urban areas is waste management, which has adversely affected Lahore, the second most populated city in Pakistan. Even one of the best housing societies in Lahore, like WAPDA Town are no exception. The waste management issue in the housing society is primarily caused by residents disposing of waste at inappropriate locations including open plots, near electricity poles or at street corners. Open garbage dumps, which are exposed to stray animals and rain, lead to waste-related diseases in the society. To handle rising concerns over this matter, WAPDA Town management recently ran a campaign with the title "Clean WAPDA Town". The campaign aimed to educate residents about proper disposal of waste by placing banners bearing motivational cleanliness messages throughout the housing society. Unfortunately, this campaign did not have any positive impact on the issue. Meanwhile, the residents raised complaints about waste spreading due to severe lack of waste bins.

The passiveness of the society administration to solve this issue was mainly due to budget constraints. Hence, the administration was unable to figure out the appropriate count and location for placing waste bins in any block of the housing society. To solve this problem, firstly a relatively small but congested block of G5 was selected. Then, through research, a detailed methodology was developed with the proposition that lack of waste bins was the main issue behind improper disposal of waste by residents. Finally, the survey data coupled with Geographical Information System (GIS) and multi-criteria decision-making techniques helped in identifying the optimal locations for placement of waste bins. The proposed methodology of waste bin placement can improve the cleanliness of the block and eventually can play a significant role in city-wide waste management.

The rest of the paper is organized as follows: Section II discusses in detail the methodology used for evaluating the locations for waste bin placements. Different alternative locations for bin placement were chosen using a Global Positioning System (GPS) survey. Finally, using a multi-criteria evaluation technique, the alternatives were ranked depending on how appropriate they were considered. Section III describes the results obtained from the methodology in terms of spatial context. At the end, Section IV lists the benefits gained through this work and briefly proposes a validation approach as future work.

II. METHODOLOGY

This research work aims at solving the waste management issue in WAPDA Town, for which a door-to-door survey was carried out in G5 block. The approximate area of this block is 67000 m^2 which includes 337 houses and 18 empty plots. The survey questionnaire results from 80 households showed that almost 96% of residents of the block were unsatisfied with waste management. Moreover, 65% of residents pointed out that the issue of waste management was due to lack of waste bins in the block. Through street survey, it was found that only one large bin, provided by the management, was placed in the block near a commercial area. Placement of new bins was seemingly the obvious solution, but due to the budget constraints, the management could place only a limited number of such bins.

This transforms the issue under consideration into a decision-making problem, where a selected number of options are to be chosen from a set of available alternatives (bin placement locations) based on certain factors. Being a spatial problem, GIS can facilitate this process. GIS combines spatial data with quantitative and qualitative information [4] and it has been quite extensively used in solving municipal solid waste management issues [7][8][12]. Some highly unstructured social problems require decision making by the municipal administration. For such cases, the fusion of GIS with decision making has formed the domain of Multi Criteria Spatial Decision Making (MCSDM) [13]. The MCSDM has been effectively used in solving various spatial waste management issues [5][6]. The application of MCSDM for waste management is mainly focused on the following matters:

i decision making for the selection of most appropriate landfill site selection [5][6]

ii optimizing waste collection procedures [7][12]

iii reallocation of existing waste bins [7]

The major shortcoming in existing research work is that these waste management practices have been focused primarily on dumping of garbage after collection from waste bins. Nothing substantial has been discussed about cleanliness issues of the study area due to improper waste dumping by the residents. Moreover, the study areas in prior works have been mostly quite large in geographical extent [5][6][7], and hence the specific issues at the block level of a municipal society are overlooked. This has led to the selection of less than optimal criteria for decision making related to waste management. Our research work attempts to fill in these shortcomings by working on a relatively small area of G5 block and focusing on waste disposal issues caused by residents. Through multiple surveys, the root cause of improper waste dumping was found to be lack of available waste bins. With this finding, the primary objective of the current work has been to improve waste management of WAPDA Town at the grass root level by proposing the most appropriate locations for placement of waste bins.

After narrowing down the problem, a GPS survey was done in the G5 block. The Android application GPS Logger [14] was used for surveying and the results collected 14 GPS points of improper waste dumping. The collected GPS points were converted into shapefile and visualized in ArcGIS Desktop 10.2 [9]. These GPS survey locations were taken as alternatives for placement of waste bins. For the evaluation of alternatives, seven different criteria were selected, as listed in Table 1. The choice of criteria was dependent on the sources of garbage generation and dumping specifically for the G5 block. Primary sources of garbage generation include houses and commercial areas. Moreover, the primary target locations for garbage dumping by residents includes empty plots, poles, roads, and existing bins. Another criterion named ‘proposed bins’ considers the distance between the bin under consideration and the nearest proposed bin. This criterion is of vital importance, since too close or too far placement of new bins would significantly affect the waste dumping practices of the block’s residents.

For the evaluation of criteria, data was prepared by the combination of GPS surveys and digitization over geo-referenced satellite imagery, as shown in Figure 1. The data for criteria C1 (Houses), C3 (Roads and streets), C4 (Empty plots) and C5 (Commercial areas) was prepared by digitizing in ArcGIS Desktop 10.2. There were 337 houses, 18 empty plots, 3 commercial points and 17 road segments. The data layers prepared using ArcGIS Desktop were stored in Shapefile format. The data for C2 (Poles), C6 (Existing bins) and C7 (Proposed Bins) was prepared using GPS survey points. There were 56 poles, 14 points of improper waste dumping and only one existing bin. The improper waste points were considered as proposed bin locations (alternatives). The average accuracy of GPS points was 5-7 meters. The GPS points acquired were in Keyhole Markup Language (KML) format, which were then converted into Shapefile format to be used in ArcGIS Desktop. The geometry type of data layers for C2, C5, C6 and C7 was set as point, for C3 as polyline, and for C1 and C4 as polygon. The coordinate system for data layers was set to World Geodetic System 1984 (WGS84) [15].

After the data preparation, a pairwise comparison technique was used to assign weights to the criteria [10][11]. The criterion C1 (Houses) bear the highest weight because G5 being a congested block has a high ratio of garbage generation per unit area. For waste dumping, the places found to be most prone were roads, empty plots and poles. Hence, their weights are comparatively high. All the selected criteria, their reasoning and calculated weights are given in Table 1. It is noteworthy to mention that the higher the value of a criteria, the more it favors the alternative.

The next step was to define an appropriate coverage area for each alternative. For this purpose, the Thiessen polygon tool in ArcGIS Desktop was used. The Thiessen polygon takes as input the alternative points and outputs the polygon enclosing each alternative. Polygons are generated in such a way that any location within a specific polygon is closer to the alternative within the polygon than to any other alternative point (as shown in Figure 2). In other words,

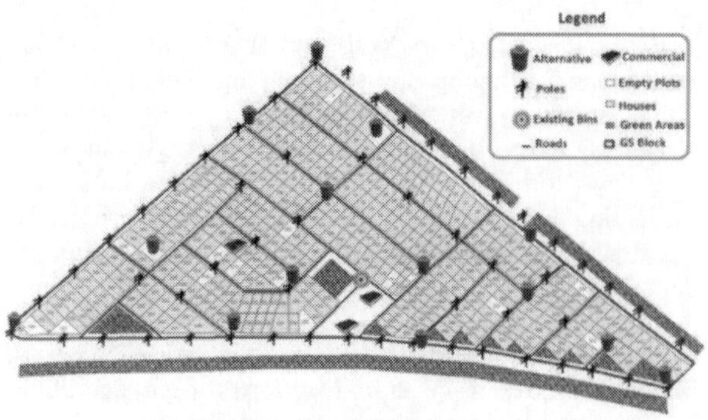

Figure 1. Block G5 detail map.

these polygons partition the available area according to alternatives and hence serve as base service area for evaluation of selected criteria.

For the most accurate ranking of waste bins (alternatives), the well-known multi-criteria decision-making technique of AHP was used, which focuses on ranking alternatives based on specific criteria with assigned weights [11]. Finally, different geo-processing tools from ArcGIS Desktop were used to evaluate the value of each criteria.

For determining the values of C1-C5, the Spatial Join tool in ArcGIS Desktop was used. It counted the value of specific criteria (e.g. no. of poles) within the geographical extent of base service layer and assigned it to the alternative enclosed within it. Then, the value of the criteria (for each alternative) was normalized to fall between 0 and 1. To calculate the values of C6 and C7, the Near tool in ArcGIS Desktop was used. It calculated the distance from each alternative to the nearest existing bin and proposed bin (alternatives), respectively. The values of all criteria are finally represented as individual attributes in the alternative data layer.

Lastly, using the formula of Weighted Sum Model (WSM), the final value of each alternative was calculated.

$$WS\,(Ax) = \textstyle\sum y\,(Ax(Cy) * W(Cy) \qquad (1)$$

where,

WS(Ax) = Total weighted score of Alternative x

Ax (Cy) = Score of Alternative x for Criteria y

W(Cy) = Weight of Criteria y

Sorting the value of alternatives in descending order lists the optimal locations for waste bin from best to worst. Figure 3 summarizes the proposed methodology in terms of three phases namely, exploratory, empirical and analysis, while Figure 4 briefly depicts the phases of decision making.

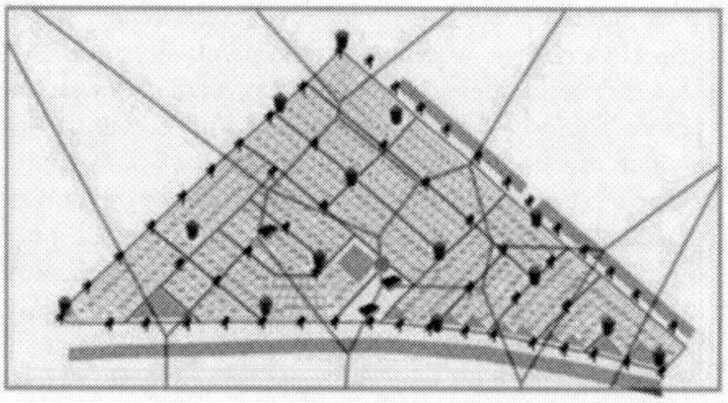

Figure 2. Thiessen polygon map.

III. RESULTS

The final weighted score of alternatives was used to spatially visualize waste bin locations with symbols of different sizes. The size of the symbol is proportional to its importance. The larger the size of an alternative (yellow circles), the better location it represents for waste bins, as shown in Figure 5. Moreover, each alternative location is serially labeled (in descending order) based upon its final weighted score. From the Figure 5, it can be analyzed that the alternatives which are spatially near the center of the block are better for being selected as waste bin locations i.e. alternatives labeled 1, 2, 3 and 4. On the other hand, alternatives labeled 12, 13 and 14 are the least optimal locations. It can be inferred from this analysis that the G5 block is affected by improper waste dumping mostly at the center, caused by congested housing and narrow roads. Hence, priority should be given to bin placements at these locations that are highly prone to improper waste dumping by the residents.

IV. CONCLUSION AND FUTURE WORK

Waste management is a major environmental issue in developing countries including Pakistan. Limited maintenance budget has adversely affected WAPDA Town residents, due to lack of available waste bins. GIS in collaboration with multi-criteria decision-making techniques helps the management in efficiently determining the location of waste bins. The proposed solution has a two-fold advantage. Firstly, due to the generic nature of the required dataset, this spatial decision solution can be applied to other blocks of the society or in various metropolitan areas of Lahore city. Secondly, altering the criteria and their weights, various outputs can be retrieved. This helps in achieving flexible decision making. According to the budget constraints of a specific area, management can choose the top locations for bin placement. The goal achieved through this work is a well-researched solution to the cleanliness issue in WAPDA Town. All previous efforts have been in

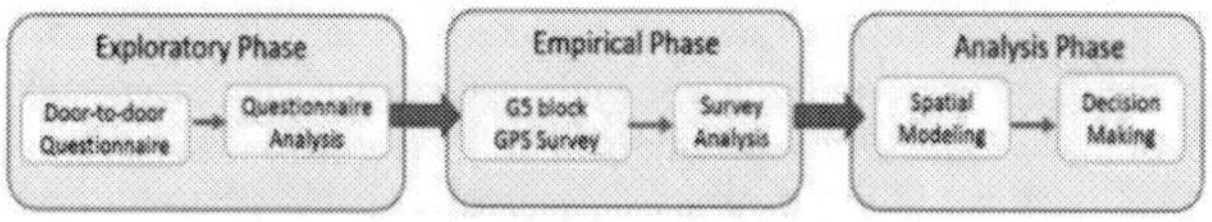

Figure 3. Proposed methodology chart.

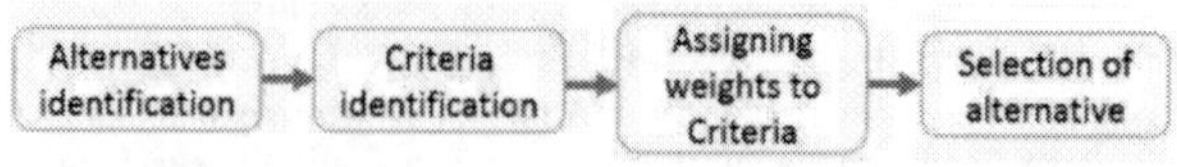

Figure 4. Decision making process.

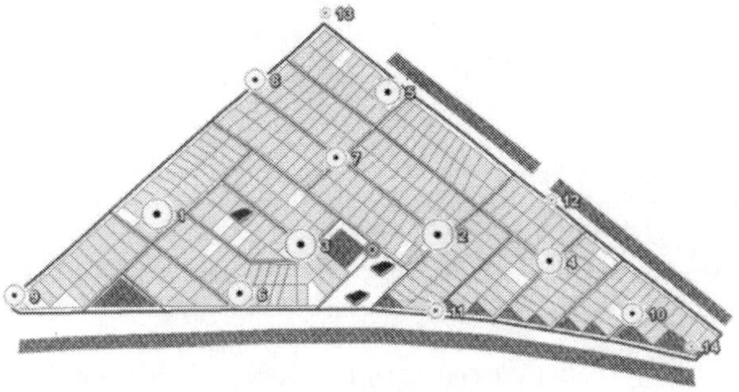

Figure 5. Decision making result.

vain due to lack of any statistical data and analytical calculations, while the current research work includes both, the surveyed data and spatial analytics.

In the next phase of this research work, actual placement of waste bins is expected at locations retrieved through the proposed solution. Upon placement of bins, further analysis would be carried out to measure any improvement in improper waste dumping by residents in the vicinity of the bin. Reduction of improper waste dumping will authenticate the selection of criteria and their weights; else brainstorming would be done for altering these parameters. This iterative process will eventually mature the spatial decision-making procedure for waste management. Lessons learned from these outcomes can be used to cater waste management issues in other blocks or municipal societies of Lahore city.

Since the final weighted score is a direct measure of the importance of the waste bin location, another future prospect could be to place waste bins of different sizes depending upon the calculated score. This will, in turn, help in efficient utilization of the financial resources of the administration.

TABLE I. CRITERIA DESCRIPTION

Code	Criteria	Weights	Description
C1	Houses	0.42	Each house represents specific amount of daily waste.
C2	Poles	0.09	Waste dumbing is done by residents near electric poles.
C3	Roads and streets	0.12	Accessibility of alternative through main road and streets
C4	Empty plots areas	0.18	Waste dumbing is done by residents inside empty plots.
C5	Commercial areas	0.04	Commercial areas generate more waste as compared to houses
C6	Existing bin	0.06	Distance from the nearest existing waste bin.
C7	Proposed Bin	0.09	Distance from the nearest proposed waste bin (alternative)

REFERENCES

[1] Zhu Minghua et al., "Municipal solid waste management in Pudong New Area, China," Waste Management no. 29, pp. 1227-1233. Crown Copyright 2008 Published by Elsevier Ltd.

[2] P. V. Gorsevski, K. R. Donevska, C. D. Mitrovski, and J. P. Frizado, "Integrating multi-criteria evaluation techniques with geographic informationsystems for landfill site selection: A case study using ordered weighted average," Waste Management no. 32, pp. 287-296, 2011 Elsevier Ltd.

[3] Q. Hamid, M. H. Chauhdry, S. Mahmood, and M. S. Farid, "Arc GIS and 3D Visualization of Land Records: A Case Study of Urban Areas in Punjab," in National Academy Science Letters, vol. 39, no. 4, pp. 277-281, August 2016.

[4] D. K. Themistoklis, P. K. Dimitrios, and P. H. Constantinos, "Siting MSW landfills with a spatial multiple criteria analysis methodology," doi:10.1016/j.wasman.2005.04.002.

[5] I. Mahamid and S. Thawaba, "Multi criteria and landfill site selection using GIS: a case study from Palestine," The Open Environmental Engineering Journal, 2010.

[6] M. A. Alanbari and Q. Al-Mseiab, "Landfill Site Selection Using GIS and Multicriteria Decision Analysis," Engineering no. 6, pp. 526-549, 2014.

[7] C. Chalikas and K. Ladaridi, "A GIS based model for the optimisation of municipal solid waste collection: the case study of Nikea, Athens, Greece," WSEAS Transactions on Environment and Development, vol. 5, no. 10, pp. 640–650, 2009

[8] H. Abdulai, R. Hussein, E. Bevilacqua, and M. Storrings, "GIS Based A and Analysis of Municipal Solid Waste Collection System, in Wa, Ghana," Journal of Geographic Information System, no. 7, pp. 85-94, 2015.

[9] ArcGIS Desktop by ESRI. (February 23, 2018). Retrieved from http://desktop.arcgis.com/en/.

[10] Pairwise comparison. (February 23, 2018). Retrieved from https://en.wikipedia.org/wiki/Pairwise_comparison.

[11] Pairwise comparison. (February 23, 2018). Retrieved from https://en.wikipedia.org/wiki/Analytic_hierarchy_process.

[12] A. Kallel, M. M. Serbaji, and M. Zairi, "Using GIS-Based Tools for the Optimization of Solid Waste Collection and Transport: Case Study of Sfax City, Tunisia," Journal of Engineering, vol. 2016, article ID 4596849, 7 pages, 2016. doi:10.1155/2016/4596849.

[13] E. Triantaphyllou, "Multi-Criteria Decision Making Methods," Multi-criteria Decision Making Methods: A Comparative Study. Applied Optimization, vol 44. Springer, Boston, MA.

[14] "GPS Logger for Android" (March 11, 2018). Retrieved from https://play.google.com/store/apps/details?id=com.mendhak.gpslogger.

[15] "World Geodetic System" (March 11, 2018). Retrieved from https://en.wikipedia.org/wiki/World_Geodetic_System.

National Geoinformation System Development in the Republic of Uzbekistan

Muzaffar Djalalov
SUE UNICON.UZ
Ministry for the development of information technologies and communications
Tashkent, Republic of Uzbekistan
email: m.jalalov@gmail.com

Abstract – **Geoinformation systems (GIS) are widely being implemented all over the world. They are helping in solving many economic and industrial issues. This paper describes how a national geoinformation system is being developed in Uzbekistan, as well as, policies, standards and technologies that are used to build a nationwide GIS infrastructure. Moreover, the national GIS concept is being analyzed and we propose a 5 year development plan based on modern international demands and trends.**

Keywords-GIS; Cadastre; National concept; Standardization.

I. INTRODUCTION

The National Geographic Information System (NGIS) creation in Uzbekistan has been carried forward by the strong will of the Republic of Uzbekistan as a part of the economic reform to use land and natural resources more efficiently based on a rapid information technologies (IT) development and application of the information and communication technologies (ICT) inside and outside of the Republic of Uzbekistan. The NGIS shall support the decision makers of Uzbekistan in different sectors of the government such as territorial development, land administration, environmental protection, social development, etc.

A. The rapid development of ICT in the Republic of Uzbekistan

The wide developments of ICT and computerization have been a global tendency of the world development for the last decades. Especially, the rapid development the ICT industry has been a driving force of the economic development with job creation and attraction of investment. Also, management effectiveness can be maximized and cost reduction in information exchange between market's participants can be expected by combining IT with production/management activities.

In the "Program for Computerization and Information-Communicative Technologies Development for 2002-2010" [1] and in the resolution of the President of the Republic of Uzbekistan "On measures for further development of a national information and communication system of the Republic of Uzbekistan" [2], the Government of Uzbekistan emphasized the significance of the economic development and improvement in the nation's well-being through ICT. In addition, Uzbekistan agencies are encouraged to attract foreign loans and grants for this program in the Resolution of the Cabinet of Ministers in 2002.

B. Rising necessities for utilization of natural resource

Abundant land and natural resources are important elements of Uzbekistan. In order to protect and allow reasonable usage of natural and land resources, the economic potential of the land must be analyzed. This can be done if there is enough information of the status and the usage pattern of the land, including natural resources and their infrastructures. Thus, the need for the construction of a national geographic information system is being emphasized.

In line with the public priorities of Uzbekistan, the project aims to develop and build the NGIS, which is the most efficient tool of the complex presentation and the analysis of the information about territorial development of Uzbekistan.

The NGIS will allow analyzing and valuing in real time different actual and reliable cartographic and other data in order to support the decision makers in different spheres: territorial development, land administration, environmental protection, social development, etc.

C. The proven economic and technical effects from research and studies

By introducing the geographic information technologies and systems, many research and studies have proven that it has many benefits over the economic and technology sectors. Protection and rational use of natural resources also benefit from similar effects.

Positive financial results of Cadastre services' activity provide additional income to the budget at the expense of the land correction and the other real property taxation.

D. Achieve the economic reform through IT application

Uzbekistan is seeking a development of the economic and the national welfare. In order to achieve this, Uzbekistan government considers ICT industry as a strategic method. Uzbekistan government particularly emphasizes national geographic information system creation.

Further, Section II gives the main idea on the GIS project in Uzbekistan and its directions, Section III describes components of each subsystem and designations, and Section IV discusses the target and the architecture of the project.

II. UNDERSTANDING THE OBJECTIVE

The NGIS target goals are to provide the basic foundation and the basic platform support of "E-government" system of Uzbekistan. The implementation of the NGIS application at the government level including ministries, departments and local administration, will gradually utilize for "e-government" system.

The NGIS shall be a basic information resource of future e-government system. The NGIS and its components should be integrated with other state information of e-government systems.

The main objective of project is to develop and build the NGIS of Uzbekistan which collects and manages the data regarding the rational use as well as natural resources preservation in order to support timely and transparent the decision making for balanced socio-economic development across country and sectors.

The NGIS will increase the level of public authorities' information awareness and enhance the reasonability of the administrative the decision-making process.

The objective summary and system description are as follows, and are followed by the objectives of each project components:

- Establishment of State Satellite Geodetic Network.
- Digital Base Map Delivery and DPW Installation.
- Implementation of Information Analytical Centers and Automatic Working Stations.
- Development of pilot system for the National System of Cadastre and Real Property Registration (NSCRP).
- The NGIS Standardization and Master Plan.

III. THE OBJECTIVES FOR EACH SUB-SYSTEM

The main objective of project is to develop and build the NGIS of Uzbekistan which collects and manages the data regarding the rational use as well as natural resources preservation in order to support timely and transparent the decision making for balanced socio-economic development across country and sectors. It will become a basic platform part of e-government system which Uzbekistan government plans:

(a) Public administration: the NGIS will increase the level of public authorities' information awareness and enhance the reasonability of the administrative the decision-making process.

(b) Accuracy: New state satellite geodetic network will create conditions for position prompt fixing of objects with high accuracy.

(c) Integration: Unified NSCRP will provide an opportunity to render public services by the interactive system "one stop shop" [3-4].

(d) E-government: With the implementation of the NGIS application at the governmental level, Project aims to be gradually utilized for E-government system.

(e) Governmental Authority Users: The actual end users by Project are the Central Information-Analytic Centers (IAC), 14 Regional IACs of the NGIS, and Situation Centers (Emergency) for state and regional governmental authorities

A. *Establishment of State Satellite Geodetic Network*

The general definition of a CORS Network is the terrestrial infrastructure (equipment and software) designed to deliver Positioning Service based on the National GNSS technology. It is intended to cover the whole region of Uzbekistan with different levels of accuracy.

A new state satellite geodetic network will create conditions for position prompt fixing of objects with high accuracy. Also, various public services shall be created. These services will cover a wide range of applications, not just for geodesists, but also for public users and end users.

B. *Digital Base Map Delivery and DPW Installation*

The digital cartographic basis objectives are quickly and accurately establishing the basis for the latest digital cartography for the basis of land management.

The digital cartography map can be used in various sectors of the government (economy, science, national defense and etc.) which will increase the business processes efficiency and improve the quality of public services.

Private sectors, job creation, productivity enhancement and other various effects can be expected.

C. *Implementation of IAC and AWS*

The actual end users by project are IAC, the 14 Regional IACs of the NGIS, and the Situation Centers (Emergency) for the state and regional governmental authorities. Therefore, IAC building objectives and AWS are improving the efficiency of the administration tasks using the results of the NGIS for the actual end users of the system.

D. *Development of pilot system for NSCRP*

Unified computer-based NSCRP will provide an opportunity to render public services by an interactive system "one stop shop". By developing pilot system for NSCRP, land/real estate information can be realized and statistical information of land use can be calculated as well. Policy information on land use development and monitoring system for land use status, standard, procedure and other technical element shall be established as well. It is important to develop one's own system rather than purchasing a ready solution (Table 1)

TABLE I. COMPARATIVE ANALYSIS BETWEEN PACKAGE- AND CUSTOM-BUILT SOFTWARE

Parameter	***Packaged Software***	***Custom-built Software***
Development period	Dependent on degree of customization agreed upon by vendor and Purchaser, deployment may be immediate	8 to 12 months, including detailed functional analysis
Degree of compliance with required business processes and rules	Depends on software, average ranges from 50% to 75%	Almost 100%

Parameter	*Packaged Software*	*Custom-built Software*
Total cost of ownership	Initial license costs may be high; Maintenance fees will depend on the type of maintenance agreement;	No licenses required; Development costs usually lower than the license costs. If creation of an IT department is needed, then the cost can be higher. Delayed implementation may lead to high costs
IPR ownership	Vendor owns source code, including those developed during	Purchaser owns source code
Maintenance and upgrades	Maintenance and upgrade is more or less assured, but subject to payment of annual maintenance fees	Maintenance subject to agreement with developer or may be done by Purchaser's IT unit, when present; Upgrades are not usually available;
Flexibility	Limited to the extent that the vendor would allow	Highly flexible, as required by Purchaser
Integration with other legacy systems	Limited	Integration parameters can be included in the functional specifications and design of the system

E. The NGIS Standardization and Master Plan

The main benefits that can be gained from the standardization will be budget waste prevention and synergy creation. Standardization means establishing a common system and enabling a range of different users to share data or the system. This will provide efficiency and interconnectedness between projects and users.

Therefore, the standardization objectives are to define the standardization object, standardization method, standardization procedures and standardization organization. It is necessary to establish what will be standardized, which method will be used for the standardization, which procedure will be used for the standard and who will establish and define standardization.

IV. UNDERSTANDING OF THE TARGET SYSTEM

Based on the above project work scope, the concept diagram of the target system is shown in Fig. 1.

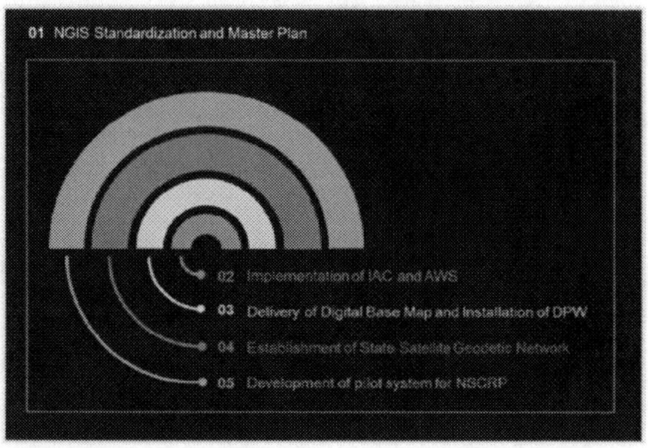

Figure 1. Conceptual Diagram of the Targeted System - Overall

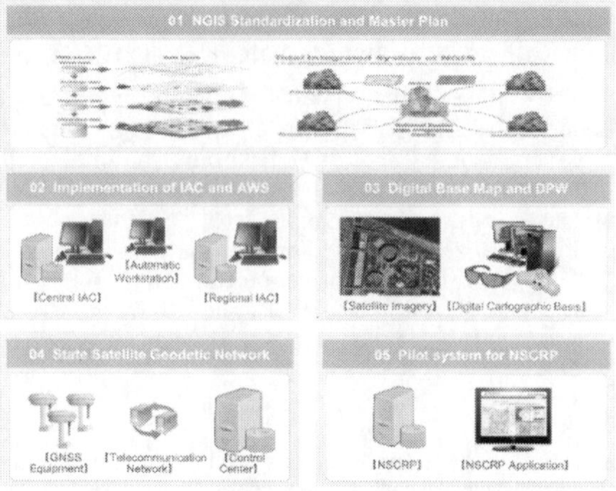

Figure 2. Conceptual Diagram of the Targeted System - Concrete

The first thing to establish within this project is the NGIS standardization. The satellite image based digital map can be produced with the standardized procedures and methods where it can be used for base map in various GIS applications. Accurate location information collected from GNSS CORS and digital map can be combined and integrated into a central information analysis center. Integration of all various GIS information can be collected, classified, refined and analyzed by the user of the Central IAC to create new contents and services which then results in service quality improvement of public services and the application of the digital map within the governmental level (Fig. 2).

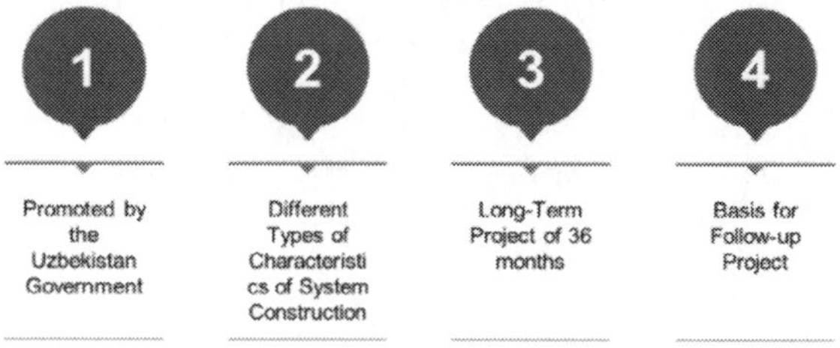

Figure 3. Characteristics of the project

For the successful project implementation, it is important to have a clear project understanding. Therefore, it is important to derive project characteristics based on the objectives and project background (Fig.3).

V. EXPECTED RESULTS

Project completion will provide the end users with convenience in the NGIS service. In addition, the end-user agencies will benefit from the higher efficiency in their business management through automation. In particular, the government will get increased control, management and monitoring ability by the rational use of the geographical information provided by the NGIS.

A. Scientific the decision-making by the use of centralized geographic information

The NGIS supports the rational state policy required for development and land preservation and natural resources through the view of current status of the nation-wide geographic information and the expectations. Various methods for geospatial analysis will help the decision-makers to shape systemic and scientific policies with visibility and accuracy.

B. Reduced processing time and efforts in public sector by the common use of geospatial information

The sharing of gathered information based on the sole standard will enable the central IAC to oversee the full extent of data as well as the regional IACs to interact through interface.

The common use of the geospatial information among different government agencies enhances synergy in public sector and will no longer allow government spending for duplicated efforts to construct individual piece of information by agency.

C. The economic effect creation by the introduction of value-added service

Once gathered, integrated national GIS information will promote various GIS-applied sectors in the private sector. Small and medium-sized companies will obtain business opportunities to get involved in public and private sectors respectively.

Increased opportunities will generate technology development and the accumulation of GIS-related skills and knowhow in the business.

Value-added jobs new creation will contribute to the moderation of unemployment problem.

D. Convenient service for end-users

The digital cartographic base and the 3rd dimension information regarding land will be provided as the form of 'One-stop Shop' service. The geographical information inputted in the existing public service for citizens will greatly improve citizens' convenience.

The easy access and use of a geographic information will give individual end-users, private or public, to process the digital map to be fit for each one's purpose.

REFERENCES

[1] The Resolution of the Cabinet of Ministry of the Republic of Uzbekistan "Program for Computerization and Information-Communicative Technologies Development for 2002-2010". May, 2002, pp.78-90.

[2] The Resolution of the President of the Republic of Uzbekistan "On measures for further development of a national information and communication system of the Republic of Uzbekistan". June, 2013, p.35.

[3] The Law of the Republic of Uzbekistan "Geodesy and Cartography". April, 1997, pp.105-149

[4] The Resolution of the Cabinet of Ministry of the Republic of Uzbekistan "On the establishment and maintenance of a Unified System of State Cadasters". February, 2005, pp.1-3.

Motion Planning in 3D Environments Using Visibility Velocity Obstacles

Oren Gal, Yerach Doytsher
Mapping and Geo-information Engineering
Technion - Israel Institute of Technology
Haifa, Israel
e-mail: {orengal,doytsher}@technion.ac.il

Abstract—**In this paper, we present a unique method combining visibility analysis in 3D environments with dynamic motion planning algorithm, named Visibility Velocity Obstacles (VVO). Our method is based on two major steps. The first step is based on analytic visibility boundaries calculation in 3D environments, taking into account sensors' capabilities including probabilistic consideration. In the second step, we generate VVO transferring visibility boundaries from the position space to the velocity space, for each object. Each VVO represents velocity's set of possible future collision and visibility boundaries. Based on our analysis in velocity space, we plan our trajectory by selecting robot's future velocity at each time step, tracking each specific target by considering visibility constraints as an integral part of the velocities space. We formulate the tracked target in the environment as part of our planner and include visibility analysis for the next time step as part of our planning in the same search space. We define visibility aspects as part of velocity space, where all the objects are modeled from the visibility point of view. We introduce a potential trajectory planner combining unified 3D visibility analysis for target tracking as part of dynamic motion planning.**

Keywords- Visibility; Motion planning, 3D; Urban environment; Spatial analysis.

I. INTRODUCTION

Trajectory planning has developed alongside the increasing numbers of Unmanned Aerial Vehicles (UAVs) all over the world, with a wide range of applications such as surveillance, information gathering, suppression of enemy defenses, air to air combat, mapping buildings and facilities, etc.

Most of these applications are involved in very complicated environments (e.g. urban), with complex terrain for civil and military domains [5]. With these growing needs, several basic capabilities must be achieved. One of these capabilities is the need to avoid obstacles such as buildings or other moving objects, while autonomously navigating in 3D urban environments.

Path planning problems have been extensively studied in the robotics community. These problems include finding a collision-free path in static or dynamic environments, i.e., environments having moving or static obstacles. Over the past twenty years, many kinds of path planning methods have been proposed, such as starting roadmap, cell decomposition, and potential field [6].

In this paper, as far as we know for the first time, we present visibility aspects as part of velocity space, where all the objects are modeled from visibility point of view. We introduce potential trajectory planner combining unified 3D visibility analysis for target tracking as part of dynamic motion planning. In the first part, we formulate visibility boundaries problem and introduce analytic solution. Later on, we present the VVO method, demonstrated with visibility boundaries with cars, pedestrians and buildings visibility boundaries. In the last part, we suggest pursuer planner using VVO for UAV test case.

II. RELATED WORK

Path planning becomes trajectory planning when a time dimension is added for dynamic obstacles [7][8]. Later on, a vehicle's dynamic and kinematic constraints have been taken into account, in a process called kinodynamic planning [9]. All of these methods focus solely on obstacle avoidance.

Trajectory planning for air traffic control and ground vehicles has been well studied [10], based on short path algorithms using 2D polygons, 3D surfaces [11]. UAVs navigation has also been explored with vision-based methods [12], with local planning or a predefined global path [13].

UAV path planning is different from simple robot path planning, due to the fact that a UAV cannot stop, and must maintain its velocity above the minimum, as well as not being able to make sharp turns.

The visibility problem has been extensively studied over the last twenty years, due to the importance of visibility in Geographic Information System (GIS) and Geomatics, computer graphics and computer vision, and robotics [1][3]. Accurate visibility computation in 3D environments is a very complicated task demanding a high computational effort, which could hardly have been done in a very short time using traditional well-known visibility methods [15]. The exact visibility methods are highly complex, and cannot be used for fast applications due to their long computation time. Previous research in visibility computation has been devoted to open environments using Digital Elevation Model (DEM) models, representing raster data in 2.5D (Polyhedral model), and do not address, or suggest solutions for, dense built-up areas. Most of these works have focused on approximate visibility computation, enabling fast results using interpolations of visibility values between points, calculating point visibility with the Line of Sight (LOS) method [16]. Other fast algorithms are based on the conservative Potentially Visible Set (PVS) [17]. These methods are not always completely accurate, as they may render hidden objects' parts as visible due to various simplifications and heuristics.

III. VISIBILITY BOUNDARIES ANALYSIS

We extend our previous work [2], developed for a fast and efficient visibility analysis for buildings in urban environments, and consider also a basic structure of cylinders, which allows us to model pedestrians and trees. Based on our probabilistic visibility computation of dynamic objects, we test the effect of these by using data gathered from Web-oriented GIS sources to update our estimation and prediction on these entities.

Dynamic objects such as moving cars and pedestrians, directly affect visibility in urban environments. Due to modeling limitations, these entities are usually neglected in spatial analysis aspects. We focus on three major dynamic objects in an urban case: moving cars and pedestrians. Each object is modeled with 3D boxes or 3D cylinders, which allow us to extend the use of our previous visibility analysis in urban environments presented for static objects [2].

1) Moving Car

3D Modeling: As we mentioned earlier, Web-cameras in urban environments can record the moving cars at any specific time. Image sources such as web cameras, like other similar sensors sources, demand an additional stage of Automatic Target Detection (ATD) algorithms to extract these objects from the image [19]. In this research we do not focus on ATD, which must be implemented when shifting from the research described in the paper toward an applicable system.

The common car structure can be easily modeled by two 3D boxes, as can be seen in Figure 1, which is similar to the original car structure presented in Figure 1.

We define the Car Boundary Points (CBP) as the set of visible surfaces' boundary points of 3D boxes modeling the car presented in Figure 1. Each box is modeled as 3D cubic $C_{car}(x, y, z)$ as presented extensively in [2] for a building model case.

Car Boundary Points (CBP) - we define CBP of the object i as a set of boundary points $j = 1..N_{CBP\_bound}$ of the visible surfaces of the car object, from viewpoint $V(x_0, y_0, z_0)$, where the maximum surface's number is six and each surface defined by four points, $N_{CBP\_bound} \leq 24$, described in (1).

Figure 1. Car Modeling Using 3D Boxes

In Figure 2, the car is modeled by using two 3D boxes. Visible surfaces colored in red, the CBP marked with yellow points.

$$CBP_{i=1..N_{CBP\_bound}}(x_0, y_0, z_0) = \begin{bmatrix} x_1, y_1, z_1 \\ x_2, y_2, z_2 \\ .. \\ x_{N_{CBP\_bound}}, y_{N_{CBP\_bound}}, z_{N_{CBP\_bound}} \end{bmatrix} \quad (1)$$

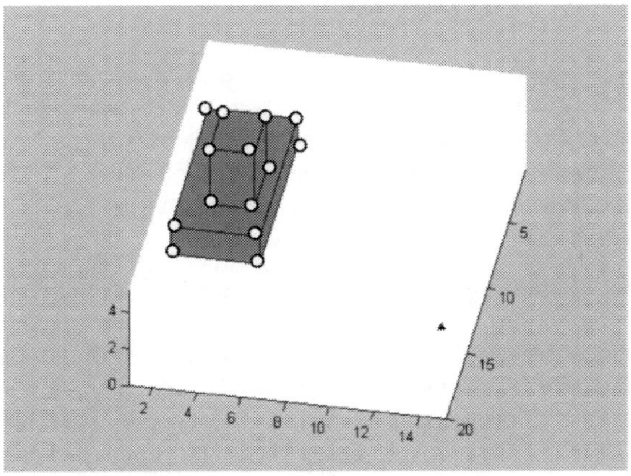

Figure 2. Modeling Car Using 3D Boxes (CBP Marked with Yellow Points)

Probabilistic Visibility Analysis

Visibility has been treated as a Boolean values. Due to incomplete information and the uncertainties of predicting the car's location at future times, visibility becomes much more complicated.

As it is well known from basic kinematics, CBP can be estimated in future time $t + \Delta t$ as shown in (2):

$$CBP_i(t + \Delta t) = CBP_i(t) + V(t)\Delta t + \frac{A(t)\Delta t^2}{2} \quad (2)$$

Where $V(t)$ is the car velocity vector $V(t) = (v_x v_y)^T$, and the acceleration vector $A(t) = (a_x a_y)^T$. Estimation of a car's location in the future based on a web camera is not a simple task. Driver behavior generates multi-decision modeling, such as car-following behavior, gap acceptance behavior, or lane-change cases including traffic flow, speed etc.[20].

Our probabilistic car model is based on microscopic simulation models that were properly calibrated and validated using VISSIM simulation [20]. The average speed in urban environments is about 45 [km/hr], from a minimum of 40 [km/hr] up to a maximum of 50 [km/hr]. In the situation of a free driving case, which is the common mode in urban environments [21], the acceleration of a family car can change between 1 to 3.5 $\left[{}^{m}/_{sec^2}\right]$, and on average 2.5 $\left[{}^{m}/_{sec^2}\right]$.

As can be seen from several validations of car and driver estimation, velocity and acceleration are distributed as normal ones, and lead to normal location distribution in (3):

$$\begin{gathered} V(t) \sim N(\mu = 45, \sigma^2 = 10) \\ A(t) \sim N(\mu = 2.5, \sigma^2 = 1) \\ CBP(t + \Delta t) \sim \sum N \end{gathered} \tag{3}$$

In time step t, where the car's location is taken from a Web-camera, visibility analysis from $CBP(t)$ is an exact one, based on our previous visibility analysis [2], as seen in Figure 2. Visibility analysis becomes probabilistic for future time $t + \Delta t$, applying the same visibility analysis for $CBP(t + \Delta t)$ presented in Figure 3.

In Figure 3, the car's location from a Web-camera appears in the bottom left side. For $\Delta t = 2[sec]$, the car's location is marked by two 3D boxes, where CBP for each of them is the boundary of visible surfaces marked in red. The probability that the visible surfaces, which are bounded by CBP, will be visible in future time is based on the last update taken from the web application (depicted with arrows in Figure 3), computed by using two different random normal PDF values for V and A.

*2) **Pedestrians***

3D Modeling: Pedestrian modeling can be done in high resolution, but due to ATD algorithms capabilities, pedestrians are usually bounded by a 3D cylinder and not as an exact detailed model [19]. For this reason, we model pedestrians as 3D cylinders, which is somewhat conservative but still applicable.

Pedestrian can be easily modeled by 3D cylinders, as seen in Figure 4 (marked in red), which is similar to the output from ATD methods tested on a Web-camera output recognizing walkers in urban environments.

We extend our previous visibility analysis concept [2] and include new objects modeled as cylinders as continuous curves parameterization, $C_{Peds}(x, y, z)$ in (4). Cylinder parameterization can be described as:

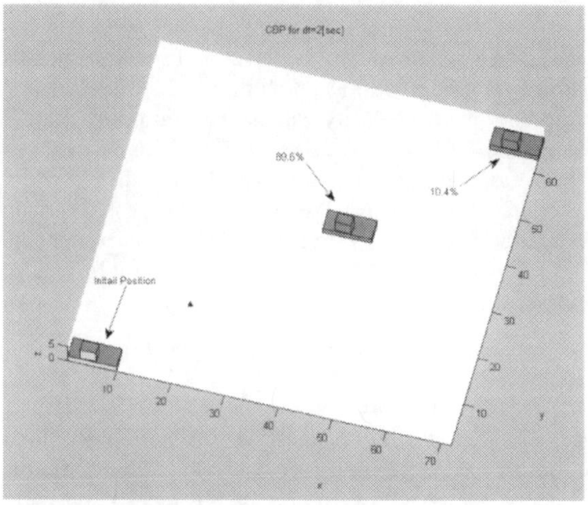

Figure 3. Probabilistic Visibility Analysis for CBP

$$\begin{aligned} &C_{Peds}(x, y, z) = \begin{pmatrix} r\sin(\theta) \\ r\cos(\theta) \\ c \end{pmatrix} \\ &0 \le \theta \le 2\pi \\ &c = c + 1 \\ &0 \le c \le h_{peds\_max} \end{aligned} \tag{4}$$

Figure 4. Modeling Pedestrians in Urban Scene Using Cylinders (Colored in Red)

We define the visibility problem in a 3D environment for more complex objects in (5):

$$C'(x, y)_{z_{const}} \times (C(x, y)_{z_{const}} - V(x_0, y_0, z_0)) = 0 \tag{5}$$

where 3D model parameterization is $C(x, y)_{z=const}$, and the viewpoint is given as $V(x_0, y_0, z_0)$. Extending the 3D cubic parameterization, we also consider the cylinder case. As can be noted, these equations are not related to Z axis, and the visibility boundary points are the same for each x-y cylinder profile.

The visibility statement leads to a complex equation, which does not appear to be a simple computational task. This equation can be efficiently solved by finding where the equation changes its sign and crosses zero value; we used analytic solution to speed up computation time and to avoid numeric approximations. We generate two values of θ generating two silhouette points in a very short time computation in (6). Based on an analytic solution to the cylinder case, a fast and exact analytic solution can be found for the visibility problem from a viewpoint.

$$\theta = \arctan\left(-\frac{-r - \frac{\left(-vy\, r + \sqrt{vx^4 - vx^2 r^2 + vy^2 vx^2}\right) vy}{vx^2 + vy^2}}{vx}, -\frac{-vy\, r + \sqrt{vx^4 - vx^2 r^2 + vy^2 vx^2}}{vx^2 + vy^2} \right) \quad (6)$$

We define the solution presented above as x-y-z coordinates values for the cylinder case as **Pedestrian Boundary Points** (PBP). PBP are the set of visible silhouette points for a 3D cylinder modeling the pedestrian in (7):

$$PBP_{i=1..N_{PBP\_bound}=2}(x_0, y_0, z_0) = \begin{bmatrix} x_1, y_1, z_1 \\ x_{N_{PBP\_bound}}, y_{N_{PBP\_bound}}, z_{N_{PBP\_bound}} \end{bmatrix} \quad (7)$$

IV. VISIBILITY VELOCITY OBSTACLES (VVO)

The visibility velocity obstacle represents the set of all velocities from a viewpoint, occluded with other objects in the environment. It essentially maps static and moving objects into the robot's velocity space considering visibility boundaries.

The VVO of an object with circular visibility boundary points such as the pedestrians case, PBP, that is moving at a constant velocity v_b, is a cone in the velocity space at point A. In Figure 5, the position space and velocity space of A are overlaid to illustrate the relationship between the two spaces. The VVO is generated by first constructing the Relative Velocity Cone (RVC) from A to the boundaries of the object, i.e., PBP, then translating RVC by v_b.

Each point in VVO represents a velocity vector that originates at A. Any velocity of A that penetrates VVO is an occluded velocity that based on the current situation, would result in an occlusion between A and the pedestrian at some future time. Figure 5 shows two velocities of A: one that penetrates VVO, hence, an occluded velocity, and one that does not. All velocities of A that are outside of VVO are visible from the current robot's position as the obstacle denotes as B, stays on its current course.

The visibility velocity obstacle thus allows determining if a given velocity is occluded, and suggesting possible changes to this velocity for better visibility. If PBP is known to move along a curved trajectory or at varying speeds, it would be best represented by the nonlinear visibility velocity obstacle case discussed next.

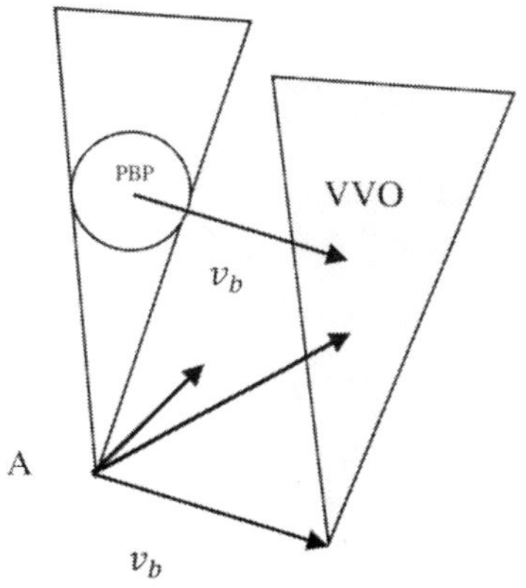

Figure 5. Visibility Velocity Obstacles

The VVO consists of all velocities of A at t_0 predicting visibility's boundaries related to obstacles at the environment at any time $t>t_0$. Selecting a single velocity, v_a, at time $t = t_0$ outside the VVO, guarantees visibility to this specific obstacle at time t. It is constructed as a union of its temporal elements, VVO(t), which is the set of all absolute velocities of A, v_a, that would allow visibility at a specific time t.

Referring to Figure 6, v_a that would result in occlusion with point p in B at time $t > t_0$, expressed in a frame centered at $A(t_0)$, is simply in (8):

$$v_a = \frac{VBP_i}{t-t_0} \quad (8)$$

where r is the vector to point p in the blocker's fixed frame, and visibility boundaries denoted as Visibility Boundary Points (VBP). The set VVO(t) of all absolute velocities of A that would result in occlusion with any point in B at time $t > t_0$ is thus in (9):

$$VVO(t) = \frac{VBP_i(t)}{t-t_0} \quad (9)$$

Clearly, VVO(t) is a scaled B for two dimensional case with circular object, located at a distance from A that is inversely proportional to time t. The entire VVO is the union of its temporal subsets from t_0, the current time, to some set future time horizon t_h in (10):

$$VVO(t) = \bigcup_{t=t_0}^{t_h} \frac{VBP_i(t)}{t-t_0} \quad (10)$$

The presented VVO generate a warped cone in a case of 2D circular object. If VBP(t) is bounded over $t = (t_0, \infty)$, then the apex of this cone is at $A(t_0)$.We extend our analysis to 3D general case, where the objects can be cubes, cylinders and circles. The mathematical analysis with visibility boundaries is based on VBP presented in the previous part for different kind of objects such as buildings, cars and pedestrians.

We transform the visibility's boundaries into the velocity space, by moving the VBP to the velocity space, in the same analysis presented for 2D circle boundaries.

Following that, we present a 3D extension for VBP case, transformed to the velocity space.

Given two objects, VBP_1, VBP_2 will create a VVO representing VBP_2 (and vice-versa) such that VBP_1 wishes to choose a guaranteed collision-free velocity for the time interval τ, and visibility boundary in velocity space.

In case of cars, buildings and pedestrians where visibility boundaries can be expressed by geometric operations of 3D boxes, analyzed in the same concept and formulation presented so far, as can be seen in Figure 6.

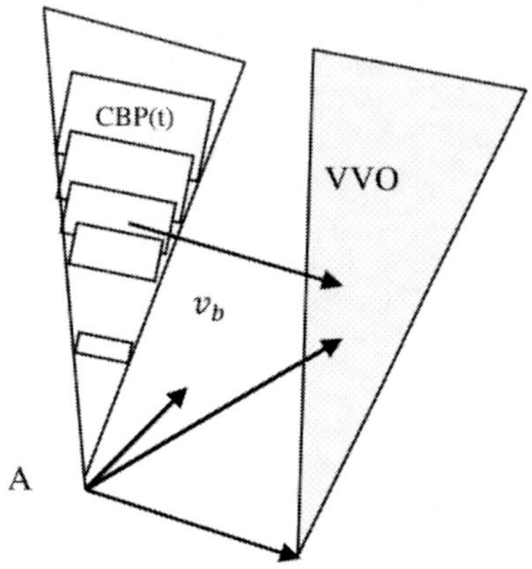

Figure 6. Visibility Velocity Obstacle for visibility boundaries consist of 3D boxes

V. PURSUER PLANNER USING VVO

Our planner, similar to previous work [22] is a local one, generating one step ahead every time step reaching toward the goal, which is a depth first A* search over a tree. We extend previous planners which take into account kinematic and dynamic constraints [9][14] and present a local planner for UAV as case study with these constraints, which for the first time generates fast and exact visible trajectories based on VVO, tracking after a target by choosing the optimal next action based on velocity estimation. The fast and efficient visibility analysis of our method allows us to generate the most visible trajectory from a start state q_{start} to the goal state q_{goal} in 3D urban environments, which can be extended to real performances in the future. We assume knowledge of the 3D urban environment model, and by using Visibility Velocity Obstacles (VVO) method to avoid occlusion, planner is based on exploring maximum visible node in the next time step and track a specific target.

1) Attainable Velocities

Based on the dynamic and kinematic constraints, UAVs velocities at the next time step are limited. At each time step during the trajectory planning, we map the AV, the velocities set at the next time step $t+\tau$, which generate the optimal trajectory, as it is well-known from Dubins theory [18].

We denote the allowable controls as $u=(u_s,u_z,u_\phi)$ as U, where $V \in U$.

We denote the set of dynamic constraints bounding control's rate of change as $\dot{u}=(\dot{u}_s,\dot{u}_z,\dot{u}_\phi) \in U'$.

Considering the extremal controllers as part of the motion primitives of the trajectory cannot ensure time-optimal trajectory for Dubins airplane model [18], but is still a suitable heuristic based on time-optimal trajectories of Dubin - car and point mass models.

We calculate the next time step's feasible velocities $\tilde{U}(t+\tau)$, between $(t,t+\tau)$ as shown in (11):

$$\tilde{U}(t+\tau)=U \cap \{u \mid u=u(t) \oplus \tau \cdot U'\} \quad (11)$$

Integrating $\tilde{U}(t+\tau)$ with UAV model yields the next eight possible nodes for the following combinations in (12):

$$\tilde{U}(t+\tau)=\begin{pmatrix}\tilde{U}_s(t+\tau)\\ \tilde{U}_z(t+\tau)\\ \tilde{U}_\phi(t+\tau)\end{pmatrix}=\begin{pmatrix}u_s^{min},u_s(t)+a_s\tau\\ -u_s^{max}\tan\phi^{max},u_s(t)\tan u_\phi(t)+u_s^{max}\tan a_\phi\\ u_z^{max},u_z(t)-a_z\tau\end{pmatrix} \quad (12)$$

At each time step, we explore the next eight AV at the next time step as part of our tree search, as explained in the next sub-section.

2) Tree Search

Our planner uses a depth first A* search over a tree that expands over time to the goal. Each node $(q,\dot{q})$, where $q=(x,y,z,\theta)$, consist of the current UAVs position and velocity at the current time step. At each state, the planner computes the set of AV, $\tilde{U}(t+\tau)$, from the current UAV velocity, $U(t)$. We ensure the visibility of nodes by computing a set of Visibility Velocity Obstacles (VVO).

The search method is based on exploring nodes which are outside of VVO. The safe node with the lowest cost, which is the next most visible node, is explored in the next time step. This is repeated while generating the most visible trajectory, as discussed in the next sub-section.

Attainable velocities profile is similar to a trunked cake slice, due to the Dubins airplane model with one time step integration ahead. Simple models attainable velocities, such as point mass, create rectangular profile [4].

3) Cost Function

Our search is guided by minimum invisible parts from viewpoint V to the 3D urban environment model, with minimal difference between robot's velocity v_a and tracked target v_{tck} .

The cost function is computed for each visible node $(q, \dot{q}) \ni VVO$, i.e., node outside VVO, considering UAV velocities at the next time step in (13):

$$w\big(q(t+\tau)\big) = abs(v_a(q(t+\tau) - v_{tck}(q(t+\tau)) \quad (13)$$

VI. Conclusions

This paper proposes an online motion planning algorithm in 3D environments for tracking a target, taking into account visibility analysis. The planner is based on local search and includes dynamic and kinematic constraints as a complete part of the planner. Visibility boundaries which are based on analytic solution for several kinds of objects in 3D urban environments, also include uncertainty and probabilistic factors. Each VVO represents velocity's set of possible future collision and visibility boundaries. Based on our analysis in velocity space, we plan our trajectory by selecting future robot's velocity at each time step, tracking after specific target considering visibility constraints as integral part of the velocities space. We formulate the tracked target in the environment and include visibility analysis for the next time step as part of our planning in the same search space.

References

[1] G. Elber, R. Sayegh, G. Barequet, and R. Martin, "Two-Dimensional Visibility Charts for Continuous Curves," in Proc. Shape Modeling, MIT, Boston, USA, 2005, pp. 206-215.

[2] O. Gal, and Y. Doytsher, "Fast and Accurate Visibility Computation in a 3D Urban Environment," in Proc. of the Fourth International Conference on Advanced Geographic Information Systems, Applications, and Services, Valencia, Spain, 2012, pp. 105-110.

[3] O. Gal, and Y. Doytsher, "Fast Visibility Analysis in 3D Procedural Modeling Environments," in Proc. of the, 3rd International Conference on Computing for Geospatial Research and Applications, Washington DC, USA, 2012.

[4] P. Fiorini, and Z. Shiller, "Motion Planning in Dynamic Environments Using Velocity Obstacles," Int. J. Robot. Res.17, 1998, pp. 760–772.

[5] Office of the Secretary of Defense, Unmanned Aerial Vehicles Roadmap, Tech. rep., December 2002.

[6] J.C. Latombe, "Robot Motion Planning," Kluwer Academic Press, 1990.

[7] M. Erdmann, and T. Lozano-Perez, "On Multiple Moving Objects," Algorithmica, 2, 1987, pp. 477–521.

[8] T. Fraichard, "Trajectory Planning in a Dynamic Workspace: A 'State-Time Space' Approach," Advanced Robotics, vol. 13, 1999, pp.75–94.

[9] S.M. LaValle, and J. Kuffner, Randomized Kinodynamic Planning. In Proc. IEEE Int. Conf. on Robotics and Automation, Detroit, MI , USA, 1999, pp. 473–479.

[10] Z.H. Mao, E. Feron, and K. Bilimoria, "Stability and Performance of Intersecting Aircraft Flows Under Decentralized Conflict Avoidance Rules," IEEE Transactions on Intelligent Transportation Systems, vol. 2, 2001, pp.101–109.

[11] J. Bellingham, A. Richards, and J. How, "Receding Horizon Control of Autonomous Aerial Vehicles," in Proceedings of the IEEE American Control Conference, Anchorage, AK, USA, 2002, pp. 3741–3746.

[12] B. Sinopoli, M. Micheli, G. Donata, and T. Koo, "Vision Based Navigation for an Unmanned Aerial Vehicle," in Proc. IEEE Int'l Conf. on Robotics and Automation, 2001.

[13] J. Sasiadek, and I. Duleba, "3D Local Trajectory Planner for UAV," Journal of Intelligent and Robotic Systems, vol, 2000, pp. 191–210.

[14] S.A. Bortoff, "Path Planning for UAVs," In Proc. of the American Control Conference, Chicago, IL, USA, 2000, pp. 364–368.

[15] H. Plantinga, and R. Dyer, "Visibility, Occlusion, and Aspect Graph," The International Journal of Computer Vision, vol. 5, 1990, pp. 137-160.

[16] Y. Doytsher, and B. Shmutter, "Digital Elevation Model of Dead Ground," Symposium on Mapping and Geographic Information Systems (Commission IV of the International Society for Photogrammetry and Remote Sensing), Athens, Georgia, USA, 1994.

[17] F. Durand, "3D Visibility: Analytical Study and Applications," PhD thesis, Universite Joseph Fourier, Grenoble, France, 1999.

[18] H. Chitsaz, and S.M. LaValle, "Time-Optimal Paths for a Dubins Airplane," in Proc. IEEE Conf. Decision and Control., USA, 2007, pp. 2379–2384.

[19] Y. Song: "The research of a new Auto Target Recognition directed Image compression," in 3th Int. Congress on Image and Signal Processing (CISP), 16-18 Oct, 2010, China.

[20] J. Archer: "Methods for the Assessment and Prediction of Traffic Safety at Urban Intersections and their Application in Micro-simulation Modeling," Centre for Traffic Simulation Research, CTR, Sweden. Technical Report, 2010.

[21] R. Wiedemann, and U. Reiter, "Microscopic Traffic Simulation: The Simulation System Mission, Background and Actual State," Project ICARUS (V1052), Final Report, Brussels CEC.2: Appendix A, 1992.

[22] O. Gal, and Y.Doytsher. "Patrolling Strategy Using Heterogeneous Multi Agents in Urban Environments Using Visibility Clustering," Journal of Unmanned System Technology, ISSN 2287-7320, 2016.

A Case Study for a Multitemporal Segmentation Approach in Optical Remote Sensing Images

Wanderson Costa*, Leila Fonseca*, Thales Körting*, Margareth Simões†‡ and Patrick Kuchler‡§
*National Institute for Space Research (INPE)
São José dos Campos, SP, Brazil - 12227-010
Email: {wanderson.costa, leila.fonseca, thales.korting}@inpe.br
†Embrapa Solos
Rio de Janeiro, RJ, Brazil - 22460-000
Email: margareth.simoes@embrapa.br
‡UERJ/FEN/DESC/PPGMA, Rio de Janeiro, RJ, Brazil
Email: geo.calvano@gmail.com
§Cirad, UMR Tetis, Montpellier, France

***Abstract*—Continuous observations from remote sensors provide high temporal and spatial resolution imagery, and better remote sensing image segmentation techniques are mandatory for efficient analysis. Among them, one of the most applied segmentation techniques is the region growing algorithm. Within this context, this paper describes a study case for a multitemporal segmentation that adapts the traditional region growing technique. Our method aims to detect homogeneous regions in space and time observing a sequence of optical remote sensing images. Tests were conducted by considering the Dynamic Time Warping distance as the homogeneity criterion to grow regions. A case study on high temporal resolution for sequences of Landsat-8 vegetation indices products provided satisfactory outputs.**

Keywords–Multitemporal Segmentation; Image Processing; Geoprocessing; Remote Sensing; Dynamic Time Warping.

I. Introduction

As satellite products have a repetitive data acquisition and its digital format is suitable for computer processing, remote sensing data have become the main source for application of change detection and observation of land use and land cover during the last decades [1]. Satellite image analysis plays a key role for detecting land use/cover changes in different biomes. The extensive amount of remote sensing data, combined with information from ecosystem models, offers a good opportunity for predicting and understanding the behaviour of terrestrial ecosystems [2].

If the satellite image analysis is performed using only per-pixel techniques, inherent information of the objects in the scene is discarded, such as shape, area and statistical parameters. In order to exploit this information, there are segmentation algorithms, which partition images in regions whose pixels present similar properties [3] [4]. Using a homogeneity criterion between the image pixels, the identified regions are treated as objects from which characteristics can be extracted to be used in the analysis.

Change detection based on time series is advantageous compared to the pure observation of image sequences, since the series takes into account information regarding temporal dynamics and changes in the landscape rather than just observing the differences between two or more images collected on different dates [2]. With the amount of multitemporal and multiresolution images growing exponentially, the number of image segmentation applications is recently increasing and, simultaneously, new challenges arise. Hence, there is a need to explore new segmentation concepts and techniques that make use of the temporal dimension [5] [6].

Many of the recent segmentation processes based on objects have paid attention to high image spatial resolutions whereas, so far, there are few studies adapted to multitemporal data [7]. In this paper, we describe a case study for a segmentation applied to time series of remote sensing images. The algorithm integrates regions in order to detect objects that are homogeneous in space and time. This approach aims to overcome the dlimitations of the snapshot model [8], that analyses each time step independently. The technique adapts the segmentation based on spatial region growing [9]. A case study was conducted using time series of Landsat-8 Operational Land Imager (OLI) scenes by applying multitemporal segmentation using the Dynamic Time Warping measure [10] as the homogeneity criterion.

With this context, this work can contribute to the segmentation of remote sensing data in geographic information systems from the construction of thematic maps as output of the segmentation process, since it is possible to generate a layer of information from the input data, representing homogeneous regions with similar properties over time.

The rest of the paper is organized as follows. In Section II, we present a brief description of remote sensing image segmentation and related works applied in change detection. In Section III, we discuss the use of satellite image time series. The Dynamic Type Warping is described in Section IV. The methodological procedures are depicted in Section V. In Section VI, we discuss the results obtained in this work. Finally, we describe the conclusion and future work in Section VII.

II. Remote Sensing Image Segmentation

Segmentation is a basic and critical task in image processing whereby the image is partitioned into regions, also called objects, whose pixels are similar considering one or more properties [8]. Overall, it is expected that the objects of interest are automatically extracted as a result of segmentation. Features can be extracted from these objects and used later for data analysis.

One of the most applied segmentation techniques in remote sensing is the region growing algorithm [9]. This is a simple iterative approach that groups pixels or sub-regions into larger regions depending on how similar they are, using some similarity criteria. The technique starts with a set of pixels called *seeds* and, from them, grows regions by adding neighbour pixels with similar properties.

The threshold definitions in region growing segmentation are a key step due to their direct influence on the accuracy of the output. The similarity threshold analyses if the pixel value difference or the average difference of a set of neighbouring pixels is smaller than a given threshold. The area threshold is another common parameter and it takes into account the minimum size of the regions that will be individualized by the algorithm. Setting these values enables the user to control the outcome in an interactive way, depending on the goal and study area. In general, the threshold is reached after several tests among possible combinations of the algorithm. The tests continue until the result of the segmentation is suitable for a particular purpose.

Several segmentation techniques applied in change detection are still derived from the traditional snapshot model [6], observing only the differences between discrete dates [11]–[13]. However, a thorough literature review revealed just a few studies that adapted methods based on objects for applications with multitemporal data [7].

Some object-based techniques aim at performing the segmentation generating one output for each time instance and then comparing the objects changes over time [13]–[17]. In other studies, the objects are defined in the first image, and then their differences are analysed in subsequent image [12] [18] [19].

Another approach has included the time as an additional factor within the segmentation, being used with the spatial and spectral image features [7]. However, many studies that applied this segmentation approach have used a limited number of multitemporal images [20]–[24] and they did not make use of time series of high temporal resolution images [6].

III. Satellite Image Time Series

Detection of changes based on time series is advantageous compared to the analysis of each image in a sequence independently, since the series take into account information regarding temporal dynamics and changes in the landscape rather than just observing the difference between two or more images collected on different dates [2]. However, a large amount of time series data has been generated over the past years, which forces the remote sensing community to rethink processing strategies for satellite time series analysis and visualization.

The time series of vegetation indices, for example, can be used to analyse seasonality for cover monitoring purposes. In the analysis and characterization of vegetation cover, for example, vegetation indices are used for seasonal and inter-annual monitoring of biophysical, phenological and structural vegetation parameters. Figure 1 illustrates the time series generation of a given vegetation index for a pixel $p(x, y)$. For each pixel, a time series can be observed, representing the variation of the vegetation index over time.

Vegetation indices represent improved measures of spatial, spectral and radiometric surface vegetation conditions. One of most used indices is the Normalized Difference Vegetation Index (NDVI), based on the reflectance of red and near-infrared wavelengths [25].

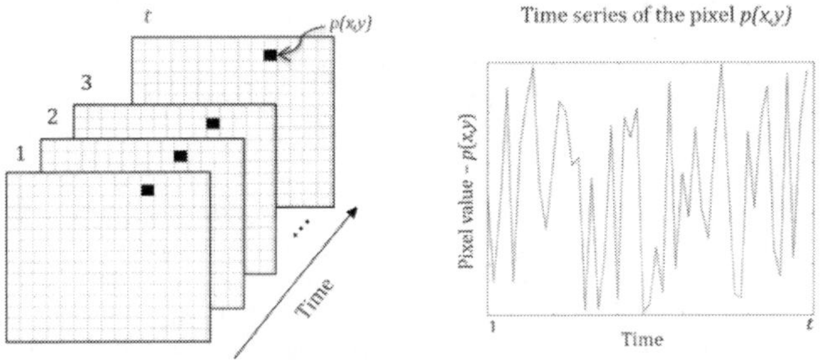

Figure 1. Example of a time series for the pixel $p(x, y)$.

IV. Dynamic Time Warping

Dynamic Time Warping (DTW) is one of the most used measures to quantify the similarity between two time series [26]. Originally designed to treat automatic speech recognition [10] [27], DTW measures the optimal global alignment between two time series and exploits temporal distortions between them.

The choice of a good similarity measure plays a key role since it defines the way to treat the temporality of data. The main change detection analysis in remote sensing images consists in comparing the data to estimate the similarity between them [28]. In many cases, the similarity is computed using a distance measure between two instances.

Among the known distances, DTW has the ability to realign two time series, so that each element of the first series is associated with at least one of the second series. With DTW, two time series out of phase can be aligned in a nonlinear form (Figure 2). Providing the cost of this alignment, DTW highlights similarities that the Euclidean distance is not able to capture, comparing shifted or distorted time series [28].

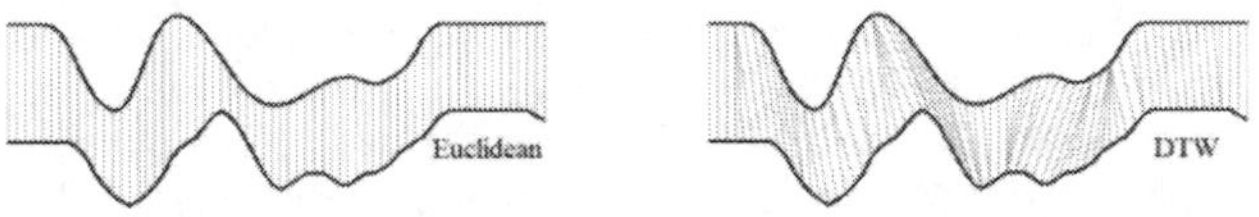

Figure 2. DTW nonlinear alignment allows a more intuitive distance to be calculated. Source: Adapted from [29].

Let A and B be two time series of length m and n, respectively, where $A = \langle a_1, a_2, \cdots, a_n \rangle$ and $B = \langle b_1, b_2, \cdots, b_m \rangle$. The first step for calculating the DTW measure between A and B is to build a matrix of size $n \times m$, where each matrix element (i, j) corresponds to a distance measured between a_i and b_i. This distance, $\delta(a_i, b_j)$ can be calculated using different metrics, such as the absolute difference $d(a_i, b_i) = |a_i - b_i|$ or the Euclidean distance.

The values of the matrix elements are calculated from left to right and from bottom to top. The algorithm adds the distance value δ of the elements in that position of each series. The elements receive the lowest value from the previous adjacent elements to the left, down and diagonal, as in (1).

$$D(a_i, b_j) = \delta(a_i, b_j) + \min \begin{cases} D(a_{i-1}, b_{j-1}), \\ D(a_i, b_{j-1}), \\ D(a_{i-1}, b_j) \end{cases} \quad (1)$$

Once the matrix is completely filled, the next step is to find the best path between the start and end values of the matrix that results in the optimal alignment value. For this, the search for the path starts from $D(a_n, b_m)$ (top right), always adding the lowest element in the neighborhood, until the first element at bottom left.

The DTW measure has been the subject of studies for geoprocessing and analysis of satellite images time series. Petitjean et al. [26] [28], for example, used DTW to compare time series affected by clouds. Maus et al. [30] presented a weighted version of DTW for land cover and land use classification.

V. Methodology

The proposed spatio-temporal segmentation by region growing is diagrammed in Figure 3. Our proposed method

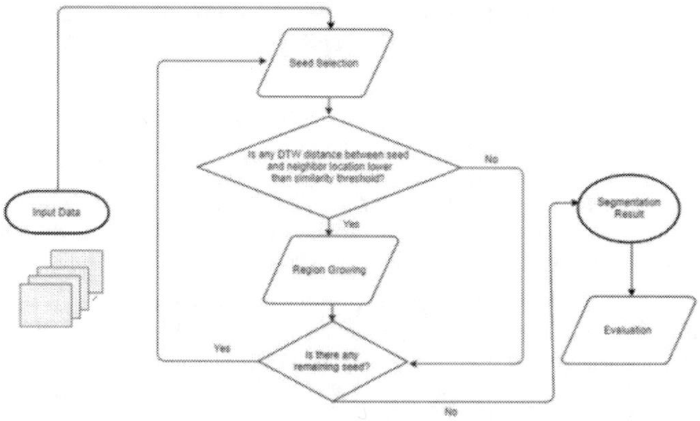

Figure 3. Flowchart of the proposed methodology.

adapts the traditional region growing technique in order to detect regions that present similar properties over time. The methodology uses the DTW distance as a part of the region growing process. The algorithm can be expressed by the following steps:

1) Select a sequence of images as input data.
2) Set similarity and area thresholds.
3) Determine the seed set.
4) Compute the DTW distance between the time series of the seeds and their neighbors. If the absolute difference between the DTW value of the time series of the seed and the time series of the neighbor is less than the similarity threshold, the neighbor is considered similar and it is added to the region.
5) Continue examining all the neighbors until no similar neighbor is found. Label the obtained segment as a complete region.
6) Observe the next unlabelled seed and repeat the process until all the pixels are labelled in a region.
7) For each segment whose size is less than the area threshold value, merge the segment with the neighbouring segment with the largest common boundary.

A case study was conducted by considering the DTW measure as homogeneity criterion in the algorithm. For each image, each pixel corresponds to a NDVI value, so that the values of this ordered sequence of images result in a time series. These collected time series are used in DTW calculation between the seed and its neighbouring pixels. The user determines the length and periodicity of the time series from the input data. The segmentation algorithm was written using R language.

For the acceptance or rejection of a given threshold in a remote sensing image segmentation result, the resulting segments were compared with a remote sensing image at the same location of the scene in the end of the time series. The seed set, processing order and location of the seeds were set randomly by the algorithm. The similarity threshold was reached using the same seed set and processing order of the seeds in all tests.

VI. Results and Discussion

Our technique was used to evaluate a central-western area in Brazil. The study area encompasses a region in the state of Mato Grosso (MT), located in Nova Cannã do Norte City, illustrated in Figure 4. A sequence of 27 images obtained from NDVI Landsat-8 OLI between April 10, 2016 and May 31, 2017 were used, with temporal resolution of 16 days. All images have a dimension of 155 $\times$ 132 pixels, with spatial resolution of 30 m.

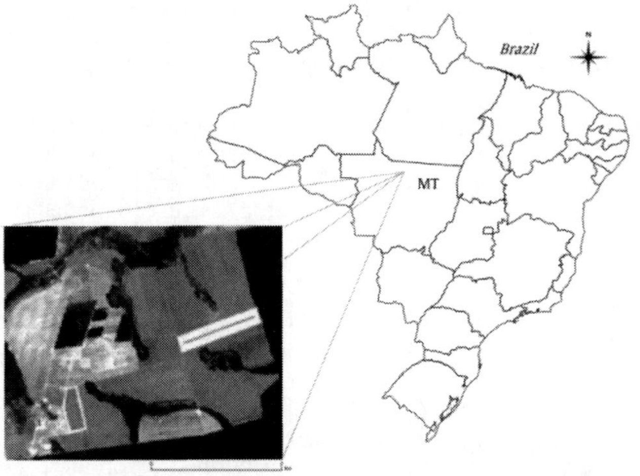

Figure 4. Study area. Landsat-8 (R4G3B2) imagery of the study area.

The study was conducted in the Gamada Farm, which is supervised by the Brazilian Agricultural Research Corporation (EMBRAPA). Wet and dry seasons are well defined in the region. The dry season occurs from May to August, whereas about 95% of the annual rainfall is concentrated between September and April. During the analysed year, the farm contained areas of native forest and pasture, in addition to regions with several types of crops, such as sugarcane, maize, rice and soybean. This area was chosen because it presented regions with homogeneous properties in the described period, according to information provided by EMBRAPA.

After several tests, the similarity and area thresholds were chosen so that the agricultural, pasture and native forest areas could be separated from the other neighboring targets. The expected segmentation output includes segmented areas with similar geo-objects presenting homogeneity over time. The similarity threshold was defined empirically, based on visual inspection of the results. For the segmentation result presented in Figure 5, the similarity threshold was set to 0.061. The processing time using this threshold value was 143 seconds. The area threshold was used to eliminate sliver polygons that the algorithm generates in boundary areas. This is due to the low spatial resolution of the images that influences the pixel values in edge areas. In addition, we set this threshold to 60,000 m^2 to disregard small regions derived from noise caused by the high presence of cloud cover in the image sequence.

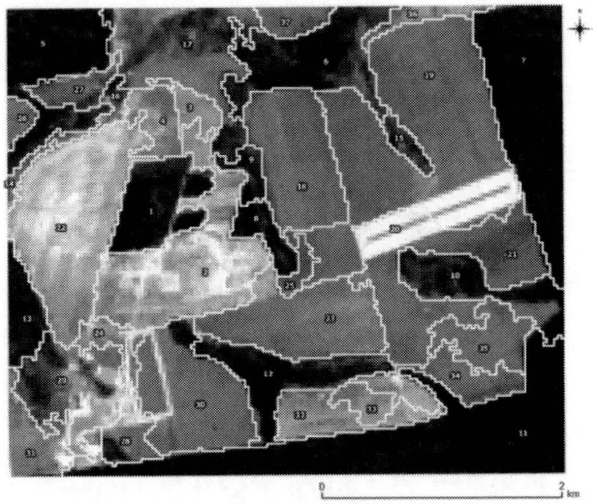

Figure 5. Segmentation output (yellow outlines) for the study area. The segments are superimposed on a Landsat-8 image (R4G3B2).

Evaluating the result of an image segmentation is difficult because, currently, no standard assessment techniques exist [31]. For this test, we compared the segmentation result to a Landsat-8 image, evaluating the output based on photo-interpretation of the satellite image. Visually, the proposed method was able to create similar-shaped segments, representing similar-sized groups of geo-objects, such as native forests, croplands and pasture areas.

The farm contains a region of Integrated Crop-Livestock-Forestry (ICLF) system. At the time of the study, Gamada Farm had crop rotation consisted of Brachiaria pasture grass (*Urochloa Brizantha*) interchangeable with soybean, rice+soybean, maize+soybean, Brachiaria+soybean, pasture, sugarcane and native forest. The region containing the ICLF system was detected by our technique, corresponding to the segment labelled 1 in Figure 5.

Additionally, our algorithm was able to create segments that presented regions with similar seasonal dynamics over the analysed period, distinguishing pastures regions (segments 2-4), native forest areas (5-17) and croplands (18-37). It is important to notice that some large agriculture areas were divided into sub-regions. Some of them were regions with different harvest periods and the method performed this separation between the areas during the analysed year.

However, since the proposed method is based on region growing technique, the algorithm contains some disadvantages. Different seed sets, for example, cause different results in segmentation. In addition, there is the dependence of processing order of the seeds, which is particularly noticeable when the regions are small or have some similar properties. In addition, DTW calculation demands a high computational cost.

The case study was encouraging and demonstrates the potential of the proposed multitemporal segmentation in dealing with time series generated by images of optical remote sensing images. However, one factor that reduces the quality of the segments is the noise in the time series derived from cloud cover.

VII. Conclusion

The proposed multitemporal segmentation brings a new way of interpreting data by means of analysing contiguous regions in time. In order to illustrate the potential of the method, we presented a study case on NDVI time series derived from Landsat-8 OLI products. We compared the segments generated by the proposed algorithm based on photo-interpretation, observing similarities between the segmentation results and the superimposed image.

Further analysis is needed to apply this approach in regions with higher temporal resolutions and to test different indices and spatial resolutions of Landsat-like image time series. However, the DTW computation and the use of the temporal dimension increases the complexity of processing compared with the segmentation of satellite images which considers only a single date.

Acknowledgment

The authors would like to acknowledge the financial support of CAPES, FAPESP e-sensing program (grant 2014/08398-6), FUNCATE MSA BNDES 14.2.0929.1, Project H2020-MSCA-RiSE-2015 Odyssea (EU 691053) and CAPES/COFECUB Programme for the GeoABC Project (n. 845/15) as well as information support of Embrapa Agrossilvipastoril and Embrapa LabEx Europe.

References

[1] E. F. Lambin and M. Linderman, "Time series of remote sensing data for land change science," Geoscience and Remote Sensing, IEEE Transactions on, vol. 44, no. 7, 2006, pp. 1926–1928.

[2] S. Boriah, "Time series change detection: algorithms for land cover change." Ph.D. dissertation, University of Minnesota, 160 p., 2010.

[3] T. Blaschke, "Object based image analysis for remote sensing," ISPRS Journ. of Photog. and Remote Sens., vol. 65, no. 1, 2010, pp. 2–16.

[4] L. S. Bins, L. M. G. Fonseca, G. J. Erthal, and F. M. Ii, "Satellite imagery segmentation: a region growing approach," Simpósio Brasileiro de Sensoriamento Remoto, vol. 8, no. 1996, 1996, pp. 677–680.

[5] J. Schiewe, "Segmentation of high-resolution remotely sensed data-concepts, applications and problems," International Archives of Photogrammetry Remote Sensing and Spatial Information Sciences, vol. 34, no. 4, 2002, pp. 380–385.

[6] V. Dey, Y. Zhang, and M. Zhong, "A review on image segmentation techniques with remote sensing perspective," ISPRS, vol. XXXVIII, July 2010, pp. 31–42.

[7] J. A. Thompson and B. G. Lees, "Applying object-based segmentation in the temporal domain to characterise snow seasonality," ISPRS, vol. 97, 2014, pp. 98–110.

[8] R. M. Haralick and L. G. Shapiro, "Image segmentation techniques," in Tec. Symp. East. Arlington, VA: Int. Soc. Opt. Photon., 1985, pp. 2–9.

[9] R. Adams and L. Bischof, "Seeded region growing," IEEE Trans. Patt. Anal. Mach. Intell., vol. 16, no. 6, 1994, pp. 641–647.

[10] H. Sakoe and S. Chiba, "A dynamic programming approach to continuous speech recognition," in Proc. 7th Int. Cong. on Acoust., vol. 3. Budapest: Akademiai Kiado, 1971, pp. 65–69.

[11] T. De Chant and M. Kelly, "Individual object change detection for monitoring the impact of a forest pathogen on a hardwood forest," Photogrammetric Engineering & Remote Sensing, vol. 75, no. 8, 2009, pp. 1005–1013.

[12] D. Duro, S. Franklin, and M. Dubé, "Hybrid object-based change detection and hierarchical image segmentation for thematic map updating," Photog. Eng. & Remote Sens., vol. 79, no. 3, 2013, pp. 259–268.

[13] C. Gómez, J. C. White, and M. A. Wulder, "Characterizing the state and processes of change in a dynamic forest environment using hierarchical spatio-temporal segmentation," Remote Sens. of Env., vol. 115, no. 7, 2011, pp. 1665–1679.

[14] J. Im, J. Jensen, and J. Tullis, "Object-based change detection using correlation image analysis and image segmentation," Int. Journ. of Remote Sens., vol. 29, no. 2, 2008, pp. 399–423.

[15] I. Niemeyer, P. Marpu, and S. Nussbaum, "Change detection using object features," in Object-Based Image Analysis, ser. Lecture Notes in Geoinformation and Cartography, T. Blaschke, S. Lang, and G. Hay, Eds. Springer Berlin Heidelberg, 2008, pp. 185–201.

[16] P. Xiao, M. Yuan, X. Zhang, X. Feng, and Y. Guo, "Cosegmentation for object-based building change detection from high-resolution remotely sensed images," IEEE Trans. Geosci. and Remote Sens., vol. 55, no. 3, 2017, pp. 1587–1603.

[17] X. Zhang, P. Xiao, X. Feng, and M. Yuan, "Separate segmentation of multi-temporal high-resolution remote sensing images for object-based change detection in urban area," Remote Sens. of Env., vol. 201, 2017, pp. 243–255.

[18] T. Blaschke, "Towards a framework for change detection based on image objects," Göt. Geo. Abhand., vol. 113, 2005, pp. 1–9.

[19] A. D. Pape and S. E. Franklin, "MODIS-based change detection for Grizzly Bear habitat mapping in Alberta," Photog. Eng. & Remote Sens., vol. 74, no. 8, 2008, pp. 973–985.

[20] S. Bontemps, P. Bogaert, N. Titeux, and P. Defourny, "An object-based change detection method accounting for temporal dependences in time series with medium to coarse spatial resolution," Remote Sens. of Env., vol. 112, no. 6, 2008, pp. 3181–3191.

[21] B. Desclée, P. Bogaert, and P. Defourny, "Forest change detection by statistical object-based method," Remote Sensing of Environment, vol. 102, no. 1, 2006, pp. 1–11.

[22] L. Drăguţ, D. Tiede, and S. R. Levick, "ESP: a tool to estimate scale parameter for multiresolution image segmentation of remotely sensed data," International Journal of Geographical Information Science, vol. 24, no. 6, 2010, pp. 859–871.

[23] L. Drăguţ, O. Csillik, C. Eisank, and D. Tiede, "Automated parameterisation for multi-scale image segmentation on multiple layers," ISPRS, vol. 88, 2014, pp. 119–127.

[24] Z. Zhou, J. Huang, J. Wang, K. Zhang, Z. Kuang, S. Zhong, and X. Song, "Object-oriented classification of sugarcane using time-series middle-resolution remote sensing data based on adaboost," PloS one, vol. 10, no. 11, 2015, p. e0142069.

[25] C. J. Tucker, "Red and photographic infrared linear combinations for monitoring vegetation," Remote Sens. of Env., vol. 8, no. 2, 1979, pp. 127–150.

[26] F. Petitjean, J. Inglada, and P. Gançarski, "Satellite image time series analysis under time warping," IEEE Trans. Geosc. and Remote Sens., vol. 50, no. 8, 2012, pp. 3081–3095.

[27] H. Sakoe and S. Chiba, "Dynamic programming algorithm optimization for spoken word recognition," in IEEE Trans. Acoust. Speech and Signal Proc., vol. 26, no. 1. New York, NY: IEEE, 1978, pp. 43–49.

[28] F. Petitjean, J. Inglada, and P. Gançarski, "Clustering of satellite image time series under time warping," in Int. Workshop on the Anal. of Multi-temp. Remote Sens. Trento, Italy: IEEE, 2011, pp. 69–72.

[29] S. Chu, E. Keogh, D. Hart, and M. Pazzani, "Iterative deepening dynamic time warping for time series," in Proceedings of the 2002 SIAM International Conference on Data Mining. Philadelphia, PA: Society for Industrial and Applied Mathematics, 2002, pp. 195–212.

[30] V. M. et al., "A time-weighted dynamic time warping method for land-use and land-cover mapping," IEEE Journ. Sel. Top. in App. Earth Observ. and Remote Sens., vol. 9, no. 8, 2016, pp. 3729–3739.

[31] M. V. D. Eeckhaut, N. Kerle, J. Poesen, and J. Hervs, "Object-oriented identification of forested landslides with derivatives of single pulse lidar data," Geomorphology, vol. 173174, 2012, pp. 30–42.

An Approach for Assessing Array DBMSs for Geospatial Raster Data

Janne Kovanen*, Ville Mäkinen† and Tapani Sarjakoski‡
Finnish Geospatial Research Institute,
National Land Survey of Finland
Email: *janne.kovanen@iki.fi, †ville.p.makinen@nls.fi, ‡tapani.sarjakoski@nls.fi

Abstract—**The increasing quantity and use of high-resolution raster data has put its management in the forefront of development. In this paper, we describe an approach that can be used to assess the capabilities of Array Database Management Systems (DBMSs) regarding the management and processing of raster data. The paper presents a framework that can be used to compare the functionalities of Array DBMSs and benchmark them. The main feature of the framework is assessing functionality using both targeted test cases and benchmarking. This assessment is followed by leveraging the gained experiences to assess non-functionality using characteristics from existing quality models. The framework can be extended by further DBMSs, benchmarks and additional hardware resources. The assessment was first implemented for the community editions of SciDB and rasdaman. The study presents some key initial observations regarding the particular Array DBMSs.**

Keywords–array DBMS; software assessment; benchmarking; SciDB; rasdaman.

I. INTRODUCTION

Array Database Management Systems (DBMSs) have been proposed as a solution for data that naturally – or with a meagre conversion – fits on a regular multi-dimensional grid. Their significance has especially been noticed in the era of the Big Data phenomenon. Climate data, high-resolution rasters and sensor time series represent data that may suit an array data model. For example, the pixels of a raster can be mapped to cells in the array, and the four axes of climate data can correspond to a geographic location, altitude and time.

Array-oriented management solutions have been available for several decades; for instance, the development of Hierarchical Data Format (HDF) [1] and NetCDF [2] data formats and libraries started in the late 1980s. Their contemporary implementations, however, only conceptually resemble their earliest versions.

In addition to the aforementioned machine-independent data formats, SciDB [3], rasdaman [4], Ophidia [5] and TileDB [6] represent modern, domain-independent solutions. Domain-specificity may be gained by using associated components (e.g., Petascope [7] for rasdaman or H5IM for HDF5), third-party interface layers (e.g., scidb4geo [8] for SciDB) or with application-specific solutions. An alternative to domain independence is to use ready-made raster-centric solutions, like PostGIS's raster type [9] or the GeoRaster feature of Oracle Spatial and Graph [10].

A. *Previous work*

The diversity of prospective systems makes analysing and comparing them a challenging task for both developers and management. To help with reasoning, comparison studies have been published. Merticariu, Misev and Baumann [11] compared the sequential performance of rasdaman, SciDB and SciQL [12] using randomly generated artificial dense eight-bit data. They came to the conclusion that, in general, their rasdaman implementation outperformed the others by one to two orders of magnitude if really small queries or data ingestions were not taken into account. Liu et al. [13] compared the performance of the file-based NetCDF-4 and SciDB regarding three-dimensional spatio-temporal rainfall data. Their study found the uncompressed NetCDF-4 to be more efficient than SciDB.

The published comparisons assess the different Array DBMSs concerning relevant functions; however, they primarily look at the systems from the performance point of view using benchmarking. The most extensive work on database benchmarking has been performed by the non-profit TPC [14]. Its benchmarks evaluate performance with use cases from different areas of business – like stock brokerage – and execution scenarios, which vary in parallelism and complexity. None of the TPC benchmarks are, however, relevant for array DBMS. The Standard Science DBMS Benchmark (SS-DB), instead, is a benchmark developed by Cudre-Mauroux et al. [15], which was designed with astronomy in mind but may be used as a generic benchmark for scientific 1D–3D array data. Cudre-Mauroux et al. used it to compare the performance of MySQL and SciDB, the outcome of which was that overall SciDB performed two orders of magnitude faster.

While the execution time is important, several other quality characteristics also affect whether an Array DBMS meets the needs of stakeholders. A plethora of models for software quality have been published (e.g [16]–[18]). A comparison of models is presented by Miguel [19]. The models have different purposes by which they can be classified as definition, assessment or prediction models of quality [20]. The quality of software can even be validated as being up to standards: the International Organization of Standardization (ISO) has a full series (ISO/IEC 25000) of standards for software quality and its evaluation. For instance, the standard ISO/IEC 25010:2011 [21] defines a dual model that splits quality into in-use quality and internal/external product quality. Figure 1 outlines the two-level characteristics included in the latter.

This paper presents an approach to assess array DBMS. In Section II, we propose a framework to assess them that includes the criteria used for evaluation and benchmarking. Next, in Section III, we describe how the framework was used to evaluate two different Array DBMSs, the used hardware and some of the initial key findings. Finally, in Section IV, we discuss some issues and conclude the paper.

II. THE ASSESSMENT METHOD

In an optimal situation, a rigorous assessment can be performed based on a set of application-specific user requirements that represent the needs of stakeholders. However, in the case of Array DBMSs, the number of potential stakeholders is so high that it is impossible to determine all the requirements. Moreover, it is not enough to assess their functionality based

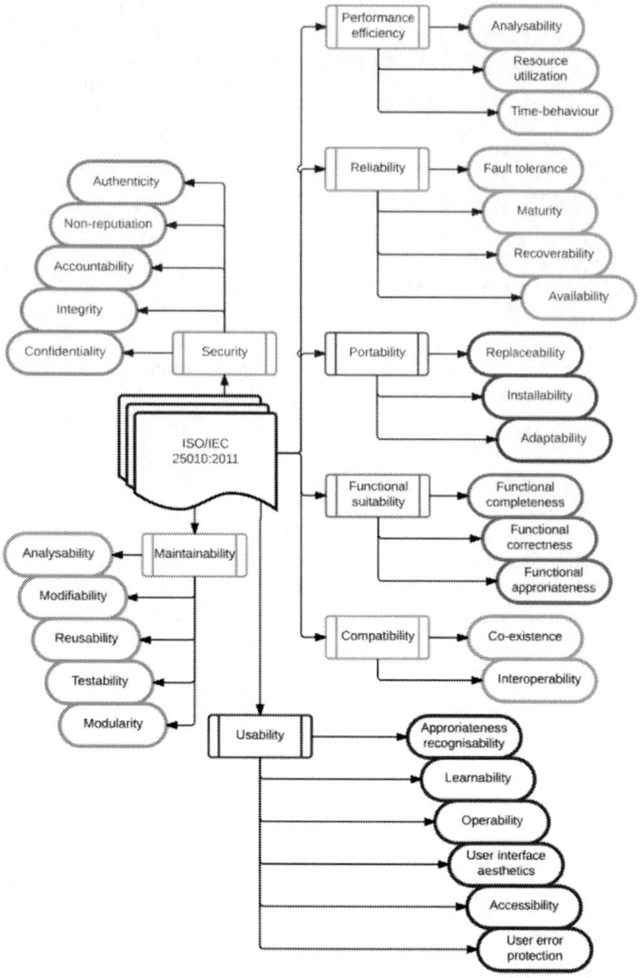

Figure 1. The characteristics and sub-characteristics of the ISO/IEC 25010:2011 product quality model.

on the documentation alone because of the rapid evolution that DBMSs are undergoing. For this reason, instead of using existing quality models as such, we divided the assessment into three parts: two parts concerning functionality and one part non-functionality.

Functionality is first reviewed against the documentation based on a set of criteria. Next, the found functionality is validated using an open web client. The client can be run from anywhere to verify that the statements regarding functionality are valid. The client is implemented using Jupyter Notebook [22], which is an open-source web application integrating live code, visualisations and accompanying text that uses Markdown language. The validation tests are written in Python and made small enough that they can be performed within a reasonable time limit. The test data is created on the fly by the web client or by using an array generator query. Hence, different instances of the same Array DBMS can be validated simply by changing the access parameters, like IP address, username and password.

Secondly, functionality is benchmarked on the server side. In this way, we can run long-lasting queries without worrying about network connection problems, and we do not need to speculate on how extensively the network transfers affect the timing. Nevertheless, benchmarking is affected by the chosen DBMS parameters and internal communication between nodes. As many users will not go through the burden of finding the optimal parameter combination, the benchmarking is run with the default settings. Bare bones results can be complemented by those gained from better performing configurations or external third-party software as long as they can be clearly distinguished and the default results are also included in the comparison.

The last part – evaluating non-functionality – is initiated after both parts concerned with functionality have been executed. This is to gain an initial understanding of the relevant quality characteristics (like reliability, maintainability and usability) through real use.

A. *The criteria for comparison*

Software, including Array DBMSs, can be assessed qualitatively using the experts of a particular field. Alternatively, the assessment may follow a predefined criteria list that scores several aspects of the software in a quantitative manner. The benefit of criteria is that they may be used by different people against diverse software. Criteria may be domain-specific or look at the software from a more general point of view. For example, the criteria of the Software Sustainability Institute [23] specialise in code quality, usability and overall sustainability.

Domain-specific criteria are based on the needs or concerns of a particular problem domain's potential stakeholders. Good criteria are also objective and unbiased; for example, no single software should be used as a reference. In the case of Array DBMSs, domain-specific requirements have been listed by Stonebraker et al. [24] and Xie [25]. The user concerns brought up by Stonebraker et al. are especially related to those raised by scientists and scientific data. Xie, on the other hand, looks at the requirements of a raster-specific DBMSs, which also apply in large part to generic array databases. Some of them are only relevant for spatial data though, like raster algebra and analytics, re-projection and cartographic modelling. As the most important characteristics, Xie picks out scalability and performance, and suggests that a database preferably has in-built analytics capabilities in order to achieve the required performance.

We split the criteria into functional and non-functional parts. The non-functional criteria first assess general software properties, like dependencies, hardware requirements, licensing, operating system support, source code access, means of installation, documentation, logging, memory-use, and error-handling. Next, other non-functional qualities are evaluated using existing quality models as a guideline.

The functional criteria are decomposed into 1) general DBMS capabilities, 2) a data model and schemas, and 3) a processing model. We also include geospatial capabilities as a domain-specific subgroup of the criteria. The general DBMS criteria assess the functionality that may be available with any type of data, like data compression, interfaces, support for accelerators and user-defined functions. The data model and schemas concentrate on array-specific capabilities, like restrictions of the data type, the density of data, the regularity of data bounds, uncertainty and multiple representation. The processing model looks at what operations the arrays can be used for – like aggregation, algebraic, bitwise, logical, moving window and string operations – but also transcendental functions, subsetting and joining. The criteria are then converted into questions to be answered in a consistent way; for example, the following questions are made regarding the array-specific dimensionality:

- What is the maximum number of dimensions?
- Is it possible to name the dimensions? Is it mandatory to name the dimensions? Can a dimension be renamed?
- Can a dimension be added or removed?
- Can the data be scaled by an integer for a dimension; that is, can a cell be duplicated a number of times before moving to the next cell?
- Can the bounds (lower/upper) of a dimension be changed after being defined?
- Can a dimension be used for time? Are time zones supported? Can time be treated as a continuous dimension or does it need to be treated as a discrete quantity; for example, if a time series is initially stored at one-second resolution, can data be added, that is defined, with millisecond accuracy in between old values?

B. Benchmarking

For benchmarking, we used two datasets, both licensed under CC BY 4.0 and having coordinates in the ETRS-TM35FIN projected coordinate reference system. KM10 [26] data represents the digital elevation model (DEM) of Finland in 10-metre resolution. It is composed of 1,509 GeoTiff files with a combined size of 9.7 GB. The data is two-dimensional with elevations being 16-bit floating point numbers, and it contains null values, which are coded -9,999. The benchmarking includes ingestion, export, cropping, operations (average, minimum), the moving average and simultaneous queries. The operations are performed on different sized square areas up to $60{,}000 \times 60{,}000$ cells. The moving average query is performed with different window sizes, ranging from 3×3 to 51×51 cells. The performance is measured by computing average values for cells within different windows. For each window size, several areas of different sizes, starting from 100×100 cells, are used. Regarding ingestion, it is performed in the format preferred by the DBMS; the time to translate to the format is not included in the timing.

The second dataset is CORINE [27]–[29], which represents the land cover classification of Finland for three different years (2000, 2006 and 2012). It is used for three-dimensional benchmarking. The resolutions of the original data are 25 and 20 metres, but in the benchmarking these are converted to a uniform five metres, allowing cell-by-cell comparisons to be made. The benchmarks include ingestion, counting the number of filtered cells and counting changes between two years. Filtering is done by area, timestamp and attribute value.

III. Evaluation Case

We performed an assessment of the rasdaman community (version 9.5.0) and SciDB Community Edition (version 16.9). For rasdaman, we installed Petascope, the Semantic Coordinate Reference System Resolver (SECORE) [30] and their dependencies like Apache Tomcat [31] and PostgreSQL [32]. As the storage backend for rasdaman, we selected SQLite [33]. For SciDB, to store its metadata, we installed PostgreSQL.

A. Software and hardware used in validation

Concerning hardware, the evaluation was performed using an Infrastructure as a Service (IaaS) [34], where each node was composed of six virtual CPUs (2 GHz; 4096 KB cache from Intel Xeon E312xx (Sandy Bridge)) and 15.6 GB of RAM. The CPUs are over-committed and thus require the benchmarking to be run several times in order to give a good estimate. The network bandwidth between servers was validated to be 8 Gb/s with iPerf [35]. The servers have an 80GB root disk that is stored on a central storage system. Additional disks were added as required. The operating system was decided to be the latest version of Ubuntu, which was supported by the DBMS; version 16.04 was used with rasdaman and version 14.04 with SciDB.

Logging was set to warning level as the more detailed levels affected the running time. In the case of multiple rasdaman nodes (peers), each node was given its own replicated data source. The option of using a centralised data storage was not tested. Neither did the tests consider the option of splitting the data into separate arrays and distributing those to different nodes.

B. Functional comparison

We performed the functional comparison according to the presented criteria. As the information source, we used publicly accessible documentation. We also tried to use scientific literature, but it turned out to be too imprecise or it referred to planned functionality.

As we expected, the fast evolution of DBMSs seems to make it hard to keep the documentation up to date. It also turned out that developing both a commercial and a community version side by side is a really challenging task. For example, in SciDB, some functionality was marketed as being available in the community edition but actually was not. Meanwhile, some functionality of the enterprise edition was found in the community edition. Most troubling, however, was realising that the disclaimers of some code in the community edition required an enterprise license. This applied, for example, to the support of complex numbers, which is provided as a user-defined type.

Next, we created a validation client for each DBMS with Jupyter Notebook. In the clients, we used application-specific declarative languages, and the queries were passed to the DBMSs from their web interfaces. To access rasdaman, we used its web service that forwards requests in rasdaman query language (rasql). In the case of SciDB, we used shim [36]. It allows the execution of arrays managing queries using SciDB's Array Functional Language (AFL), which has a SQL-like syntax. However, we could not use operations defined in SciDB's Array Query Language (AQL), because it is not supported by shim.

Validating every functionality found in the documentation would have required us to implement a complete unit testing framework for both DBMSs. Hence, we chose to direct the testing towards the 1) basic functionality, 2) the most demanding functionality and 3) the most recent functionality. This approach paid off regarding finding problems. In particular, the late addition of null values in rasdaman turned out to be problematic. At worst, their use in data types corrupted the whole database. Without the validation, the problems of the functionality would not have been found. Moreover, isolating problem sources gave significant input for the non-functional assessment.

C. Performance evaluation

The performance evaluation was executed using bash scripting on the server side. For each DBMS, a single server instance was run. If the Array DBMS supported multiple nodes, then distributed instances were also tested; hence, we had three different configurations: sequentially on a node, parallel on a node and parallel on four nodes. We did not assess additional software, whether from the same author as the DBMS or a third-party, but acknowledged them and their potential in the functional comparison.

1) The KM10 benchmark: The KM10 data was stored in two dimensions (*E*, *N*) with an attribute containing the elevation as a floating point value. The data was stored without overlap. On SciDB, the chunk size was selected to be 2,400 × 1,200 cells and the history of array modifications was removed during ingestion.

On both DBMSs, the data was ingested from CSV files. For rasdaman, the files only contained elevation values, not coordinates. For SciDB, the files contained coordinates and elevations for the cells for which data existed. The uncompressed data sizes were 76.8 and 84.5 GB for rasdaman and SciDB respectively. Figure 2 represents the ingestion speed. For rasdaman, it includes the time (3,039 s) required to set the initial null values into blocks sized 10,000 × 10,000 cells. This had to be performed because otherwise the DBMS has zeros as null values, which is unacceptable in the case of a DEM.

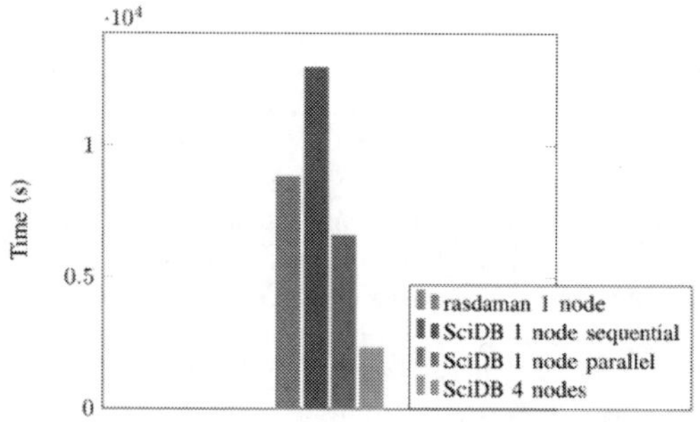

Figure 2. The ingestion time of the KM10 digital elevation model.

The data was exported from rasdaman using the CSV format, but in the case of SciDB we had to use its CSV+ format because the data contained empty cells. Initially, the servers had no swap memory, but it was added to enable testing rasdaman operations, because they failed when the RAM ran out. For example, rasdaman failed the 30,000 × 30,000 cell crop test without swap; still, not even an unlimited swap helped it in the execution of the 60,000 × 60,000 sized query. Figure 3 illustrates the time required for export from KM10.

In the moving window calculations, for each window size, the execution times with different analysis areas were scaled to comparable units and averaged out. The results are shown in Figure 4. The execution times with rasdaman showed little variation with respect to the size of the analysis area. On the other hand, the largest area analysed with rasdaman was 5,000 × 5,000 cells, whereas with SciDB 10,000 × 10,000 and 28,000 × 28,000 sized areas were analysed with single node and cluster installations respectively, with window sizes of up to 21 × 21 cells.

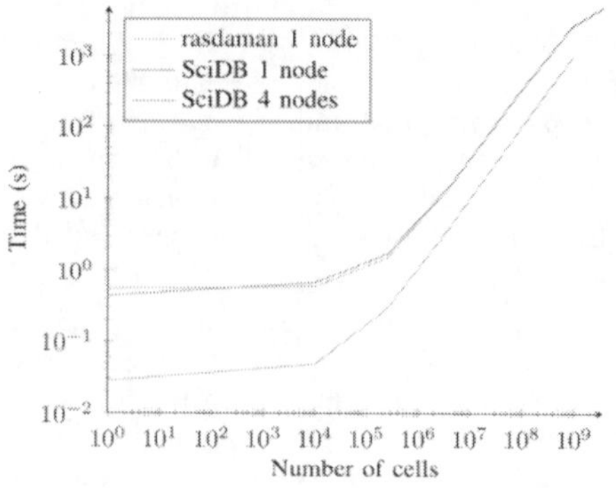

Figure 3. The time required for export from the KM10 digital elevation model.

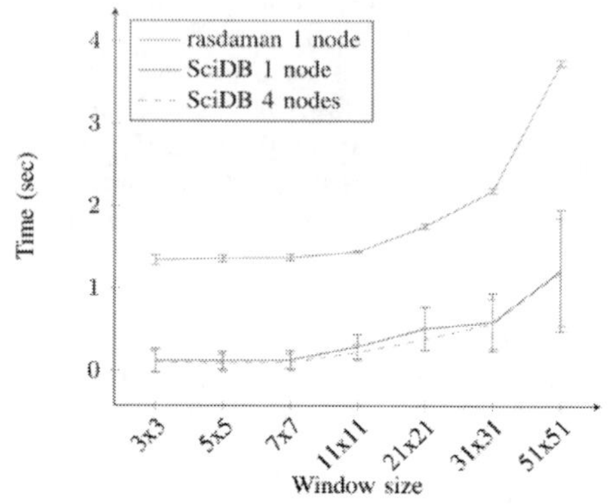

Figure 4. The time required for computing the moving window average for 10,000 cells with the KM10 digital elevation model.

2) The CORINE benchmark: On SciDB, the CORINE data was stored in three dimensions (*E*, *N*, *year*) and the land cover code was stored as a 16-bit unsigned integer. The chunk size was selected to be 2,000 × 2,000 × 1 cells. The data was stored without overlap. The history of array data was not stored.

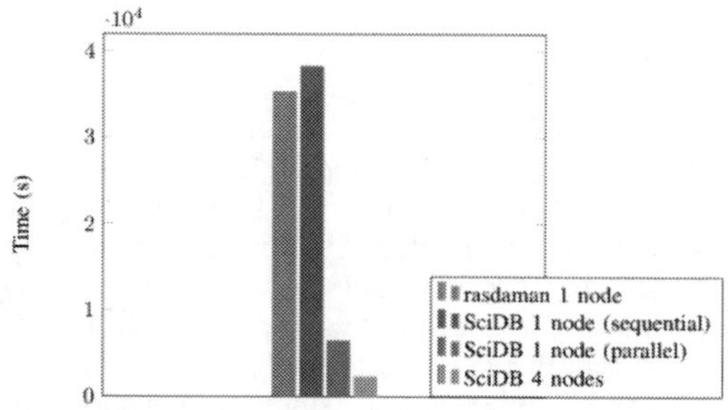

Figure 5. The ingestion time of the CORINE data.

The data ingestion of CORINE followed the same pattern as with KM10 (Figure 5). Between the DBMSs, the gap of sequential input got smaller than with the KM10. Similarly, the parallel and multi-node versions of SciDB performed better. A reason for this may be that in rasdaman the data was imported without using the scale function, because the source argument of the function must fit into the server's main memory, and according to the documentation, only nearest neighbour interpolation is supported for scaling. In SciDB, we used the xgrid function for scaling.

In both tests related to counting, the DBMSs behaved similarly: rasdaman handled smaller queries better, whereas SciDB performed faster with larger areas. The main difference that could be found was in the use of multiple processors and nodes. For example, SciDB was almost seven times faster regarding the largest area on one node regarding the query that counted the number of cells filtered by area, timestamp and attribute value (Figure 6). This correlates with the number of processors; likewise, with four nodes, SciDB became over three times faster than on one node.

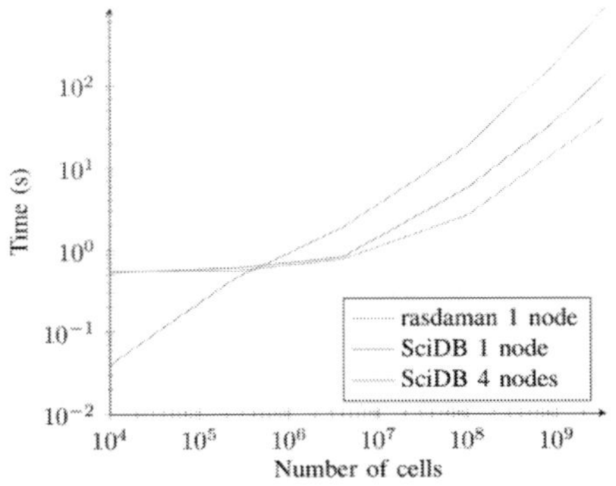

Figure 6. Counting the number of cells filtered by area, timestamp and attribute value from the CORINE data.

The difference between the DBMSs became larger when the complexity of the task grew. For example, SciDB was over 50 times faster in computing the changed cells between two timestamps from the CORINE data (Figure 7) regarding the largest query that rasdaman could manage.

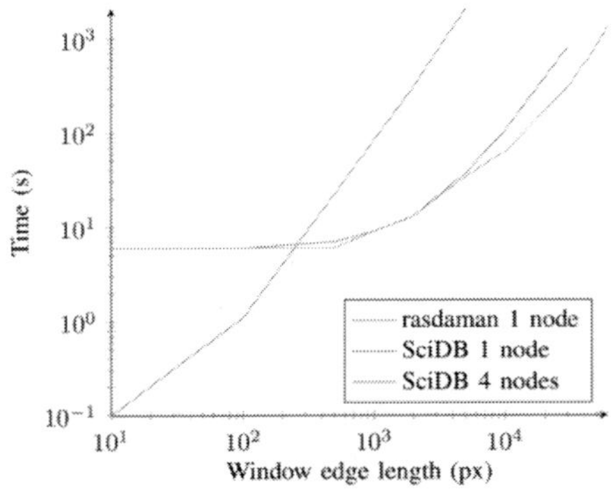

Figure 7. Counting the changed cells between two timestamps from the CORINE data.

IV. Conclusions, Discussion, and Future Work

In this paper, we addressed the assessment of Array DBMSs. We proposed performing the assessment in two consecutive steps: functional and non-functional steps. We also proposed executing the assessment of functionality by validating it against its documentation in an efficient manner, which especially targets error-prone areas but also evaluates the basic functionality. The used approach allows others to re-evaluate the assessed systems and to expand it to other Array DBMSs.

We also performed an initial trial of the approach on two Array DBMSs, which showed that the DBMSs have achieved a good level of functionality and performance. However, they struggle keeping up their documentation regarding both the languages and capabilities of their model. Inconsistency between the documentation and the behaviour reduce the usability and creditability of the systems.

The DBMSs are evolving at such fast pace that our approach will face the same challenge as the SS-DB benchmark: it has not been updated to work with the latest DBMS versions. A potential group of actors to keep the validation up to date are the authors of the DBMSs themselves. However, that creates a dilemma – will they be able to make an independent evaluation that disregards their agenda? We doubt this, mainly because the developers are already putting in effort to create unit tests and moving towards continuous integration which should reveal the problems that they have thought of.

If the authors of the Array DBMSs do not update the benchmarks and the validation scripts after making changes to the query languages or interfaces, our approach may require a TPC-kind of actor with sufficient resources to take ownership of the assessment. One candidate for this role is the Research Data Alliance (RDA) because Array DBMSs are well suited for research-focused data. However, the RDA (or any other party taking responsibility) will need a user pool to define the requirements to be evaluated and possibly even to develop test cases that the DBMSs can aim at passing. The creation of the test cases and the performance evaluation would be even simpler if the languages and interfaces used by the DBMSs become harmonised at some point.

Acknowledgement

The paper is based on the research carried out in the collaboration project "Evaluation and demonstration of Array DBMSs using national geospatial data", part of the EU-funded RDA EU3 project (grant agreement number 653194). The IaaS used in the work was funded by the Academy of Finland through "Finnish Grid and Cloud Infrastructure" (urn:nbn:fi:research-infras-2016072533; grant number 283818).

References

[1] The HDF Group, "HDF group history," https://support.hdfgroup.org/about/history.html, [accessed: 2018-01-23].

[2] Unidata, "NetCDF," http://www.unidata.ucar.edu/software/netcdf/, Boulder, CO: UCAR/Unidata Program Center, [accessed: 2018-01-23].

[3] Paradigm4 Inc., "SciDB," http://www.paradigm4.com, [accessed: 2018-01-23].

[4] rasdaman GmbH, "rasdaman," http://www.rasdaman.org, [accessed: 2018-01-23].

[5] CMCC Foundation, "Ophidia," http://ophidia.cmcc.it, [accessed: 2018-01-23].

[6] TileDB Inc., "TileDB," http://tiledb.io, [accessed: 2018-01-23].

[7] A. Aiordăchioaie and P. Baumann, "PetaScope: An open-source implementation of the OGC WCS geo service standards suite," in Scientific and Statistical Database Management: 22nd International Conference, SSDBM 2010, Heidelberg, Germany, June 30–July 2, 2010. Proceedings, M. Gertz and B. Ludäscher, Eds. Springer Berlin Heidelberg, 2010, pp. 160–168.

[8] M. Appel, "scidb4geo," http://github.com/appelmar/scidb4geo, [accessed: 2018-01-23].

[9] "PostGIS," http://postgis.net, [accessed: 2018-01-23].

[10] Oracle Corporation, "Oracle Spatial and Graph," http://www.oracle.com/technetwork/database/options/spatialandgraph/, [accessed: 2018-01-23].

[11] G. Merticariu, D. Misev, and P. Baumann, "Towards a general array database benchmark: Measuring storage access," in Big Data Benchmarking: 6th International Workshop, WBDB 2015, Toronto, ON, Canada, June 16-17, 2015 and 7th International Workshop, WBDB 2015, New Delhi, India, December 14-15, 2015, Revised Selected Papers, T. Rabl, R. Nambiar, C. Baru, M. Bhandarkar, M. Poess, and S. Pyne, Eds. Springer International Publishing, 2016, pp. 40–67.

[12] Y. Zhang, M. Kersten, M. Ivanova, and N. Nes, "SciQL: Bridging the gap between science and relational DBMS," in Proceedings of the 15th Symposium on International Database Engineering & Applications, ser. IDEAS '11. New York, NY, USA: ACM, 2011, pp. 124–133.

[13] H. Liu, P. van Oosterom, C. Hu, and W. Wang, "Managing large multi-dimensional array hydrologic datasets: A case study comparing NetCDF and SciDB," Procedia Engineering, vol. 154, no. Supplement C, 2016, pp. 207–214, 12th International Conference on Hydroinformatics (HIC 2016) - Smart Water for the Future.

[14] TPC, "Active TPC benchmarks," http://www.tpc.org/information/benchmarks.asp, [accessed: 2018-01-23].

[15] P. Cudre-Mauroux et al., "SS-DB: A standard science DBMS benchmark," in 4th Extremely Large Databases Conference October 6-7, 2010, 2010, [accessed: 2018-01-23].

[16] B. W. Boehm, J. R. Brown, and M. Lipow, "Quantitative evaluation of software quality," in Proceedings of the 2nd International Conference on Software Engineering, ser. ICSE '76. Los Alamitos, CA, USA: IEEE Computer Society Press, 1976, pp. 592–605.

[17] J. A. McCall, P. K. Richards, and G. F. Walters, "Factors in software quality," Rome Air Development Center, Air Force Systems Command, Griffiss Airforce Base, New York 13441, Tech. Rep. RADC-TR-77-369, November 1977.

[18] R. G. Dromey, "A model for software product quality," IEEE Software, vol. 13, no. 1, 1995, pp. 33–43.

[19] J. P. Miguel, D. Mauricio, and G. Rodríguez, "A review of software quality models for the evaluation of software products," International Journal of Software Engineering & Applications (IJSEA), vol. 5, no. 6, 2014, pp. 31–53.

[20] F. Deissenboeck, E. Juergens, K. Lochmann, and S. Wagner, "Software quality models: Purposes, usage scenarios and requirements," in 2009 ICSE Workshop on Software Quality, 2009, pp. 9–14.

[21] "ISO/IEC 25010:2011. systems and software engineering – systems and software quality requirements and evaluation (SQuaRE) – system and software quality models," International Organization for Standardization, Geneva, CH, Standard, 2011.

[22] Project Jupyter, "The Jupyter Notebook," http://jupyter.org, [accessed: 2018-01-23].

[23] M. Jackson, S. Crouch, and R. Baxter, Software Evaluation: Criteria-based Assessment, https://www.software.ac.uk/sites/default/files/SSI-SoftwareEvaluationCriteria.pdf, 2011, [accessed: 2018-01-23].

[24] M. Stonebraker et al., "Requirements for science data bases and SciDB," in CIDR 2009, 2009.

[25] Q. Xie, "The design of a high performance earth imagery and raster data management and processing platform," ISPRS - International Archives of the Photogrammetry, Remote Sensing and Spatial Information Sciences, vol. XLI-B4, 2016, pp. 551–555.

[26] National Land Survey of Finland, "Korkeusmalli 10 m, 20.04.2017," http://kartat.kapsi.fi, [accessed: 2018-01-23].

[27] Finnish Environment Institute, "CORINE maanpeite 2012, 20 m, 30.9.2014," http://www.syke.fi/fi-FI/Avoin_tieto/Paikkatietoaineistot, [accessed: 2018-01-23].

[28] ——, "CORINE maanpeite 2006, 25 m, 15.6.2010," http://www.syke.fi/fi-FI/Avoin_tieto/Paikkatietoaineistot, [accessed: 2018-01-23].

[29] ——, "CORINE maanpeite 2000, 25 m, 11.5.2010," http://www.syke.fi/fi-FI/Avoin_tieto/Paikkatietoaineistot, [accessed: 2018-01-23].

[30] D. Misev, M. Rusu, and P. Baumann, "A semantic resolver for coordinate reference systems," in Web and Wireless Geographical Information Systems: 11th International Symposium, W2GIS 2012, Naples, Italy, April 12-13, 2012. Proceedings, S. Di Martino, A. Peron, and T. Tezuka, Eds. Berlin, Heidelberg: Springer Berlin Heidelberg, 2012, pp. 47–56.

[31] The Apache Software Foundation, "Apache Tomcat," http://tomcat.apache.org, [accessed: 2018-01-23].

[32] The PostgreSQL Global Development Group, "PostgreSQL," http://www.postgresql.org, [accessed: 2018-01-23].

[33] SQLite Development Team, "SQLite," http://www.sqlite.org, [accessed: 2018-01-23].

[34] CSC – IT Center for Science Ltd., "Pouta user guide," https://research.csc.fi/pouta-user-guide, [accessed: 2018-01-23].

[35] "iPerf," https://iperf.fr, [accessed: 2018-01-23].

[36] Paradigm4 Inc., "shim," http://github.com/Paradigm4/shim, [accessed: 2018-01-23].

Towards Modelling Privacy Risks in Geo-Social Networks

Alia I. Abdelmoty

School of School of Computer Science & Informatics,
Cardiff University, Wales, UK
Email: AbdelmotyAI@cardiff.ac.uk

Abstract—**"Social privacy" concerns how individuals manage self-disclosure, availability, and access to information about themselves by other people when using social-driven applications. To manage social privacy, one needs to understand the level of threat implied by his information disclosure and be able to relate it to the scope of visibility granted for this information. This paper argues that the risk to personal privacy comes from the implicit information embedded in the relationships between the different elements of data collected on these networks. A proposal is made to explicitly represent such relationships and use them to model the level of threat to personal privacy on these networks. Exposure of this information will enable users to be aware of their own data and to make informed decisions on their sharing behaviour online.**

Keywords–Location Privacy; Geo-Social Networks; User Profiles.

I. Introduction

The proliferation and affordablity of location tracking-enabled devices are allowing individuals to accumulate an increasing amount of personal information, such as their mobility tracks, geographically tagged photos and events. Embracing these new location-aware capabilities by social networks has led to the emergence of Geo-Social Networks (GeoSNs) that offer their users the ability to geo-reference their submissions and to share their location with other users. Subsequently, users can use location identifiers to browse and search for resources. GeoSNs include Location-Enabled Social Networks (LESNs), for example, Facebook, Twitter, Instagram and Flickr, where users' locations are supplementary identification of other primary data sets, and Location-Based Social Networks (LBSNs), for example, Foursquare and Yelp, where location is an essential key for providing the service.

In addition to location data that describe the places visited by users, GeoSNs also records other personal information, such as user's friends, reviews and tips, possibly over long periods of time. User's historical location information can be related to contextual and semantic information publicly available online and can be used to infer personal information and to construct a comprehensive user profile [1] [2]. Derived information in such profiles can include user activities, interests and mobility patterns. Users may not be fully aware of what location information are being collected, how the information are used and by whom, and hence can fail to appreciate the possible potential risks of disclosing their location information. Methods of exposing both the explicitly collected and implicitly derived information from user location are needed to enable users' awareness, and to allow users to make informed decisions about sharing their data online.

In this paper, the type of information stored in user profiles on GeoSNs are considered as a folksonomy structure of user, place and tag entities. A layer of privacy risk levels is proposed to label the relationships between these entities in the folksonomy graph, based on the degree of associations between them. A lot of work has been done recently on exploring the content of information shared by users on GeoSNs. On the other hand, a lot of work is ongoing to explore the privacy threats posed by sharing this information online. In this paper we combine both lines of research and propose a new approach to associating the information shared with its possible privacy risks. By representing the implicit content in the user profile data, application can help users appreciate the possible privacy risks associated with their sharing behaviour and thus allow them to make informed decisions on disclosing their information. The work presented here is a first step towards building privacy-aware GeoSNs.

An overview of related work is presented in Section II. In Section III, the geo-folksonomy data model is used to store the information collected by the GeoSNs. The model is extended with the proposed privacy levels information. A framework for a privacy-enabled GeoSN is also presented. In Section IV, example user profiles, defined using the enriched geo-folksonomy model, are described. Conclusions and an overview of future work are given in Section V.

II. Related Work

Significant interest is witnessed recently in studying the value and utility of location information in GeoSNs for the purpose of user and place profiling. Here, we review some of the methods used for extracting the explicit and implicit content of the data generated on these networks and some of the work done on user profiling with this information.

Some works utilised publicly available information from GeoSNs in order to derive or predict users' location. In [3], Twitter users' city-level locations were estimated by exploiting their tweet contents with which it was possible to predict more than half of the sample set within 100 miles of their actual place. Similarly, Pontes et al. [4] examined how much personal information can be inferred from the publicly available information of Foursquare users and found the home cities of more than two-thirds of the sample within 50 kilometres. Sadilek et al. [5] investigated novel approaches for inferring users' location at any given time by knowing the GPS positions of their friends on Twitter. For almost 84% of users the exact locations were derived even when setting their location data as private, where an accuracy of 57% was accomplished by using information of only two friends.

Sharing location information on GeoSNs can be utilised to analyse and predict spatiotemporal user behaviour including their interests, activities, mobility patterns as well as future movement. Location-Centric Profiles (LCPs) are proposed in [6] that contain aggregated statistics extracted from profiles of users who visited a given location on GeoSNs. These were provided for the venue owner as a way for monitoring their business. Vosecky [7] modelled users' interests shared on microblogs in relation to their corresponding disclosed locations. Users' geographic location from Twitter was extracted from the locations directly tagged by them or from those mentioned in their tweets [7]. Users' geographical regions of interests are then derived that represent clusters of personal activity.

Rossi and Musolesi [8] proposed and tested three approaches for identifying users by exploiting their check-in information on LBSNs, particularly spatiotemporal tracks, frequency of visit, and users' social ties. Evaluation results showed that only a small amount of check-in information was adequate to identify users with high accuracy, where almost 80% of users were successfully identified in some datasets. Zhong et. al. [9] were pioneers in exploiting the predictability aspect of location check-ins in order to develop location-to-profile framework that infers demographics of users. In particular, they derived enriched check-ins' semantics based on three main factors, namely, spatiality, temporality and location knowledge such as customer review sites and social networks. A series of experiments were carried out on the dataset that revealed the feasibility of deriving users' demographics from their check-in information, where gender and educational background attributes provided the best outcomes followed by age, sexual orientation, marital status, blood type and zodiac sign. More recently, researchers have exploited GeoSNs to explore the personality aspect by examining the reciprocal relationship between users and spatiotemporal features. In Chorley et. al. [10], a study was conducted to understand human behaviour in terms of examining the relationship between the location types visited by Foursquare users and their personality. A five-factor personality model was proposed and correlations were observed between the personality traits and Foursquare check-in attitude.

The above studies show a significant potential for deriving personal information form GeoSNs and the implication of possible privacy threats to users of these applications. A lot of work considered methods of user profiling with personal location information collected on GeoSNs, but no works have yet considered the privacy implications of building such profiles and how to address the threat for the users of these networks.

III. The Geo-Folksonomy Model

In this work, we use a folksonomy data model to represent user-place relationships and derive tag assignments from users' actions of check-ins and annotation of venues [1]. In particular, tags are assigned to venues in our data model in two scenarios as follows.

1) A user's check-in results in the assignment of place categories associated with the place as tags annotated by this user. Thus, a check-in by user u in place r with the categories (represented as keywords) x, y and z, will be considered as an assertion of the form $(u, r, (x, y, z))$. This in turn will be transformed to a set of triples $\{(u, r, x), (u, r, y), (u, r, z)\}$ in the folksonomy.
2) A user's tip in the place also results in the assignment of place categories as tags, in addition to the set of keywords extracted from the tip. Thus, in the above example, a tip by u in r with the keywords $(t_1, \cdots, t_n)$, will be considered as an assertion of the form $(u, r, (x, y, z, t_1, \cdots, t_n))$, and is in turn transformed to individual triples between the user, place and tags in the folksonomy.

The data collected by the GeoSN can be represented as a geo-folksonomy, which can be defined as a quadruple $\mathbb{F} := (U, T, R, Y)$, where U, T, R are finite sets of instances of users, tags and places respectively, and Y defines a relation, the tag assignment, between these sets, that is, $Y \subseteq U \times T \times R$.

A geo-folksonomy can be transformed into a tripartite undirected graph, which is denoted as folksonomy graph $\mathbb{G}_{\mathbb{F}}$. A geo-Folksonomy Graph $\mathbb{G}_{\mathbb{F}} = (V_{\mathbb{F}}, E_{\mathbb{F}})$ is an undirected weighted tripartite graph that models a given folksonomy $\mathbb{F}$, where: $V_{\mathbb{F}} = U \cup T \cup R$ is the set of nodes, $E_{\mathbb{F}} = \{\{u, t\}, \{t, r\}, \{u, r\} | (u, t, r) \in Y\}\}$ is the set of edges, and a weight w is associated with each edge $e \in E_{\mathbb{F}}$.

The weight associated with an edge $\{u, t\}, \{t, r\}$ and $\{u, r\}$ corresponds to the co-occurrence frequency of the corresponding nodes within the set of tag assignments Y. For example, $w(t, r) = |\{u \in U : (u, t, r) \in Y\}|$ corresponds to the number of users that assigned tag t to place r.

A. *Privacy-oriented Geo-Folksonomy Model*

Here, a possible model is proposed of the levels of privacy threats with respect to the user geo-profile. Two variables contribute to the level of threat to user's privacy on social networks, namely, the amount and content of the disclosed information, and the visibility scope of this information. Here, we focus on the data content and isolate the visibility variable, i.e. we assume that all data in a user profile is available to potential adversaries. This is not an unreasonable assumption given that the application owns all the user data sets it collects. The scope of visibility can be used to control access to user's data in a privacy-oriented system design, which is the subject of future work.

With respect to data content, the level of risk to personal privacy can be quantitatively assessed using the amount of data disclosed by the user; the level of risk is directly proportional to the amount of data disclosed. The more data stored about the user's spatio-temporal history, the more inferences that can be made in the profile. Data have three explicit dimensions: spatial, social and temporal. Reasoning with the relationships between these dimensions can result in the inference of implicit personal information that the user may not have wished to disclose. For example, reasoning along the spatio-temporal dimension can reveal patterns of presence or absence from places and the degree of attachments to place, etc. An abstract "traffic-light" model is proposed here to communicate the level of risk to user's privacy on GeoSNs. Three levels are defined as follows.

- Green: safe to disclose the information,
- Amber: caution; disclosing the information can result in moderate privacy implications, and,

- Red: danger; disclosing the information can result in risky privacy implications.

The levels are mapped to the degree of association computed between the entities in the geo-folksonomy, namely, between different entities (user and place, user and tag, place and tag), as well as between similar entities (a user and other users, place and other places, and tags). The familiar "traffic light" metaphor is used to enable a quick and accurate interpretation of the communicated information to users.

Every edge e in the geo-folksonomy graph is given a privacy label $vc = Green|Amber|Red$, that is a function of the pre-assigned weight on the edge. Thus, for example, $vc(t,r) = f(w(t,r))$ and $vc(u,r) = f(w(u,r))$, etc. Note that as the weights on the edges are dynamic, the labels used can also change over time. For example, a label may initially be green, and then can change to amber or red as the frequency of the user visits to the place increases. Note also that the function used for assigning the privacy labels can be more realistically defined by considering the pattern of association in addition to the frequency. For example, a periodic tag assignment by the user is more revealing of the user's behaviour than a random assignment for the same frequency.

Figure 1 depicts the overall process of user profile creation. The process starts with data collection of check-ins and tip data from the GeoSN, that are then processed to extract users, places and tags and their associated properties. The modelling stage includes the definition of relationships between the three entities and the computation of weights on the edges of the folksonomy graph using co-occurence methods. The privacy-level detection module takes the folksonomy graph as input and computes the privacy levels for all the edges in the graph. The enriched folksonomy graph is then used to create the different user profiles. The user similarity module uses the generated profile to compute similarity vectors for users in the data set. The privacy notification and feedback module uses the generated privacy levels to present the data to the user through the user interface.

IV. Privacy-aware User Geo-Profiles

The geo-folksonomy can be used to represent a user's spatial and semantic association with place. A spatial user profile represents the user's interest in places, while a tag-based profile describes his association with concepts associated with places in the folksonomy model. Similarity between users can be measured on the basis of their spatial or semantic profiles. Spatial profiles gives a measure of user preferences in places, while semantic profiles, on the other hand, is a conceptual measure of user interests.

A. *Basic User Profiles*

Spatial User Profile

A spatial user profile $P_R(u)$ of a user u is deduced from the set of places that u visited or annotated directly.

$$P_R(u) = \{(r, w(u,r)) | (u,t,r) \in Y, \quad w(u,r) = |\{t \in T : (u,t,r) \in Y\}|\}$$

$w(u,r)$ is the number of tag assignments, where user u assigned some tag t to place r through the action of checking-in or annotation. Hence, the weight assigned to a place simply corresponds to the frequency of the user reference to the place either by checking in or by leaving a tip. We further normalise the weights so that the sum of the weights assigned to the places in the spatial profile is equal to 1. We use $\overline{P_R}$ to explicitly refer to the spatial profile where the sum of all weights is equal to 1, with $\overline{w}(u,r) = \frac{|\{t \in T:(u,t,r) \in Y\}|}{\sum_{i=1}^{n}\sum_{j=1}^{m}|\{t_i \in T:(u,t_i,r_j) \in Y\}|}$, where n and m are the total number of tags and resources, respectively. More simply, $\overline{w}(u,r) = \frac{N(u,r)}{N_T(u)}$, where $N(u,r)$ is the number of tags used by u for resource r, while $N_T(u)$ is the total number of tags used by u for all places.

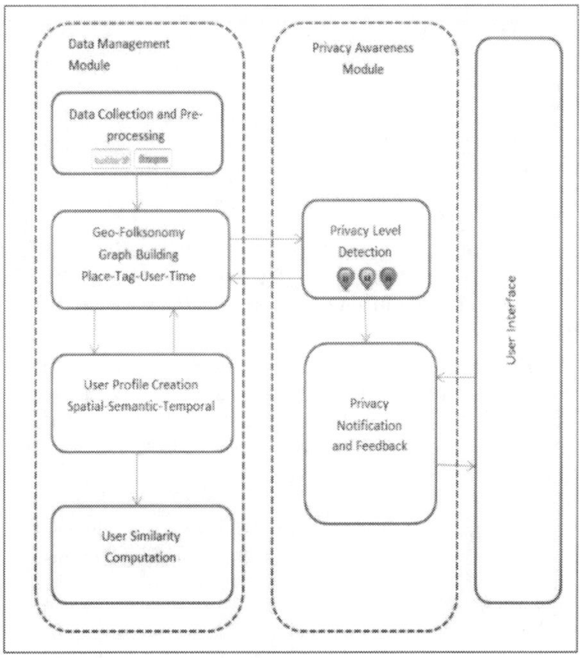

Figure 1. Framework of the privacy-enabled GeoSNs.

Correspondingly, we define the tag-based profile of a user; $P_T(u)$ as follows.

Semantic User Profile

A semantic user profile $P_T(u)$ of a user u is deduced from the set of tag assignments linked with u.

$$P_T(u) = \{(t, w(u,t)) | (u,t,r) \in Y, \quad w(u,t) = |\{r \in R : (u,t,r) \in Y\}|\}$$

$w(u,t)$ is the number of tag assignments where user u assigned tag t to some place through the action of checking-in or annotation.

$\overline{P_T}$ refers to the semantic profile where the sum of all weights is equal to 1, with $\overline{w}(u,t) = \frac{N(u,t)}{N_R(u)}$, where $N(u,t)$ is the number of resources annotated by u with t and $N_R(u)$ is the total number of resources annotated by u.

Temporal versions of the profiles can be recorded by considering snapshots of the geo-folksonomy at different points in time. For example, a basic spatio-temporal profile can be represented as follows.

A spatiotemporal (ST) user profile $P_{Rt_c}(u)$ of a user u is deduced from the set of places that u visited or annotated directly.

$$(P_R(u))_{t_c} = \{(r, w(u,r)_{t_c}) | (u,g,r) \in Y,$$
$$w(u,r)_{t_c} = |\{g_{t_c} \in G : (u,g,r) \in Y\}|$$

$w(u,r)_{t_c}$ is the number of tag assignments in the time slot t_c, where user u assigned some tag g to place r through the action of checking-in or annotation.

B. *User Profile Example*

Here an example is given of a sample user profile created from the experiment data set used in this work. This user checked in 600 different venues, with associated 400 venue categories.

Figure 2 shows the spatial profile for this user. The dots in the figure represent the weight assigned to place (representing the edge between the user and the place) in the profile. Weights are clustered into 4 equally spaced groups and are mapped to the three noted privacy levels. A simple function for splitting the range of levels is used in this case. However, more intelligent methods for identifying this function can be envisaged, particularly when considering the temporal dimension of the data.

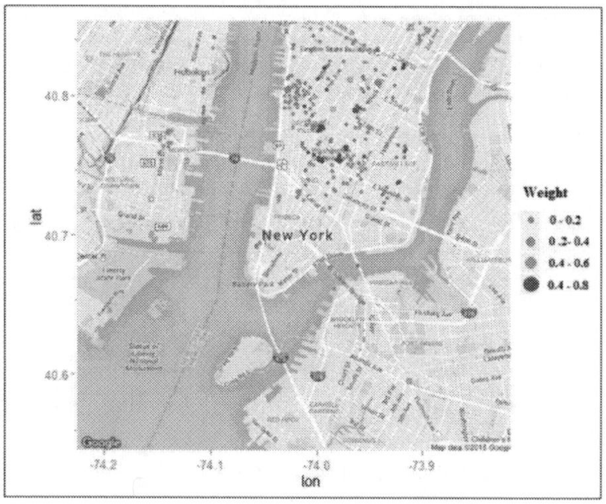

Figure 2. A sample spatial user profile and the corresponding privacy levels.

V. Conclusion

The proliferation of GeoSNs and the large-scale uptake by users suggest the urgency and importance of studying privacy implications of personal information collected by these networks. User profiling is a common method used by online applications to understand users's behaviour and preferences for the purpose of improving their quality of service. However, information implicit in location-based user profiles can reveal personal information about users that can pose real privacy risks. This paper highlights the importance of raising users' awareness of the information they share on GeoSNs. A proposal is made to extend user profiles by explicit representation of the level of risk to personal privacy associated with the information they contain. It is suggested that the level of threat is directly related to the strength of association between the data elements contained in these profiles and that a simple model reflecting this degree of association will be helpful in raising the user awareness of privacy implication of location disclosure. Future work will consider the following:

- Evaluating the proposed methods using realistic sample data sets.
- Exploring different methods of defining the thresholds for the defined levels of risk, e.g. by considering the patterns of association, in addition to the frequency.
- In-depth treatment of the temporal dimension and how to represent dynamic change of the proposed model.

References

[1] S. Mohamed and A. I. Abdelmoty, "Spatio-semantic user profiles in location-based social networks," International Journal of Data Science and Analytics, vol. 4, no. 2, 2017, p. 127142.

[2] F. Alrayes and A. Abdelmoty, "Privacy concerns in location-based social networks," in GEOProcessing 2014: The Sixth International Conference on Advanced Geographic Information Systems, Applications, and Services. IARIA, 2014, pp. 105–114.

[3] Z. Cheng, J. Caverlee, and K. Lee, "You are where you tweet: a content-based approach to geo-locating Twitter users," in Proceedings of the 19th ACM international conference on Information and Knowledge Management CIKM '10, 2010, pp. 759–768.

[4] T. Pontes, M. Vasconcelos, J. Almeida, P. Kumaraguru, and V. Almeida, "We know where you live?: privacy characterization of foursquare behavior," in UbiComp '12 Proceedings of the 2012 ACM Conference on Ubiquitous Computing, 2012, pp. 898–905.

[5] A. Sadilek, H. Kautz, and J. Bigham, "Finding your friends and following them to where you are," in Proceedings of the fifth ACM international conference on Web Search and Data Mining, WSDM '12, 2012, pp. 723–732.

[6] B. Carbunar, M. Rahman, N. Rishe, and J. Ballesteros, "Private location centric profiles for geosocial networks," in Proceedings of the 20th International Conference on Advances in Geographic Information Systems. ACM, 2012, pp. 458–461.

[7] J. Vosecky, D. Jiang, and W. Ng, "Limosa: A system for geographic user interest analysis in twitter," in Proceedings of the 16th International Conference on Extending Database Technology. ACM, 2013, pp. 709–712.

[8] L. Rossi and M. Musolesi, "It's the way you check-in: identifying users in location-based social networks," in Proceedings of the second edition of the ACM conference on Online social networks. ACM, 2014, pp. 215–226.

[9] Y. Zhong, N. J. Yuan, W. Zhong, F. Zhang, and X. Xie, "You are where you go: Inferring demographic attributes from location check-ins," in Proceedings of the Eighth ACM International Conference on Web Search and Data Mining. ACM, 2015, pp. 295–304.

[10] M. J. Chorley, G. B. Colombo, S. M. Allen, and R. M. Whitaker, "Visiting patterns and personality of foursquare users," in Cloud and Green Computing (CGC), 2013 Third International Conference on. IEEE, 2013, pp. 271–276.